JUDGE THIS BOOK BY ITS COVER

Ron Young
with Steve Olivas

D1600267

JRNYman Publishing
Nashville, Tennessee

TABLE OF CONTENTS

PROLOGUE

Life is so…weird.

I celebrated a birthday a few days before starting this book. I turned 62. Not a huge milestone birthday. But every time I finish another year, I look over my life and wonder how it all got to here.

And it is fuckin' weird.

During my childhood, every waking decision was about how to cope with the insanity that was my home life. Then I discovered music and drugs—and the healing power of both. The decisions I made were about hedonism; fun and freedom at all cost.

Then I entered the "rock star" phase of life and fought to make career decisions for myself. The record label and its corporate machinery were accustomed to taking charge and treating the talent like it was an expendable cog in the gearing. My life was spent half raging against the machine, half wanting to make the fans happy, and half hustling to keep the SS Hedonism afloat.

And half figuring out how fractions work.

Soon thereafter, I was shot out the ass end of the entertainment industry and right into a war. My body and soul were wretched with resentment and pain. I didn't know who I was. I had spent a lifetime trying to feel comfortable in my own skin…and nothing was working.

The theme of every single fucking decision I ever made was about control; controlling a chaotic world that was stronger than me. I learned from day one that giving up control and letting my guard down would lead to my devastation. From dealing with my crazy-ass alcoholic mother to navigating the narcissistic shitbags that ran the entertainment industry, I kept an ever-tightening grip on my control. Finally, I had to let go.

Had I hung on, I would have continued to avoid my pain through sex, drugs, and rock and roll.

Well, not quite. I hate to buck a good cliché, but sex is not a part of my hedonism. Yes, I was a young healthy male and loved sex just as much (maybe even more?) than the next guy. But I am also extremely monogamous. When I am in a relationship, I am committed. Plain and simple.

Call bullshit if you want, but this is the truth.

So, drugs and rock and roll. Every damn day. Had I continued down that blurry path, I would have eventually passed the point of no return. Jail. Death. A gnarly mutant toxin, cut in with the coke or heroin I was doing, that might have melted my brain into a three pound nerf ball. Could have easily been any of the above.

With sobriety comes a whole different set of decisions. I had to get a job and buy a house. I had to grow up and pay taxes. I fell in love for real and got married, which meant sharing responsibility for the future with another human being.

In a nutshell, I learned to give up some of that control and feel comfortable and confident facing whatever lies ahead. My body and mind still carry the scars of those battles long fought and lost, but I am more at peace with who I am.

Life is so fuckin' weird.

My decisions these days still involve making music. It has been the only love that understands the full history of my existence. But I also ponder things like the best food for my dogs, or when I should pick my avocados. I live in a home I would have never thought I deserved. I live with a woman who loves me for who I am, despite knowing who I am.

So fucking weird.

I spend a fair amount of time on social media, and I am constantly bombarded with news of this person or that person dying. I read these announcements and think, *Wow. That person probably woke up this morning with no idea they were going to die.*

Maybe they thought about feeding their dogs or picking avocados. But they will never have those thoughts again.

That's why I decided to write this book. Nobody knows when their last day will be, but we all know it's coming, one way or another.

I don't honestly know who the hell would want to read this book. At least my life has been interesting, and I hope you'll be entertained. Maybe you'll pick up on something that helps you in your own weird life.

So, I'll gaze out my office window and write these words for you. My goal is to finally answer a question, mostly for myself, that has popped up way too often:

Why am I so fucked up?

CHAPTER 1:
ORDER FROM CHOAS

Every superhero (and every super-villain) has an origin story. None of these origin stories are idyllic. None of the heroes or foes grew up frolicking in a field of love-warmed daisies. Their motivations were shaped and driven by tragedy more than triumph, thus blurring the line between the good guys and the bad guys. The difference is a razor thin line. Something internal pushes them toward the darkness or the light.

I won't say whether I am hero or villain; that's for you to decide. The tattoos and long hair of my youth suggest villain to some. But I do look damn good in tights and a cape.

That's not true. I should probably go back and erase all that but, fuck it. When you read a book by Ron Young, you get what you get.

Maybe that's a good place to start: my name. Over the years, I have been asked more times than I care to remember if Ron Young is my real name. Sounds a little made up, right? Like some over-simplified truncation of an ethnic name that a manager forced me to change when I got into show business.

Half true.

My Russian grandfather came to America with the last name Yonchenko. It was the early 1900s, when immigrants brought a little slice of the Old Country into American culture. As a result, the melting pot of our nation began.

Unfortunately, Yonchenko was unwieldy as a surname when you make your living introducing yourself. My dad was a salesman who had a hell of a time pronouncing and spelling his last name to everyone he shook hands with or called on the telephone.

To make life simpler for everyone, he had it legally changed. Yonchenko became Young. And this change happened long before I came along.

So yes, Ron Young is my actual birth name.

My earliest memories have nothing to do with names. They have more to do with utter madness. The setting was Queens, New York, in an immense apartment complex built by the real estate tycoon, Sam LeFrak.

I bring his name up because in an ironic twist, LeFrak went on later in life to form an entertainment and recording company. The name of his business wasn't all that creative, but "The Entertainment Company" produced songs by Barbra Streisand, Donna Summer, and Dolly Parton, among others.

When I say our apartment complex was immense, I am not being hyperbolic. There were, no joke, tens of thousands of units sprawling across entire city blocks. In fact, the development was called "LeFrak City" because his structures were responsible for housing so many New York families.

Our little slice of the LeFrak pie was home to three children —me, an older brother, and an older sister. My brother, Michael, is nine years older than me. My sister, Sandi, is ten years older. I was probably a mistake, if I'm being honest with myself. But that wasn't the biggest inner demon I had to battle growing up.

My mother was an alcoholic. A crazy fucking bitch.

I recite that angrily, but then chuckle afterwards whenever I mention it to anyone. That dichotomy really defined my childhood to a T. Still to this day, I balance anger with levity; humor (as a defense mechanism) saved my ass from drowning in rage many times. As a kid, I always struggled to reconcile loving my mother with hating my mother.

I know I chuckle. But it was brutal, man.

Our home had a lot of discord. A lot of late night screaming matches between Mom and whoever was the target of her rage. Mental abuse and physical abuse were the standard. Without exaggeration, Mom would get into fistfights with various members of the family.

Most of her aggression was aimed at my dad as I got older. She could hate him with all the bile in her heart and he would never leave her. He made it convenient for her, I suppose. He would stay gone as much as possible…which probably enraged her even further. But he remained married to her in order to support the family financially. And because she probably was blackmailing him with threats of taking custody of me in a divorce.

My brother and my sister got the fuck out as soon as they possibly could. They knew a shit-storm when they saw it, so jumped out when a door opened to the rest of their lives. Like Dad, they stayed away from the house during high school. Then they left home to create shit-storms of their own when they became of age.

Age was my curse. I was so much younger than the other two children. I was the soldier that got left behind. To add to the chaos, things got worse for Mom when I was eight years old.

* * *

We moved to a community called Bayside while I was in third grade. Michael and Sandi were already out of the house (lucky fucks) when Mom ruptured a disc in her back. I don't remember exactly what she did to twist and fall or whatever. The cause didn't really matter. What mattered was that Mom upgraded her crazy when she went from being an alcoholic, to being an alcoholic hooked on pain killers.

Wheelchair-bound, Mom's misery index was in the red zone. She would bounce from totally numbed out on pills, to crazy violent bitch, to loving affectionate mother. She also acted like she couldn't do anything for herself. She required somebody to wait on her hand and foot. Dad was never home, so I was shoved into the role of Mom's caretaker.

It doesn't take Sigmund Freud to figure this one out. I was never comfortable in my own skin because I never knew who I was. From one minute to the next, my self-image changed. In one instant, I was Mom's whipping boy, a target of her violent mouth and violent fists. Moments later, I was a sponge for her affection, soaking up her love like The Good Son.

I spent more time with her than anyone, so I became a lightning rod for the love and hate that shot through her at the speed of booze and opiates. Unlike her detached relationship with Dad, she needed me to physically care for her…so she couldn't abuse me 100% of the time.

Maybe if she only treated me like a piece of shit, and excluded all the love bombing, it would have been easier for me. At least I would have known who I was. Being a piece of shit wouldn't have been fun, but it would have been easier for me to understand than having to cope with her swinging from "You're a piece of shit" to "You're a lovely little good boy" all in the same breath.

Talk about a mind fuck.

During all this chaos, I had to figure out how to keep my head above water. Obviously, I didn't think about it like that at the time. When we're kids, we don't even consider how fucked up our lives might be. Our life is just our life; plain and simple. It's not until we get a little older that we start to compare the "normal" we knew with the "normal" that other people seemed to know.

I was in a constant state of anxiety, man. I was so scared of mom flipping from Dr. Jekyll to Mr. Hyde. It was like Robert Lewis Stevenson knew her personally when he wrote the book.

As a result, I worked hard to keep Mom stable. Being at her beck and call might keep the peace for a few extra minutes. I became a people pleaser because that was the survival skill necessary in my situation. Molding myself into whatever Mom wanted at the time was my superpower. It didn't work 100% of the time, but I was bright enough to know that it worked more often than not.

At the very least, it kept my ass from getting beat or screamed at. Most of the time.

What I really needed was some mechanism to manage the anxiety. If I didn't find an outlet, her brainsick roller coaster would have eaten me up inside. I was too young to do drugs, or to jerk off, or to do any other stress-relieving thing I found later in life. But from 1966 to 1967, several planets lined up that set me on a path toward being an entertainer. Each of these planets is just as improbable as the next, but they rocked my young world to the point of helping me learn how to escape.

That same strategy has carried me into my 60s. In fact, I still lose myself just as I did back then. I get swept away in the "high" of being in front of a crowd.

* * *

When I was six years old, I got my first taste of public notoriety. It happened in the central courtyard of our apartment complex. LeFrak designed his complexes so that every four buildings were placed in a square, with a giant, Olympic-sized pool in the center. These pools became "party central" during the summer, and ours was no different. Our pool area was packed every weekend. This was our major social event back when people would still get out and mingle with their neighbors.

On one particular weekend, a band was hired to set up and play for the throng of swimmers and sunbathers. For some reason, I got up in front of the masses, and sang "Hanky Panky" by Tommy James and the Shondells. In hindsight, I can't remember exactly why I thought this would be a good idea, but six-year-old me saw no flaw in my plan.

I had no idea what the words meant. Music was played constantly in our home, and this song hit #1 for two weeks in the United States that summer. Let's be honest—the lyrics weren't all that difficult to master. I heard it everywhere.

Seeing it performed was a different matter. Sure, musical performances were shown on television. We had *American Bandstand*. Plenty of variety shows like *The Ed Sullivan Show*, *The Mike Douglas Show*, and *The Tonight Show* had musical guests. But in 1966, there was no way puritanical TV standards and practices would have let anyone perform a tune as risqué as "Hanky Panky"!

Despite having watched performers on TV, I still didn't pick up on how to sing and dance. But I never let a lack of understanding keep me from pleasing people. I did my best to ham it up and have fun.

As it turned out, listening to a six-year-old kid singing suggestive lyrics was hilarious to the adults hanging around the pool. There was an uproarious response. Adults whooped, danced, laughed, and applauded…and I loved it.

That one cheesy song became my gateway drug. I was hooked.

Tommy James is still alive as of the writing of this book. Part of me hopes this story will find its way back to him. On the other hand, I'm not sure if I should thank him or punch him for pulling me into this career!

Later that same summer, the mayor of New York City visited our pool. Mayor John Lindsay was out and about, pressing the flesh and doing some PR among his constituents. He had beaten out William F. Buckley in the 1965 election and was busy doing whatever it is that a mayor does, which includes constant campaigning.

At one point—and I have no idea how this came about—I ended up sitting on his lap for a photo-op. He probably posed for a hundred pictures that afternoon, but mine seemed to be particularly eye-catching.

Mind you, I was far better looking back then than I am now. I flashed my dimples and tossed my cowlick; I knew how to work a crowd. I don't recall if any ladies swooned that afternoon, but in my mind's eye, they all did.

The next day, that photo was published on the front page of the *New York Post*. I was instantly the talk of the neighborhood. My parents bought several copies of that edition, cutting the photo out of one issue to hang on our wall.

My notoriety only grew from there. Because another chance event continued my forward momentum as an entertainer.

* * *

In 1963, the New York Mets needed a public relations win. This was their sophomore season, and they were coming off a disastrous inaugural year. In their previous season, they posted a 40-120 record, the worst in major league baseball since 1899. Ticket sales dropped. Their owner, the first woman to own a major league team in North America, Joan Whitney Payson, decided to be proactive in keeping the fans interested. Along with her public relations staff, she created "Banner Day."

The concept was simple. Any fan (that wanted to participate) was allowed to parade onto the field of Shea Stadium between the games of a double-header. They'd show off homemade banners declaring their love for "dem bums," the Mets' affectionate, albeit unfortunate, nickname. The Mets players would act as judges and select the banner and the fan they liked the best.

Ms. Payson's idea was a rousing success, carrying on each season for several decades.

However, the team itself still struggled. 1966 was another disastrous year for the Mets as they famously passed on Reggie Jackson in the major league baseball draft. Instead, they chose a guy who never played in the majors: Steve Chilcott.

They made a better decision for the 1967 season. They acquired future Hall-of-Famer, Tom Seaver. Two years later, Seaver helped them win the World Series against the Baltimore Orioles, giving the team a new moniker, "The Miracle Mets."

However, the Mets weren't the only guys to have "miracle" wins. I was about to join the divine.

In 1967, our apartment wasn't too far from Shea Stadium, the home of the Mets. My parents would make my brother take me to Mets games. He was fifteen and I was six; you can guess his general attitude toward hauling his kid brother through the streets of Queens.

Banner Day was still a noted Mets event, and it was one of the games Michael was required to take me to. This added insult to his super-pissed attitude. He was made to create a banner and dress up in a costume to take me on the field between games.

My brother, in an act of unprecedented creativity, momentarily set his frustration aside and came up with a great idea.

At the time, Tareyton Cigarettes had a famous print ad campaign. The tag line of the ad was, "Tareyton smokers would rather fight than switch." Magazines and newspapers that ran the ad showed a picture of a girl and guy smoking Tareyton cigarettes, both of them sporting a black eye.

With that as inspiration, we made a banner with the phrase, "Met fans would rather shrink than switch." Then, we somehow got our hands on two full-size adult Mets uniforms. I dressed up in one, with the pant legs and sleeves rolled up. We then called a friend of mine, Raymond Lawrence, and dressed him up exactly the same way.

The concept was that we "shrunk" instead of switching our team loyalty.

We three stooges proudly marched onto the Shea Stadium infield that day, showing off my big brother's witty idea.

Tom Seaver—yes, *the* Tom Seaver—and the catcher, Jerry Grote (another marquee player for the Mets) spotted us and immediately declared us the grand champions of the 1967 Banner Day. They ran onto the field, grabbed me and Raymond, and brought us into the Mets dugout to show us off to the rest of the players.

If you thought Michael was pissed before, he was snarling

16

mad when he was denied access to the dugout. Evidently, two seven-year-olds in adult Mets uniforms were cute and ferociously awesome. A surly, fifteen-year-old babysitter/brother was objectively not.

Raymond and I had photos taken with all the Mets players and got a thumbnail tour of their facilities beneath the stadium. My brother didn't get shit, save for the knowledge that he was responsible for the concept that won Banner Day.

I closely followed Banner Day each year after we won. Years later, winners were awarded huge prizes like a trip to Hawaii or a car. When we won, we received a case of tuna fish (not kidding) and a black and white television. The TV was an Admiral brand that lived on our kitchen counter for a good fifteen years. You couldn't kill that TV; it was bullet-proof. Eventually the antennae broke off and we used a coat hanger and aluminum foil to get reception.

Ah, the good old days.

As a direct result of winning Banner Day, Raymond and I were invited to appear on a major national children's television program called *Wonderama*. 1967 was the year that host Sonny Fox passed the torch to a new host named Bob McAllister, but Sonny was still there when we appeared.

The special guest star on our episode was Burt Ward, who played Robin on the original *Batman* television series. I was at the age where Batman was bigger than life to me. I can't overstate how weird it was to get interviewed on the same show with Robin the Boy Wonder.

All I remember about the interview was being asked what I wanted to do when I grew up.

I answered, "I want to be a garbage man."

Sonny Fox rolled with it. "Really? A garbage man? Whatever for?"

"So I can get dirty all the time and my mom won't make me take a shower."

The audience found that to be hysterical, and the producers saw an opportunity to turn my response into a running joke. From that interview forward, I had several cameo appearances on the episode. They would have Raymond and I walk across the set, right through the shot of whatever else was going on, carrying a trash can filled with papers. I think they also had me tell a joke.

My fifteen minutes of fame was in full swing.

Because Raymond and I appeared on *Wonderama*, our names were in the episode listing in *TV Guide*. If you're around my age, you remember how big of a deal "The Guide" was back in those days. Everyone used *TV Guide* to map out their viewing schedule for the week, read up on the latest news and gossip regarding the popular programs and the stars who played in them, and see who the guests would be on their favorite talk and variety shows.

And my name appeared in *TV Guide* next to all this.

My fucking name! In print! In a national publication!

If my parents had a choice between me winning the Nobel Prize in Medicine and me having my name appear in *TV Guide*, they would have cancelled my flight to Stockholm so fast, my head would have been spinning. This was the biggest of the big deals for me. My celebrity status in LeFrak City was now etched in concrete.

I absolutely loved and craved the spotlight after these crazy adventures.

But these were not the only examples of my burgeoning notoriety. I'll hit you with a line from late night info-mercials: "But wait! There's more!"

Remember *Candid Camera*, the TV show hosted by Allen Funt? It was a show that filmed harmless practical jokes on unsuspecting people, and was the precursor to shows like *Punk'd* and *The Jamie Kennedy Experiment*. *Candid Camera* was a perennial smash hit on CBS, reaching the peak of its power during the mid-1960s.

In late 1967, the show came to my grade school and filmed a segment using the students. The bit was simple: they gave kids two ice cream cones, then set up a scenario where the kids had to figure out how to hold the cones while opening a glass door.

Pretty clever. As I recall, I was the only student who was able to figure out how to pull it off. Thus, my vignette was one chosen to air on the show.

The fact that my school was on the program, much less that I would be chosen out of all the students to be on the aired segment, was mind boggling.

I wish I could say *Candid Camera* sought me out because I was the kid who sang "Hanky Panky" at the pool the previous summer. But alas, this one was more random than that. However, it continued to feed my addiction to entertaining people.

Within the span of just over one year, I was on two national television programs, I was in *TV Guide*, I was led into the New York Mets' dugout by their superstar pitcher, Tom Seaver, and I made the front page of the *New York Post*. I craved the moments when I could make somebody laugh or smile. It was my grammar school drug of choice.

Therefore, my star-crossed destiny of begging for attention began.

As a part of the grand paradox that is my life, I was simultaneously becoming more and more introverted. Although the world seemed to love me, I withdrew because things continued to deteriorate at home.

* * *

My mom's level of crazy was hitting a crescendo around this time. The screaming seemed constant; she would get into actual fistfights with both my brother and my dad. I pulled deeper and deeper inside of myself to escape the assault on my nervous system.

I wasn't a twitchy or jumpy kid, but I found myself walking on eggshells whenever I was home. Even during moments of peace and quiet I was still on high alert for the next catastrophe. At any given moment, and for reasons beyond my control, Mom would lose her shit and the cacophony would begin once more.

For many years, I was tossed around on a perfect storm of stress, with little hope of either clear weather or solid ground.

* * *

I don't remember why we moved from LeFrak City to Bayside. I was eight years old and not thrilled about changing schools. I was a good student back then. Truth be told, I was a good student all the way into college. Getting good grades was about the only thing I could control in my life, so I lost myself in my studies most of the time. Good grades also gave me some gold-star points with my parents. It was nice to have a steady stream of stellar report cards for Mom to be proud of. It kept me out of her crosshairs…at least temporarily.

This was about the time my siblings abandoned ship. By now, Sandi was long gone. She was an exceptionally smart student and left for college when she was just fifteen years old. She was accepted into the Pratt Institute in Brooklyn, choosing to live on campus despite being less than an hour away on the subway.

Michael chose a different route. Or to be more precise, a different route chose him. This was right in the middle of the Vietnam era. The United States entered the ground war in 1965, and the draft was running on all cylinders by 1968. Michael's draft number was eight; he was going into the service one way or the other. Michael is as tough an hombre as there is, but he was really nervous about going to war.

Our dad was a combat veteran, having served as a Naval pilot in World War II. He understood good and well what Michael's draft number meant, so he made a few phone calls. Dad pulled some strings to have Michael enlist in the Naval Reserves when he was still seventeen. By the time we moved to Bayside, Michael was stationed in Guam.

This whittled our family down to three. At eight years old, I was practically an only child with a crazy alcoholic mother at the helm. Without Sandi or Michael, the full force of Mom's alcoholic rage was turned on me and Dad.

As I mentioned earlier, Mom hurt her back soon after we moved. She was wheelchair-bound and hammered on Dilaudid (hydromorphone), or whatever pain killers and tranquilizers she was prescribed that week. Plus she downed her usual dose of booze on top of it.

It was ugly. I know I joke around a lot…but it was ugly.

Half the time she was beating me with a coat hanger or a hairbrush, and the other half of the time she was numbed out on pills and forcing me to come cuddle with and love her.

To make matters more confusing, Mom began to relish the attention she got from strangers when I pushed her around in public in her wheelchair. She learned to play the "sick role," which extended her wheelchair stay by years and years. I was pretty sure her back had healed, but she insisted upon maintaining her personal drama so she could bask in the sympathy and well-wishes of passers-by.

Until then, "truth" never seemed seem like a fluid concept to me. I had been a sharp kid, and I knew what I saw when I saw it. But then, reality started to bend just a little. What was real and what was bullshit began to swirl into a big crock-pot of insanity. My fucked-up mother was an unpredictable Jekyll-and-Hyde creature. Her back injury was healed and not healed. My workaholic dad was here but not here. I was supposed to be a kid, but I was doing all the cooking, cleaning, and caretaking.

The chaos got to me. Most of the time, I didn't know if I was coming or going; if I was angel or devil, hero or villain. I wondered if it was possible to be both at the same time. My little brain was breaking.

It's a wonder I didn't become a serial killer.

As far as you know.

Insert tension-breaking chuckle here.

21

But wait! There's more!

At this point, Dad decided he'd had enough of this shit. I can't say I blamed him. Mom made his life a big bowl of chaos soup just like she did with mine. Except Dad was an adult and had options I did not have. I was about to get left behind again. This time, it was for keeps.

Dad announced he was filing for divorce and that Mom could go fuck herself.

It scared the shit out of me. I wasn't sure of what it would be like to live alone with Mom, but I was absolutely certain it would be horrific.

However, something strange happened. I dare say it was even stranger than what was already happening. Mom used her craziness to her advantage. I didn't find this out until many years later, but behind the scenes, Mom and Dad had a come-to-Jesus conversation. Mom told Dad that if he divorced her, she would sue the shit out of him and tell the courts he constantly abused her and the kids while they were together. Her goal would be to ruin him financially and take full custody of me.

He believed her. I know I would have.

So instead, they struck a deal. Their marriage would become more of a business arrangement than a romance. Almost overnight, "Team Young" became "The Young Corporation." In exchange for Mom not fabricating a story about being a victim of long-term domestic abuse, Dad would agree to live in the same house and support her financially. They further agreed that they didn't have to sleep together or even be nice to each other. This union was to be solely transactional.

Their marriage became cold and lifeless. One hell of a template for me to learn about life and relationships.

Their new situation became my routine. I tip-toed through the fire of Mom's temper and the ice of my parents' marriage. I pushed Mom around the pool every summer and did all the chores around the apartment. I did well in school, which was both a blessing and a curse. My mother and teachers were proud, but the knuckle-dragging troglodytes in my class were pissed whenever I'd fuck up the curve on the science test.

I evolved into a weird little outcast kid. When you're ten

years old and pushing your loudmouthed lunatic drama-queen mother in her wheelchair, the other kids—even the nice ones—look at you like you're a fucking freak.

Dad was gone every day until seven or eight at night. Mom was in and out of hospitals with one phantom ailment after another. This made me the latchkey kid that creeped out my classmates.

There was no way out. I couldn't sing "Hanky Panky", sit in the Mets' dugout, or hang with the mayor in the *New York Post* anymore. There were no more appearances on national television. No more entertaining people. Hell, now everyone steered clear of me.

I needed to find my own universe to escape to.

I needed to find the universe called "Music."

CHAPTER 2:
FREEDOM

Once I hit middle school, things changed for me. I discovered the curative power of music by way of the influence from my big brother and big sister. Music wouldn't always pave a clean and virtuous road for me to walk, but it was just what the doctor ordered when I needed to escape my disastrous life.

Sandi, for her part, was a huge fan of Motown, rhythm & blues, and soul. She exposed me to all the great black artists of the fifties and sixties. To be honest, this wasn't exactly what my peers listened to. But for me, it was close enough to be familiar, yet far enough away to be novel and wondrous.

When my brother got back from the navy, he brought his taste for old-school blues music home with him. I was getting into the popular music of the day, with a particular affinity for Led Zeppelin, The Allman Brothers, and Bad Company. Michael took pride in teaching me the roots of rock and roll. He led me down the rabbit hole of Howlin' Wolf, Big Mama Thornton, and Muddy Waters. Then we explored the influence of Ray Charles, Nat King Cole, and Dinah Washington.

My appreciation of music expanded well beyond anything the other middle schoolers around me could relate to. I felt a kinship with the artists and was able to fully appreciate the evolution of the songs on the radio. My mind became both a catalogue and a timeline of the modern era of blues-tinged rock and roll.

I loved music that was soaring and passionate, from angst-riddled and painful anthems to loving and hopeful ballads. It mirrored my life and captured my spirit in a way that made the rest of the world fade into the background. Music became a part of me; every sweet note soothed the creases burning in my desperate brain.

Music made my imagination run in every direction. I loved music, and I wanted to infuse it into my desire to entertain and make people happy. The person who gave me the impetus to follow that dream was a kid named Michael Jackson.

Man, I would listen to the Jackson 5 and marvel at how someone my age could get to be on stage, singing memorable songs, dancing effortlessly, and getting so much adoration and recognition. Although Michael and I were about two years apart, I didn't know or care about that. As far as I was concerned, we were the same damn age. He wasn't an adult doing things kids either couldn't or shouldn't do. Michael was a kid, doing *exactly* what I wanted to do!

He inspired me because he made me believe I could be a young entertainer, too. He belted out the songs like an old soul. His feet glided so smoothly across the stage. His talent brought him adoring fans. To twelve-year-old Ron Young, Michael Jackson was the coolest cat in the alley.

I buried myself in music. Quite often, Mom would too. She sat on the living room carpet and drank the days away—all the while listening to classic R&B music on her hi-fi stereo. Music poured into every room of the house, filling the gaps between the staccato fits of screaming and carrying on. Completely shit-faced, Mom would sing along with Nat King Cole…probably to find a modicum of happiness in her life.

I think I've just now realized that somewhere along the way, I got "scripted" to be inebriated while enjoying music. Music and alcohol paired up in my brain as if I was one of Pavlov's dogs. I saw

Mom do it so many times, that her actions infiltrated my young psyche and set it as the "normal" way to enjoy music.

That association carried into my adulthood. I have slept through (or "passed out during") some of the greatest concerts in history. In 1973, I saw Zeppelin at Madison Square Garden as they recorded *The Song Remains the Same*. Unfortunately, it was all a fucking blur because I was so tanked up. I couldn't take it in. I barely remember being there.

Yet, I couldn't imagine going to the concert any other way. I just figured it's what people are supposed to do. I saw Mom do it over and over again while I was a kid, so why not?

* * *

Before we go on, I want to make sure you understand something very important about me. Because frankly, I know that words have power—so I don't want mine to be taken the wrong way.

I was not raised with any semblance of hate for any group of people. For all my mom's faults, I can't think of a single episode where she disparaged any individual on the basis of a general category, such as race, religion, economic status, and so on. With that in mind, in this book, I'm going to use the term "Black" instead of "African American." To me, the more current term never really made a lot of sense, anyway. Lots of Black people in America don't have African lineage. Some have Caribbean lineage, while others have a big mix of different lineages. And furthermore, lots of Black people in this big world are not American at all. So, for this book, I'm sticking with Black, and I do so with all respect.

I truly do not want to be perceived as being poised against anyone without reason. Obviously, once you demonstrate that you're an unapologetic asshole, I will absolutely have a negative opinion of you. Until then, I treat everyone with dignity and respect.

It's how I want to be treated.

Anyway, I learned what I could about Black culture and the Black community through the music I loved. Man, I still remember seeing the stories on television about the civil rights movement. I was a little kid when the Watts riot broke out in Los Angeles.

That night, I made myself dinner—which was customary for

27

me when mom was (mercifully) passed out in her room. I plopped down in front of the little black-and-white TV I won at Shea Stadium and turned on the news.

On it, I saw footage of the police ordering their dogs to attack Black people and then turning fire hoses on Black people…who were merely trying to stand up for their rights. I still remember thinking: *How can this be okay? How is it okay to sic dogs or hoses on people who aren't doing anything wrong? Not doing anything other than wanting to get something to eat, or ride a bus, or go to school?*

Early moments like that gave me a strong sense of the injustices in the world. It also alerted me to the bubble I lived in; my pure white neighborhood kept me from experiencing the full dimension of humanity. Obviously, I didn't have those words when I was seven or eight years old. But the concept was not lost on me.

I started to understand. The world is bigger than my neighborhood, and I may seem just as unusual to someone from another place as they seem to me.

Throughout my adulthood, I have been extremely sensitive to how I come across to people. I've been the long-haired biker-looking guy with sleeved arms and a fully tatted back. I may look like I fit into a certain category, but I don't. Some motorcycle clubs are notorious for being anti-Semitic or anti-gay or anti-black, but I'm not that way. It makes no sense to me to be that way.

The first interaction I had with Black people growing up was with my neighbors in our Bayside apartment complex. The only Black family on my block lived next door to us. They were a super nice pair of college professors, Woodrow and Carolyn Bovell (I can't believe I still remember their names!). I really liked Mr. and Mrs. Bovell, but remember thinking about how they must feel out of place living here.

Their son was about my age, and his name was Matthew. Matthew had multiple sclerosis, which must have furthered his feeling of being out of place. Plus, Matthew was in a wheelchair; he barely had anyone he could relate to.

I became friends with Matthew. Since my mom was in a wheelchair, I had no qualms about hanging out with him. A lot of kids probably felt uncomfortable around him for one reason or another, but I didn't. We didn't hang out a lot, but we did play together some, just by virtue of living so close to each other.

The last I heard, Matthew was living in Illinois with his wife, Tricia. I wish them very well.

My next experience of being around and interacting with Black people happened when I was in middle school. By some strange twist of fate, I ran for class president—and I won. Somebody suggested I run for president. I don't remember who or why, but I figured, Yeah, why not? So I gave a few speeches and decided on a platform that included allowing kids to play basketball at recess. The basketball issue had become a *big* deal.

To provide some context, this was during the era of busing. I lived in Bayside, a predominantly White/Italian/Irish/Jewish middle-class urban neighborhood. However, Black kids started getting bused in from other parts of the city to go to school there.

We went from having almost no Black kids in school to now having hundreds of Black kids. Some of my friends had racist parents who instructed their kids to stay away from the Black kids. I never understood that because I had no experience with that point of view. My family never had an "us versus them" mentality.

A lot of racial tension was building up in the school. Just like the dichotomy I had lived with all of my life, I was able to make friends and happily coexist in both worlds. I made friends with a lot of Black kids because we shared a common interest in both music and sports.

Basketball was really coming into its own as the sport of choice for inner city Black kids. It sounds like a trope, but that doesn't make it less true. My White friends loved baseball and football, and my Black friends loved basketball.

Our school had basketball goals set up on the playground, but nobody was allowed to play on them. I honestly have no idea how this came to be, but I thought it was stupid. The school probably lost a ball over the fence in 1942 or some shit, and the goals were shut down since then. Either way, being able to see the goals without being allowed to play on them was supremely frustrating to my new friends.

From my point of view, it had nothing to do with race. I became aware of the frustration and set about to solve the problem. In fact, I would have never even recognized the problem had it not been for my buddy, Mark Johnson.

Mark was one of the kids who got bussed in. He sat next to

29

me in homeroom, and we started to get to know each other. Over time, we grew to be good friends. Somewhere along the way, he talked about how pissed off his neighborhood buddies were about the basketball situation.

I didn't perceive it as a racial issue, despite it apparently striking quite a chord with the Black kids. What hit me was that nobody was allowed to play basketball—regardless of whether they were Black or White. I remember thinking, *Well, yeah...that IS pretty fucked up.*

I figured I would try to do something about it.

In the end, I won by a landslide. Dichotomy paid off! I was able to secure votes from "both sides of the aisle," as it were.

Apparently, I was way more popular than I gave myself credit for. I honestly had no idea who I was in the eyes of my peers. Hell, I had no idea who I was, *period*. Now, I was middle school president.

However, my presidency didn't last long.

As every dichotomy goes, the other side of Ron Young poked out its ugly head. Most of my problems in life stem from this inner duality. Like two weeks later, for example—when I got arrested.

Yup. Arrested.

In fuckin' middle school.

Not a typo.

A couple of weeks after I got elected, the racial tension in school began to boil over. The White kids would enter the building at the back of the school, but the Black kids got off the buses at the front of the school. Somewhere in the middle, a bunch of fistfights would start.

Left to their own devices, the kids would not have fucking hated each other. But the parents had to fill their kids' heads with their own bullshit.

A rumor started going around school that there was going to be a big race war on campus. Keep in mind, we were fucking twelve years old. The whole idea was bat-shit crazy—but that didn't make it less real or less tense.

I must mention that I was a member of the Boy Scouts of America. Not even kidding. In the Scouts, I learned some of the best life hacks: how to roll a joint, how to unhook a girl's bra, and how to successfully navigate a plethora of other urban life skills.

Part of the Scouting experience included camping with my troop. Two important things came out of those excursions. First, I learned how to swim across the lake (in the dark) with my friends, so we could make out with the Girl Scouts at their adjacent camp. And second, I owned a rather impressive Bowie knife.

Which led directly to my arrest.

With the prospect of a race war hanging over the school, I decided to come prepared. Any war requires the masses to be properly armed, right? One morning, I tucked the Bowie knife into my sock on the way to school.

Because I'm me, and because I have no actual practical skills when it comes to truly being a badass, I got caught before the school day could even get started. A teacher noticed the handle of my Bowie knife sticking out the bottom of my pant leg. She sent me to the principal's office, and, out of abject fear of a middle-school kid, he called the police. The police arrived and promptly arrested me.

My "permanent record" might still reflect the deadly weapons charge I think they wanted to slap on me. It was humiliating.

Thus, my run as a violent warlord came to a screeching halt. This also ended my run as middle school president. I was impeached before I even hit puberty. Probably a world record, although I have never thought to look into it.

But that was me—the guy who lived on both sides of the fence. Middle school president AND knife-wielding guerrilla. A kid who could hang out and blend with fucking anyone, man.

At the time, Queens had kids who would regularly go to temple or church, study, and stay the course. It also had kids who would do drugs and steal cars. And I was friends with all of them.

The dangerous shit was fun, but I knew I wasn't very good at it. I just hung back and hung out—part of the cool kid crowd. And we listened to great music.

Freedom, baby. Freedom.

* * *

All this coolness was in stark juxtaposition to my internal reality.

I was thrust into a bizarro world. By day, I was going to school; one bee buzzing in a hive with hundreds and hundreds of other bees. I did well with my grades, but this was the New York City Public School System. The bar wasn't set too high when it came to academics.

Then by night, I was living in a small apartment with my fucked-up mother.

I had carried the burden of "golden child" throughout my youth. All the chaos and the drinking and the screaming—I just wanted it to stop. I did everything I knew how to do to make it stop.

But it would never stop.

I didn't know it at the time, but I needed to change the internal script that choreographed my life. The script that said I needed to please everyone all the time. The script that said I should avoid conflict at all costs. Conflict leads to fistfights which lead to trips to the emergency room which leads to the police showing up which leads to more drinking which leads to more conflict and more fistfights, yadda, yadda, yadda.

When you're a people pleaser, you desperately want everyone to like you. Hell, everyone *does* like you…but no one truly respects you. This can drive you to make bad life decisions because you never stand up for what you feel is right or for what you need in a situation. Instead, you give in and accommodate the wishes and needs of others. Period.

And that was me.

A little kid has no experience or brain space to navigate this severe internal conflict: trying to love their mother while simultaneously hating her fucking guts because of the kind of person she is.

Music became the ombudsman, the mediator. It negotiated a truce between the two warring factions in my adolescent brain. It took me out of a bad place and brought me to a peaceful place. It was also the connective tissue that held my friend groups together.

Music was a huge part of culture back then. That doesn't seem to be the case anymore. I think the constant availability of all music any time (via the internet) has lessened the impact of new singles and new albums on release. Heck, radio stations don't have a fraction of the clout they used to have when it comes to influencing listeners.

Back then, music was our identity.

I remember hanging out in front of the apartment complex and talking about whichever album just came out. Then one of my friends would get their hands on the vinyl, and we would rush to their place to give it a spin.

Nobody ever came to my place, of course. I had the creepy drunk mom in the wheelchair. But that didn't stop me from spending as much time as I could at my friends' apartments. Music became the hub of everything I did socially.

As I moved through my teens, my thoughts turned almost exclusively to music. My social activities centered on it. My friends and I hung out at the music store, camped out overnight to be first in line for concert tickets, and attended the live shows together.

Freedom sounded a lot like music. And then music opened the door for freedom to be partnered with another escape: alcohol and drugs.

* * *

When I got to be fifteen or sixteen years old, getting high felt like the missing link. Stress was a constant passenger in my mind's vehicle—but drinking and getting stoned made the ride so much smoother.

I didn't have the perspective to fully understand how profoundly fucked up my domestic situation had gotten. However, my inner voice told me time and time again that something wasn't right. Drugs made it tolerable. Drugs and music made me feel...*free*.

Mom loved when I would spend time away from home with my friends or sleep over at one of their houses. It was like a vacation for her. She could drink herself into oblivion without having to worry about yelling at her kid.

That became my routine. I would hang out with my friends and listen to Led Zeppelin and smoke shitty Mexican dirt weed. Those years felt like an out-of-body experience. I floated on a hazy purple cloud while going through puberty, learning about girls, and finally feeling like I was fitting in.

Don't get me wrong; I've always had friends. I played little league and pulled pranks with my buddies at school. But I still felt like an outsider. Mom made my life awkward.

Mom made *me* awkward.

Hell, all of my friends' parents were friends with each other. Not mine. My mom was the drunk weirdo that the other adults went out of their way to avoid. No Canasta or Mahjong clubs for her.

Maybe it was all in my head. Maybe the other kids accepted me at face value, and I wasn't really as much of an outsider as I thought I was. Who the fuck knows? I might have created a weird dynamic for other kids because I felt so weird myself.

Either way, music and drugs pulled me into a realm I had never experienced before. At least, I never *thought* I had experienced before. All of a sudden it didn't matter. I was one of the guys. Truly.

It was a simpler time. When it wasn't.

So, at fifteen and sixteen years of age, freedom allowed me to look at the future. When you're in your teen years, that's the one crisis everyone around you has to face. It's a rough transitional period out of childhood and into adulthood. Everyone you know starts to pick their path. Some drop out of school. Some focus on their studies. Some join street gangs. Some get pregnant. Some are good at sports, so they double down on their long-term athletic goals.

For me, all I could think of was, *I have to get the fuck out of here.*

I knew I had to escape from my mother. I was biding my time until I could break away. I was serving a prison sentence, scrawling tally marks on the wall of my cell, counting the days until my release.

My neighborhood, for all its bumps and warts, was actually a solid, middle-class neighborhood. Many of my friends had parents who were professionals in the community, working their way into the American dream. Over time, I saw them accumulate wealth and purchase real houses just past the fringes of the apartment complexes.

They got away; they moved forward…just like I wanted to do.

I assessed my options. Progress couldn't wait until I got my driver's license…but it didn't have to. This was around the time when my friends would either buy their first car or their parents would gift them one. Freedom now grew a set of wings. We could get stoned, drive around, listen to music, and make out with girls. We were teens caught between the reckless impulsivity of childhood and the greater consequences and responsibilities of adulthood.

You could be one of the obedient, compliant ones. Or you could get in a lot of trouble.

I had my foot on both sides of the line.

At that point in my life, I still battled with what I was. Was I a hero or a villain? I did very well in school, but I was also developing an addictive personality. Dirt weed was nice for a while, but it just wasn't enough.

It paled compared to pills.

Eventually, some of the people I hung out with would show up with a handful of pills. They probably found them in prescription bottles stolen from their mother's or grandparents' medicine cabinets. We swallowed the pills, no questions asked, and then sat back and listened to the latest Black Sabbath 8-track.

I had an addict for a mother, but I knew nothing about addiction itself. I didn't understand my tendency to overindulge.

For example, a buddy of mine showed up before school one morning with some pills. I didn't know what exactly they were, so I guessed at their relative strength based on their size. They sure seemed small to me.

So I took two.

Needless to say, I never made it to school that day. I passed right the fuck out and slept in the back of my buddy's car until eight o'clock that night.

Not that he gave a shit. That idiot ignored my comatose ass and actually drove us to school. I remained passed out in the back seat of his car—*in the school parking lot*—throughout the entire day.

After school, he drove home. *His* home. With me still passed out in the back seat.

Yup. Parked at his family's apartment complex and left me in the back seat. Then he went inside to have dinner and watch TV. Not a care in the world.

Asshole.

This time, my dual identity saved my ass. Two days after I took those two little pills, I took my SATs…and I scored really well.

However, my ability to pull victory from the jaws of defeat actually turned into a long-term problem. I started to figure out that I could get away with shit my peers couldn't get away with. I had the mental horsepower to excel, despite hammering my brain with enough substances to lose an entire day to a back seat snooze-fest.

And that's the way it went until my senior year. I partied like a sailor on leave, but still managed to eek out As and Bs in all of my classes. In short, I enjoyed the fuck out of high school.

In 1977, something happened that made me realize—with clarity—that I absolutely had to get out of this place. In the end, it was a tragedy that helped me make up my mind to go to college.

* * *

When I was around seventeen years old, angel dust made its way into my world. Guys in our neighborhood started manufacturing and selling it. It would take another year for it to officially become illegal in the United States, so not many people knew a whole lot about it. Here's what I did know: that shit fucked you up. Everyone around me knew it, too. We had a front row seat to living proof of how bad that stuff was.

Because everyone knew Allen Kinitsky.

Allen was a few years older than me, but we ran in the same circles. I remember we called him Poindexter when we were kids because he wore big, thick-rimmed glasses. We played in the same little league, for goodness sake.

Then this particular drug hit the scene. Allen began to smoke angel dust, and shit got dark for him real fast. One night, he came back to the Bayside apartment he shared with his parents. His dad was asleep on the couch and his mom was awake in the kitchen.

Allen and his mother got into an argument about something. We'll never know what the argument was about because he picked up a kitchen knife and proceeded to beat and stab her to death.

Just like that, his life changed forever.

It didn't stop there.

He freaked out and realized what he had done. But instead of turning himself in or going on the lam, he went into the living room and beat and stabbed his dad to death, too. He killed both parents in an angel dust-induced haze.

According to the news, Allen laughed while he was booked for the crimes.

It. Fucks. You. Up.

As you can imagine, this news sent shock waves through the neighborhood. Allen had been a good kid, but angel dust turned him into a piece of shit. How could this happen?

And that was the turning point. Things were starting to change around me. I had to get out of there. I had to. I had to get out of there because if I didn't, I knew what would eventually happen to me.

Knowing how well I had done on the SATs, and knowing how much I liked science, I decided that college would act as my Wonka's Golden Ticket. I set about to apply myself toward mastering the next phase of life.

* * *

Following high school graduation, I chose SUNY (State University of New York) Stony Brook for college. The pre-med program was strong, which appealed to my love of science. Plus, the school was only 90 minutes away, in the middle of Long Island. The distance was far enough that I needed to live there, but close enough that I could hustle home if I had to.

SUNY Stony Brook was a public state school. My dad didn't have a lot of money, so we were deliberate to choose a school that could fit within our middle-class budget.

Dad helped me pack up my shit for the move to my dorm. In near-total silence, he drove us to the school. He parked the car, walked me into the dorm, and then down the hallway to find my room.

This was a typical freshman college dormitory in the late 1970s. My room had colored lights. The smell of weed and the howls of Led Zeppelin wafted throughout the hallway. The dorms had all the madness you would expect from a bunch of idiotic 18-year-old boys getting away from home for the first time ever.

We went back outside, still without speaking, to unload my belongings. Dad tossed them from the trunk of the car and onto the dorm's front lawn. I watched in silence, waiting to begin transferring the pile into my room. I guess Dad had other plans for himself. He must have had a plane to catch or a hot dinner date to attend.

Because my dad looked at me and said, "Well, good luck!"

And with that, he hopped into his car and sped off.

My father was apparently not much for long, drawn out, tearful goodbyes.

He fucking left me standing there.

But don't shed a tear for me following this flagrant dump-and-run. As I watched his car disappear around the corner, all I could think to myself was, *This…is…fucking…G-R-R-REAT!*

I had finally gotten away from my mom. I had full rein to be whoever the fuck I wanted to be. The guys in the dorm were smoking weed, they were listening to the music I loved, and there were girls as far as the eye could see.

I soon learned that the girls were actually even closer than I had thought. The floor on which we lived in Benedict Hall was E-0. If you walked up one flight of stairs, you found yourself on floor E-1, looking down a row of thirty rooms that were all filled with girls!

It was a glorious happenstance that I got randomly placed into Benedict Hall, Party Central of SUNY Stony Brook. It was a coed dorm, where each floor alternated between all-male and all-female students. These were the halcyon days of cocaine, Quaaludes, and disco. Free love and bad weed were the popular standards, and punk rock was making its way across the pond to the States.

Benedict Hall also had a completely functioning bar located in the dead center of the building. The bar featured a huge Bose sound system and pool tables. It opened early in the evening and stayed open until three or four in the morning. It was run by the students.

Can you believe that? Who came up with that brilliant idea? A fucking bar in my dorm!

If anyone would have pulled me aside that day and asked what I wanted to be when I grew up, I would have said, "Fucking numb and fucking laid!"

It's a wonder none of us died.

I was liberated. A kid in a candy store. I got to choose whatever the hell I wanted to be. I became completely unfettered, like someone who was paroled from the prison of his life.

I barely attended any of my classes. I pissed away the days playing pool, popping 'ludes, and snorting lines. My goals shifted from getting good grades to figuring out how to get a girl's pants off her. The little devil in my head tied up the little angel in my head and threw it into a woodchipper. For the first time in my life, I looked forward to each new day.

Alas, I wouldn't stick around long enough to see my college graduation. However, a lot of extremely cool things happened between the day I moved into Benedict Hall and the day I moved to Los Angeles.

I'm amazed I lived to tell the tale.

CHAPTER 3:
COAST TO COAST

I'm sure I had every intention of being some kind of doctor when I entered college. I didn't sign up with the exact plan of, "I'm going to blow through all my dad's money and then disappear to the West Coast!"

But dude…once the barn door opened, this wild mustang ran free.

My first roommate was a badass fifth-degree black belt in judo or ju-jitsu or some other martial art. He was cool; we got along well, given that we didn't know each other from Adam when the semester began. It was nice to be paired with a guy who could kick anyone's ass if they tried to steal our stuff or tried to fuck up our shit.

Over the semester break I changed roommates for a very brief period. Nothing against the black belt guy, but everyone switched around back in those days. The brief domestic arrangement is very blurry to me. I can't for the life of me remember the poor guy's name, but it was through this short-lived cohabitation that my academic bobsled skittered even further off course.

* * *

The community of Stony Brook is on the north side of Long Island and is a part of Suffolk County, easily one of the richest counties in America. In fact, the township of Southampton lies within a stone's throw (pardon the pun) of Stony Brook. It's part of the stretch of shoreline you have probably heard of, as it is commonly referred to as "The Hamptons."

It should come as no shock that many of the students at Stony Brook came from significant family wealth. My roommate's girlfriend was Laura Rorer, daughter of William Rorer III—grandson of William Rorer, founder of Rorer Pharmaceuticals.

This is starting to sound a lot like the gospel according to Matthew, explaining how Jesus descended from Abraham.

Two things about Rorer Pharmaceuticals: First, they were a small company until the old man developed and sold Maalox in 1949. Sales of Maalox blew the fuck up, bringing William Rorer a shit-ton of money.

Second, Rorer also developed and sold Quaaludes, a portmanteau of "quiet interlude" and Maalox. 'Ludes aren't manufactured anymore because they were a highly addictive hypnotic sedative. Super effective if you used them to cure insomnia, but also super easy to use as a date rape drug. They worked fast and tended to interfere with memory—so the FDA shut down their manufacture in 1983 (National Center, 2022).

At that time, Laura was an heiress to the Quaalude empire. Uber wealthy and uber connected, as far as her access to pills was concerned.

These were the days where disco and punk overlapped. The days of Studio 54 and CBGB. The days of the New York Dolls, The Police, and The Talking Heads. New York was both the epicenter of cool music and the epicenter of partying with recreational drugs as if there was no tomorrow.

Laura had access. She would take us to a Rorer warehouse out on Long Island, where we would grease the security guard with $500 and make off with a pallet of Quaaludes.

I shit you not. We would waltz right in and make off with twelve large bottles, 500 pills per bottle. When we would throw a party, we'd have a big bowl of Quaaludes for people to sample.

All efforts toward higher learning ceased to exist during this era of my college education. I lived at the bar, rising up the ranks of pool sharks and hustlers. I was the Pablo Escobar of Quaaludes, and the Master of Ceremonies when it came to throwing wild galas on campus.

At one point (as you an imagine), my dad got pissed. My grade point average after the first semester of my freshman year was about a 1.8. Not the worst GPA ever seen in the history of college fuckups, but certainly not stellar. It was bad enough that my dad gave me a strongly worded lecture about wasting his money and my potential.

My reaction to his lecture was to double down on the mayhem. I'm fairly certain my GPA fell into the negatives each semester after that. I don't honestly know if that's mathematically possible. If it is, I accomplished it.

As college students are wont to do, I had to ask my dad for money every time I needed something. It wouldn't have been kosher to mention that I was burning through my resources on cocaine and booze, so I kept those superfluous details to myself.

In the end, Dad cut me off. He ordered me to get a job… which I did.

I got a job as busboy in a high-end steakhouse off campus. My status as social kingpin took another leap forward because I used this job to feed the masses. Whenever one of the restaurant patrons did not finish their steak or their lobster, I would throw the remains into a to-go box. These would collect throughout the evening, padded by mistakes and other random food portions that the chefs would have no use for.

When I would return to the dorm at two in the morning, I would have about $1,000 worth of high-end food in tow. All the stoners and drunk idiots would stay up late and wait for me to return, and then descend upon the food like locusts on a wheat field.

Technically, I was working. I had a job and never showed up late for a single shift. Dad was happy because I wasn't shaking him down for cash anymore. My peers were happy because I was a steady stream of drugs and food.

And I was happy because I was making everyone else happy. People Pleasing 101.

It was absolute bedlam, man. I would be up all night partying, and then sleep through my classes the next day. My internal clock became that of a vampire—up all night, sleep all day.

I blame the administration at SUNY Stony Brook. They were the ones who stuck me in Benedict Hall, right? Had they placed me anywhere else on campus, I am certain to have been a model student, possibly graduating with a degree in electrical engineering like my old man. I would have built churches, hospitals, and rescue missions for wayward puppy dogs. I would have probably died an American hero, with government buildings, highways, and a national holiday named in honor of me. People far and near would have exalted my very name.

Ron Young! Ron Young! Ron Young!

And if you believe THAT crock of shit, I've got a bridge to sell you.

I cut back on my class load. I explained to my dad that it was really hard to wade through the pre-med curriculum. Looking back, he probably knew exactly what I was up to, but he never said a word. He was mostly interested in making sure I could support myself, no matter what that looked like. He was a bright guy and knew I had to spread my wings. If nothing else, Dad knew the score of the game at home. He understood what I had lived through to get to this point.

If there is a God, S/He certainly has a twisted sense of humor.

* * *

The 1.8 GPA wasn't going to springboard me into a good medical school. I knew those slots were extremely competitive and populated by students, whose worst semesters were light-years better

44

than my best semester.

My initial desire to be a physician had nothing to do with humanity or saving the planet. It was strictly an economic decision, since I was interested in, and good with, science. When I realized medical school wasn't in the stars for me, I considered other science-based options that paid well.

My first thought was to go into a chiropractic program. At that time, the field sounded like a lot of voodoo to me, but what the hell. Unfortunately, I fucked around too long to even have a shot at chiropractics, so I kept lowering the bar as I went along.

Next, I thought about becoming a medical researcher. That idea lasted about five minutes before The Ultimate Truth landed on me: I have to make music.

At that point, it was clear that I was never going to graduate. I had no interest in academics anymore. I was out on the town every weekend seeing great bands. There was nothing that came *close* to stirring the passions in me like music did.

During the college transition from academia to music, I met my first wife, Marlana. And once we met, things progressed very quickly between us.

She and I met at the bar in my dorm. I was certainly no flittering social butterfly back in those days. But by second semester, my friends and I knew most of the girls who lived in our dorm. The ones who liked to party, that is.

Other random Stony Brook students would drop by and hang out at our building, too. Being The Party Headquarters meant we were a beacon for anyone who wanted to unwind and relax after class. When a newbie arrived, it wouldn't take long for them to decide if this scene was right or wrong for them, and vice versa.

I first noticed Marlana on a particularly cold night on Long Island. She was fucking cute—but what really got my attention was the t-shirt she wore. It said, "Oui." As many of you degenerates will remember, Oui was the name of a particular soft core pornographic magazine which was quite popular among my peer group.

That should give you a good idea of where my head was at.

I made my move. I had some decent game back in the day. Say what you will about dorky Ron Young, but I was a smooth, silver-tongued cat in 1979, if I do say so myself.

Don't judge.

When Marlana and I first came face to face, it was like a great magnet pulled us together. It only took a couple minutes for me to realize that she was different from the hundreds or thousands of other girls who blew through this bar. Something about her was immediately special to me.

She had a great vibe; she was cool and she was beautiful.

I was smitten.

She came back to my room that night. We stayed up all night and talked and hung out and whatever.

Yeah, we whatevered. Probably more than once. We still didn't know if we had a lot in common—that wasn't what pulled us together. What we did have was strictly carnal; we were two peas in a pod.

I was in love, or whatever passes for love when you're a horny nineteen-year-old guy. She moved in with me the very next day, and we remained together for nearly twenty years.

Throughout the totality of our relationship, I put that poor woman through hell. She was with me through the absolute darkest days of my life—darker than even the ones I spent living with my crazy mother. Marlana put up with my shit for as long as she could. As long as *anyone* could.

Marlana was also with me through the absolute best days of my life. Back when music was new, fresh, and exciting. Back when life itself was still in the original shrink wrap and had that "anything is possible" smell. Back when she and I made important decisions that would shape the rest of my life.

* * *

Neither Marlana nor I were into academics. We were both very smart, but we were more into living life first-hand rather than wasting time in a windowless classroom. We loved good food, good music, and good parties. They say you're only young once, and we took full advantage of every moment we could.

Most of our time was spent away from campus. New York City was a siren song that pulled us back almost every night. We

46

went to bars and clubs and saw every live music event we possibly could. Two years flew by in the blink of a drum roll.

Meanwhile, back at Stony Brook…

I entered the final semester of my illustrious college career with a whopping .1 GPA. No need to take off your glasses and rub your eyes—you read that correctly. As Vic Perrin said at the opening of every episode of the old television series, *The Outer Limits*, "There is nothing wrong with your television set. Do not attempt to adjust the picture."

My poor dad. He had such high hopes for my career as a strait-laced professional. He had no preparation to understand the person I had become. I was growing my hair long and accumulating a growing number of tattoos. I was out of excuses for my bad grades, and I eventually quit reporting to school altogether. I was on my way into the underground world of music.

My dad would not have gotten too judgmental about my choices. He ultimately wanted for me to be happy, and I was happy in The City.

Where I wasn't happy was Stony Brook.

Stony Brook as a community was awesome. I made friends that I'm still connected to today. I loved the parties and the exciting world of freedom. But the classes and studies weren't for me. When it was time to go, it was time to go.

Marlana and I picked up and moved into New York City. We continued to go to clubs five or six nights per week. We were the ultimate music fans.

I was not a musician. I was a fan. I loved listening to the process of making music and its end result, but I had no formal training or genuine knowledge of the craft. I know that for most musicians, their childhood and adolescence was spent strumming chords on the guitar or taking piano lessons. Not me. My dad couldn't afford that shit.

Hell, I was 21 or 22 years old, and I still had no idea if I could sing. Sure, I'd sing along to the radio when we drove around in a car, but so would all my other idiot friends. I had no way of knowing if I was any good or not. I just did what everyone else did.

When people ask how I got involved in the music industry, I tell them it was destiny. I don't know that I ever had a choice in the matter. Marlana and I were going to so many clubs and seeing so many bands, I came to realize that nothing in the world moved me or stirred my passions like music did. It gave me pleasure that transcended anything else I had ever experienced.

That might sound overly dramatic, but I am my mother's son. Still, I swear to God that is absolutely how I feel. I went into music because I don't believe I could have not gone into music. I would have ended up here eventually, one way or the other.

My decision to start a musical career came about one afternoon while talking it over with Marlana. She had heard me sing many times—probably in the shower, where I am a maestro. And to her credit, she thought I was pretty good. Without her support and encouragement, I could not have mustered the courage to do it. Sure, I was cocky—but I didn't have balls of steel. What I *did* have was a great cheerleader in Marlana. The chutzpah I needed to be a performer all came from her.

It was 1980 in New York City. The City was positively vibrant in those days, exploding with a great music scene. I already mentioned one club, CBGB, which stood for Country BlueGrass and Blues. But the Mud Club, the Peppermint Lounge, Max's Kansas City, and many other venues also ushered in the new sounds and attitudes of both the musicians and the fans. Along with the emergence of punk and metal, a resurgence of blues and rockabilly hit the scene.

Rockabilly as a genre wasn't all that new. It came into its own in the early 1950s, thanks to artists like Carl Perkins, Elvis Presley, and Jerry Lee Lewis. The sound was a combination of early blues-rock (the "rock" in "rockabilly") with western swing and bluegrass (the "hillbilly" part of the word "rockabilly"). However, the popularity died down a little in the early 1960s, not long after the plane crash that killed Buddy Holly, Richie Valens, and the Big Bopper.

In the 1970s, nostalgia for 1950s music emerged in London clubs. Dave Edmunds and Nick Lowe formed the band Rockpile and brought rockabilly back to the United States. When they arrived, they wore their hair in pompadours and dressed in fifties-style clothing. This inspired new genres like psychobilly and gothabilly, which combined rockabilly and punk. Bands like The Cramps and the Stray Cats made the old sounds new again.

That's when I answered an ad in the *Village Voice* for a rockabilly lead singer. The band holding auditions was called The Kingpins, and they sounded like a good match for me.

I still had no idea if I could genuinely sing. I figured the band would judge whether or not the noises I made in time to the music qualified as "singing."

I remember almost nothing about the audition, but I got the gig. I was now a part of a great band put together by talented guys. The Kingpins were led by our guitar player and elder statesman, George Worthmore. He was supremely talented and was the real technician of the group. The rest of us were just snot-nosed punks. I was on vocals, Rich Thomas was on bass, and Brian Hudson was on drums.

photo credit: Julie Scher-Molinare

Brian came from Cleveland where he played in a punk band called The Pagans. When he got to New York City, he joined the band that became my foray into the music scene.

We were a damn good band; tight and professional, even in

49

those early days. We opened for nearly everyone who came through town. I was in hog heaven, doing the very thing I was meant to do. I was confident I had made the right decision. I still recall when the enormity of that realization gripped me.

* * *

In midtown Manhattan sits an unassuming building, with low-relief art deco panels above the windows of each floor. It is called, simply enough, The Music Building. Built in 1927 on Eighth Avenue and West 39th street, it's the largest music facility in New York, with 24/7 access to anyone who leases one of the 69 rehearsal studio apartments scattered throughout the building's twelve floors.

Because of its clientele, The Music Building was constantly filled with the most creative, vibrant, and supremely talented musicians in the world. For example, Madonna lived in the building when she was just starting out in New York.

I remember standing in the lobby waiting for the elevator one morning. I looked around and thought, *I'm home.* I inhaled the moment; it was so damn powerful, man. The significance of the moment hit me like lightning. I knew with 100% certainty this was it. This was what I would do.

The Kingpins' reputation and skill gained steam in the scene. In fact, the booking agent at The Peppermint Lounge became our manager and got us some sweet gigs opening for The Cramps, Johnny Thunders, and Bo Diddley.

Off stage, life was a freight train. I was excited to get the Kingpins gig, but that meant life shifted from fast to light speed. We popped Quaaludes, snorted coke, and hit every after-hours club we could cram into. The days bled into each other with no way to staunch the overall hemorrhage. Time both flew by and stood still; I had no awareness of it. New York City has a way of altering your perception like that.

During the day, I got jobs at Trash & Vaudeville, a famous second-hand clothing store, and The Unique Clothing Warehouse, another repository for unique threads. These jobs afforded me access to a limitless supply of amazing clothes. I had an extensive stage wardrobe of sleeveless T-shirts, tight jeans, leather jackets, loud bowling-league shirts, drainpipe trousers, and brothel creeper shoes to go with my perfect pompadour. Visually, I was the consummate front man of a rockabilly band.

The Kingpins were always decked out. We brought a sense of style and panache into the clubs as we wowed the fans packing the place that night. Those were some crazy times, man!

Personally, I was doing great. Performing made me feel comfortable in my own skin. If anything, I was far more comfortable in front of a couple hundred people than I was offstage and talking to fans one-on-one.

I often tell people that the profile of the typical music artist combines a grandiose sense of magic with a crippling sense of self-doubt. The self-doubt morphs into a tireless engine that drives the creative process.

That philosophy sounds bizarre to anyone who idolizes performers, but I've found it to be true more often than not. I got my first taste of working alongside brilliant artists during those early days performing with The Kingpins in New York.

One set of stories that best illustrates this philosophy involves the late, great Johnny Thunders. His creativity was supreme—but his insecurities drove a drug addiction that ultimately killed him.

The Kingpins opened for Johnny quite a bit during this era. Our music was the perfect pairing. His songs were a little edgier than ours, as he was definitely cut from the cloth of the New York punk scene. But we both delivered that bluesy/rockabilly sound.

If you know anything about Johnny Thunders that doesn't involve his love of music, it would probably be his penchant for partying. Heroin had been a part of New York City life since the beginning of the 1900s, with the kinds of users and the way it's consumed changing over twelve decades. It became a drug of choice for jazz musicians in the 1950s and spread to the rest of the music community from the 1960s onward. Johnny was the victim of a full-blown heroin addiction. His death in 1991 (at the young age of 38) has some controversy surrounding its circumstances, but nobody argues that drugs were definitely at the center of his demise.

The Kingpins shared a roadie (Pete) with Johnny and his band. On a handful of occasions, Pete would come find us to say that Johnny was passed out in the dressing room because he had OD'd on dope. We'd go throw water on him and do our best to walk him around—anything to get him upright for the show.

When Johnny would find himself in a financial bind, he'd tell the club owner that his guitars had been stolen. Of course, it wasn't true. But it put the owner over a barrel—he needed Johnny to perform. The owner would then loan him cash in the form of an advance of his performer's fee. Johnny, in turn, would use the cash to buy dope.

One night before a show, Pete came and told us that Johnny had gotten roughed up by a couple guys on the Lower East Side. Sure enough, Johnny was in his dressing room, royally pissed off. He'd gotten robbed, and then had the shit kicked out of him. Even worse, he hadn't scored any dope.

And such was his life. I watched it happen.

Some folks feel Johnny's death wasn't merely due to an overdose. They contend that foul play was involved. Hell, when you deal with drugs and drug dealers, you take a huge chance. Your life is what's at stake.

Addiction is hell.

* * *

By a stroke of interesting luck, the Kingpins managed to get Lenny Kaye to produce our first record. It was the very first thing I had ever recorded, and I was excited to learn that Lenny agreed to work with us. Lenny was the guitarist in the Patti Smith Group, one of the biggest names in the NY punk scene.

We respectfully asked Lenny what he would charge to work on our album, and he said he wouldn't charge us a single penny—if we helped him move his record collection to his new apartment in the Bowery.

That fucking guy! What he didn't tell us was that his new apartment was on the fifth floor, that there was no elevator in his building, and that he had over 70,000 albums. We hauled milk crate after milk crate after milk crate up those damned stairs. I think the whole move lasted five or six days. I just remember grunting up the narrow stairwell thinking, *We should have just fucking PAID this guy.*

New album in tow, The Kingpins knew we had to get out of New York and gig in new places to expand our fan base. Because our drummer Brian Hudson was from Cleveland, we piled our gear into a van and went to where he was sure he could get us a new audience.

We did a handful of extraordinary shows with a punk band called The Big Boys, which included guitarist Chris Gates. Chris went on to be signed as a part of the band Junkyard. He was also from Austin, Texas and talked us into playing gigs in the Lone Star State.

After playing a few shows with The Big Boys in Texas, we were ready to go back home to New York...until we were approached by a promoter. He presented us with an opportunity to open for a new guitarist and his two-person band. According to the promoter, this guy was on the verge of blowing up. From what I understood, he was a blues guitarist with an incredible range of jazz, rock, and blues music. He was also a very creative song writer with a playing style that was both adaptive and refined.

His name was Stevie Ray Vaughan.

Unfortunately for me, I did not read his name—I only heard his name from the promoter. In my mind, I thought, *Pfft, what a Texas Yahoo! His name is Stevie Rave-On?! Who does he think he is? Buddy Holly???*

Stevie and his promoter were both from Texas, which made his name make sense in a backwards kind of way. But our attitude was, *Yeah, what the hell. We'd be happy to open for the Yahoo.*

We showed up at a club called Fitzgerald's, in Houston. It was a nice place that held about 500 people. Except that night, there were about 50,000 bodies jammed into the place. It was packed to the rafters with exuberant people ready to have fun.

We hadn't experienced this kind of a crowd before: huge and boisterous. We were accustomed to small groups of disaffected New Yorkers who were too cool to clap—not a million cheering faces enjoying the shit out of the show and everything around it.

We did our thing and retired to the dressing room, which was just off stage left. But when Stevie took the stage, we had to come out to lay eyes on this guy. We were blown away; *Holy shit! This dude is amazing.*

And we weren't the only ones. The fans went absolutely apeshit crazy for Vaughan. He filled that place with music, the likes of which we had never heard before. His style was so unique and fluid. How could one person so cool be so on fire? The man had no choice but to succeed.

We met him after his performance, and he was a super fuckin' nice, down to earth guy. For example, while we were in Houston, we didn't have anywhere to stay. Stevie caught wind of this and invited us to stay with him. He was at a cheap, fleabag motel since no one was making any money back then. Yet, he was generous to the point of opening his door to us.

When we showed up to his room, the party was on. We drank and hung out for most of the night. Then, out of the blue, he tossed an envelope onto the bed. As the envelope skittered to a stop on the shitty bedspread, he said, "Here! This is for you guys."

I picked it up. "What's this?"

"Well listen, I know you guys only got paid about a hundred bucks tonight. We know how it feels to live hand-to-mouth and gig-to-gig, so we get you. It was a really good night for both us and the club. We'd like to share some of it with y'all. Consider this a little Texas hospitality."

There was $300 in the fuckin' envelope. We couldn't believe it. A budding—but still largely undiscovered—Stevie Ray Vaughan took money out of his own pocket so we could live a little while we were on the road.

You'd be hard-pressed to find another person so incredibly nice, empathetic, and supportive. We ended up doing three shows with him, and he did the exact same thing every night. I had nothing but respect for the man. He was a real guitar hero.

As it turns out, Stevie was a little like Buddy Holly. Both died young when their aircraft went down. Buddy Holly died in 1959 at the age of 22, and Stevie Ray Vaughan died in 1989 at the age of 35.

And the world got a little sadder after losing these two very talented artists and all-around good guys.

* * *

What a life.

I went from attending an academic university, filled with normal kids who wanted to get normal jobs and lead normal lives—to waking up each day and stepping into a river of histrionic energy. It was so much fun. But it couldn't last forever.

Once again, this time in 1984, the music scene started to change. Hip Hop became the new music in New York, and clubs repurposed themselves out of punk and rock and roll. Our punk rockabilly sound lost its home. Thus, the Kingpins disbanded.

George Worthmore is still out there, still killing it. He formed another band, The Divebombers. He also had a club in South Africa, and he did a little acting in a few movies.

Brian Hudson and I became close friends, and he was the best man at my wedding. He passed away back in 1991…not long after moving to Los Angeles.

As for Rich Thomas, he moved back to his Midwest roots. He owns a tattoo shop, a tattoo supply company, and is still scratching his musical itch. He too has "mellowed" with age.

So in 1984, I saw the writing on the wall. If I wanted to sustain a career in music, I had to move to Los Angeles. And that's exactly what Marlana and I did. We picked up, packed up, and moved across the country.

Surely, bigger things lay ahead.

CHAPTER 4:
BREAKING IN

When I moved to Los Angeles, I needed to find my musical identity…my direction. I wanted to establish myself and have a viable career. Rockabilly wasn't going to cut it on the West Coast on any major commercial level—particularly as the novelty of the Stray Cats started to wear off. Everyone getting record deals in those days was playing a new form of metal. It was infused with a strong blues influence, which did appeal to me. But the guys on stage carried an image I just could not pull off.

I acknowledge the contribution to music that 1980s metal brought to the table—big hooks, big looks, and the "monster ballad." Take a serious look at Mötley Crüe, RATT, Quiet Riot, Hanoi Rocks, and all the pioneers of the Sunset Strip music scene. They were the hedonistic answer to Ronald Reagan's conservative America. Most notably, they called out the hypocrisy of the conservative society when Dee Snider took on Tipper Gore, head-to-head, on Capitol Hill. He went up there to speak against the censorship efforts of the Parents' Music Resource Center.

But…that *look*. The aesthetic. The gender-bender androgyny. Their hair was teased out and back combed, their faces had loud makeup of near-drag queen proportions, and they stomped on stage in high heels night after night. I don't have that big of a personality.

Although the quality of the music was very polished, I just couldn't take the sound. The singers brought their pitch up to a higher key. My voice is not suited to such a high register—I'm not a castrati. I just couldn't get into that whole vibe. It wasn't my jam.

If I'm not all that, then what am I?

I'm an everyday, down-to-earth, working class kind of guy. I have a passion for motorcycles and the elbow-grease lifestyle that comes with it. I dress like a biker, tattoos and all. I wasn't one to haunt the strip clubs and I wasn't outrageous or larger than life. My voice has a natural rasp and low tonal quality that prevents me from singing in a high pitch like they did. Honestly, I just fuckin' didn't want to sing that high. It's not a good sound, especially coming out of me.

That's the direction I chose. I brought a working class, blue-collar vibe to my identity and my music. I've got the look of a motorcycle club without the dodgy element. And it worked. I went for the opposite of The 1980s Metal Scene.

The appeal and mystique of a motorcycle club is exactly what I was trying to recreate in my band. People will look at a band in a similar way they look at a motorcycle club. When the club rides by in a pack, everyone stops and stares. The onlookers secretly wish to pierce the veil and see what life is like behind that curtain. Awe-inspiring, mysterious, and powerful—but pragmatic, down-to-earth, and gritty. Just the way a band should be.

In fact, I purchased a Harley soon after arriving in California. The weather was always nice, and I was into bikes anyway. Seemed like a natural thing to do—and it was. It was fucking awesome. I wasn't in a club, but I certainly mused over the guys who were.

I got a job working the door at one of the bigger showcase clubs in Hollywood. I figured that if I was going to be in a band, I needed to get to know the owners and the talent bookers. What better place to meet other music people, too? Industry types frequented the clubs to assess the current talent, so other musicians would hang around to get noticed by the suits.

A win/win.

I got a second job working the door at another club out on the West Side. I'm amused every time I read somewhere that I worked as a bouncer in Los Angeles. Dude, I'm not a big guy. I know I looked scary, but I lack the killer instinct necessary to rush into a fight between people I don't know. I wasn't a bouncer—I was a doorman. I decided who to let in and who to leave out. Simple as that.

I wanted to build a career the blue-collar way. I embraced the lifestyle by rolling up my sleeves and getting to work. It was the only way I knew how to get things done.

In fact, the guys in Little Caesar used to help our one-and-only roadie set up the equipment. I'm not just referring to "back in the day" when we played shithole clubs. I'm including the time after we signed with Geffen, as well.

Talk about a blue-collar approach!

We were just being practical. Not only was it cheaper to go with a skeleton crew, but it didn't make sense to spend more money for more guys. We were mechanically inclined and perfectly capable of preparing the stage. Shit, with our goatees and tattoos and grimy jeans, people used to think we *were* the roadies.

Fans were so used to a rock band rolling up in a dazzling tour bus and then getting high and getting laid while the crew sets up the stage. Seeing us do the exact *opposite* shocked a lot of people.

We were just a bunch of guys taking care of business.

I loved the guys in Little Caesar. Getting us all together for the first time happened organically over a period of time.

* * *

The music scene in the mid-1980s Los Angeles was a breath of fresh air compared to what was happening New York after Hip Hop took hold. A ton of different things were happening all over the city. You had the Sunset Strip and the burgeoning glam metal movement exploding in West Hollywood. On the East side, there was a more colorful, counter-cultural movement featuring the newly conceived cow punk genre. This genre featured bands like Jason and the Scorchers, The Blasters, and other very cool post-modern punk bands populating the after-hours bars.

With such a wide swath of music being created in every corner of LA, I was never at a loss when it came to creative options. It was an exciting time to be in SoCal.

I took full advantage of everything the city had to offer, cruising from place to place on my new Harley. Soaking in the nightlife meant I was able to maintain my vampire-like schedule. I didn't see much of the sun, save for the short time it was rising and the brief window when it was setting.

That's an exaggeration of course, but I'm sure you're picking up what I'm putting down.

I played with a few different bands during this period. We would get together and rehearse, sometimes we would play a few gigs, other times we'd never make it out of the garage. The Holy

Grail for musicians back then was getting signed to a record deal. Of course, that didn't happen too often, but it didn't keep people from trying.

I met Tom Morris, Little Caesar's drummer, in one of those early bands called The Smilin' Jacks. Tom never quite matched the "tatted up-tough biker" image that Little Caesar carried. He was more of a "hang-loose surfer dude" from Santa Monica. But he was a solid drummer and a very nice, quiet, and down to earth guy. When Little Caesar came together shortly thereafter, Tom was the drummer I called.

The way it all happened was serendipitous. I had my biker look going—the goatee, the long hair, the biker vests. About this time, the popularity of Harley-Davidson bikes was picking up a lot of steam in California. Celebrities like Mickey Rourke, Sylvester Stallone, and Nicolas Cage led a renewed interest in the bikes and the motorcycle lifestyle.

Even some of our contemporaries tried to get in on the action. I won't out them publicly, but I remember a few famous pop metal bands approaching me to ask if they could use my bike for a photo shoot or a music video.

Fuckin' posers.

Kidding.

(Not really)

My career was coming together for me and ultimately for all the guys in Little Caesar. Glam metal wasn't going to work, but a new door opened in the music scene. A blue-collar mentality was generating a swell of interest; it was calling for a good ol' self-deprecating, down-to-earth, bluesy, working-man type of guy. Like me.

It happened exactly the way you'd think it would happen for us. We got together and bet on ourselves.

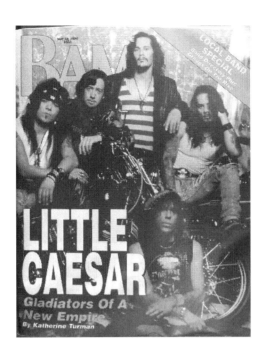

I assembled a group of guys who had the same outlook as me. I already knew Tom, so that call was easy. I got to know guitarist Loren Molinare from the club scene. He would hang out at clubs where I worked the door. We hadn't played together, but I knew he was eager to join a band and make some music.

Then came Fidel Paniagua. Loren knew him because he had dated Fidel's wife (before they were married) back in the day. Fidel was a solid family man and as loyal as they come. He was also a mechanic and managed a big custom hot rod shop in East LA. Like me, Fidel was deep into the whole motorcycle scene.

I can't remember who introduced me to Apache (a.k.a., Jimmy Hayne), but I do remember we first met at the door of Club Lingerie. Apache also had a grit that didn't fit in with the "beautiful people" on The Strip.

All these guys were talented and hard-working. More importantly, they were fun to be around and liked the same kind of music I liked. We were sick and tired of the over-produced sound of the current pop metal shit. We wanted to make good, guitar-based rock and roll again.

We were a rough looking band of rock and roll assholes. It

was an image that was both our saving grace and our tragic downfall. We didn't know it at the time, however. We were too excited just to catch the elevator on the way up.

* * *

I managed to make a deal with the suits. I approached talent buyers who booked the bands at each of the venues and presented them with a deal they couldn't refuse. I told them, "Look…give my band a support slot with a good show on a Saturday night. If we can't bring people in, don't ever book us again."

I put my dick on the table, as it were. Sure, it's a metaphor, but you never know. Those were some wild days.

But I wouldn't put my dick on just *any* table.

I knew that if we tried to generate interest by playing early-evening gigs to fifteen disinterested bar flies on a Tuesday night, we'd never get anywhere. We had to place ourselves in a position to win. Getting decision makers to see how we affected a big crowd was the most efficient way to accomplish that.

Finally, we got a slot—a headlining slot on a Saturday night. I made a few phone calls and reached out to all my biker friends, asking if they would please come out and support the band. Our first show was at a club called The Music Machine…and it was *packed*!

Incidentally, it was because of this showcase that we stumbled upon "Chain of Fools." We wanted to create a hard rock/soul vibe. Glammy, empty bullshit—where you compare your love interest to a common fruit-filled dessert—turned our stomachs. It was disposable music. We went back to basics.

From my perspective, I had always wanted to be an R&B guy in a shiny suit, singing and dancing on *The Ed Sullivan Show*. The Pips, the O'Jays, The Temptations—those cats had soul. The other guys in Little Caesar shared my affinity for that genre, so we picked our direction. A few days before the showcase, we landed on what would become our signature tune.

I threw out the idea. "Hey—what if we did an Aretha Franklin song…but play it like AC/DC?"

The seed was planted. Everyone went home and listened to

Aretha's version of "Chain." The next day, everyone came back with a tape of their own bastardized version. It was still in the early phases of development, but we all knew there was definitely something here. We liked the song, and had some really clever and creative ideas for making it our own.

We sewed together the best riffs, thus finalizing our version of the classic R&B song. We had no intention of breaking new ground with this rendition. We merely wanted to throw all of our influences into a crock pot and see what kind of tasty dish we could serve.

Everyone in the band was a fan of music long before they became a maker of music. And now, by combining improvisation and careful curation, we had a sound.

We cobbled together a few originals to go along with "Chain of Fools." Then we rehearsed until we were tight and fully prepared (ha!) for the big show.

* * *

Over 100 motorcycles lined the street in front of the club that night. Our people arrived in droves—and we fuckin' *killed* it. It was 1987, and glam metal hadn't yet swept the country. That said, glam was hot and heavy in Los Angeles. So everyone we knew locally was looking for a change back to the way it used to be—Foghat, Lynyrd Skynyrd, AC/DC, and the like.

As luck would have it, exactly the right guy was in the audience. A guy named Chuck Reed, who was the personal assistant to super producer, Jimmy Iovine.

Chuck loved what we did. He reported back to Jimmy that he found a band totally different from anything else flooding the industry. Jimmy, to his credit, was never a particular fan of pop metal. He cut his teeth with the likes of Bruce Springsteen, Tom Petty, and Patti Smith.

A few days later, I received a phone call. The voice on the other end explained that he (Chuck) had seen us at The Music Machine and wanted to introduce me to a guy.

In hindsight, I have no idea how Chuck Reed got my home number. But he stuck me on the phone with Jimmy Iovine.

Jimmy and I had a long conversation, during which I expressed loyalty to my guys. Jimmy had a reputation of breaking up the components of bands he discovered. If there was a weak link, Jimmy would oust the guy and replace him with a new one.

That was a no-fly for me. I explained that my band was like a motorcycle club. Our membership was sealed; nobody comes or goes without full consent of the club. We wanted to work with him, but he had to promise to let us be who we are.

He totally understood and agreed. After a two-hour phone call, Jimmy Iovine was our new manager. He assigned a guy named Tony Ferguson to take over our day-to-day operations, and Tony ended up staying with us for our entire run with Geffen.

Tony was fantastic. He had the best disposition to handle our band; we never got too full of ourselves with Tony at the helm. Within six months, he told us, "Enough with this playing in Hollywood bullshit. I don't want you guys burning yourselves out."

With that, he had us cherry pick the best shows to do. To his credit and his affiliations, we got real hot real quick. Every night was like an A&R-fest. Once word got out that Jimmy was our manager, every label sent their advance scouts to sniff around and do a little reconnaissance on us.

Incidentally, A&R stands for "Artists and Repertoire." An A&R guy works for a record label and scouts for new talent. They find a band or artist they think has potential, and then recommends them to the label. If the label agrees to sign the artist, the A&R guy acts as a sort of liaison between the label and the artist/manager. The A&R guy isn't necessarily the artist's friend—they represent the label in all creative matters by looking out for the label's best interest. It's the manager's job to look out for the artist.

I've always thought of A&R guys as suffering from Ben Franklin Syndrome. A lot of people will claim that Benjamin Franklin invented electricity. Franklin didn't invent electricity; he invented different ways to harness it. A&R guys like to think they created the bands they discovered—but not so. They just think of ingenious ways to harness us.

We had A&R guys crawling all over us. For me personally, this was the most surreal period of my life. Things were happening so fast that my head spun like the little girl's in The Exorcist. I didn't get much sleep for a full two years. I worked as a doorman and played music by night. I also worked as a dispatcher for a messenger service by day. My dad instilled a solid work ethic in me, which nearly killed me in the late 1980s.

But I conducted band business on the work phone during slow times at my day job. Jimmy would call and talk over planning and strategy. We discussed offers made by record labels and catch up on the overall health of the band.

A bidding war ensued. The rep from Atlantic Records said to us, "Here's a blank check. Write whatever number you want on it and let's do this."

I was giddy. They were just going to give us whatever amount we wanted to sign on! I could picture Bon Scott, AC/DC's badass original lead singer, looking down from Heaven, flashing me a thumbs up and saying, "You're one of us now, mate!"

Photo Credit: Heather Harris

It took Tony to talk me off the ledge. He reminded me that this, and other offers like it, were not free money; labels don't throw endless cash at a band out of the goodness of their hearts. These were actually big loans they were giving out. It may seem "free" in the moment, but it would turn into decades of indentured servitude in the long run. I didn't understand it back then. Bands have to pay all that money back. The label siphons "recoupable expenses" from the money a band earns from that point forward. They get paid back before the band gets paid. Period.

The band gets famous; the label gets rich.

For example, if an album sells 1,000,000 copies, we feel pretty good. The band members each get a nice platinum album to hang on their wall. Along with that, the band makes about one dollar per record. The song writers are awarded a little more per album, plus the band gets money for airplay and other things—but let's not go into the weeds with all the financials. We will stick to round numbers to make this simple.

Keeping to the example, let's say the band makes a million bucks. There are five of us in the band, so $200,000 a piece, right?

Nope.

What happens next is that the label sends us an invoice for all the money they laid out to get us to where we are. These are the "recoupable expenses." They get repaid for the advance we took, for the production costs of the album, for the music videos we shot, for the tour bus, for all the food we ate, for the hotels we stayed in, and for whatever else the label decides to use to pad their invoice.

Not only that, the artists get stuck paying for shit that has nothing to do with anything. For instance, if an A&R guy wants to take a vacation, he will make sure the band has a gig or a meeting in the city he wants to visit. He'll fly his entourage to that destination for several days' worth of frolicking. He'll meet with the band on one of the days, and then charge the entire excursion to the label, where it goes onto the expense sheet of the band he met with.

It's a dirty fucking business filled with a shit-ton of unscrupulous assholes.

Believe me, the accounting is dubious at best. We never see a breakdown of expenses while the meter is running. We just get walloped with a final reconciliation once the sales money starts pouring in. The money itself pours out from the sales and into the label's coffers.

Back to that million-selling, platinum album. Where did our million bucks go? Well, after everything is tabulated up, we get a bill for two million dollars from the label. They help themselves to ALL of our money, and then remind us that we still owe them a million bucks.

Let's not forget that debt racks up interest as time goes by. The executives bark at us, "Chop-chop! Get back out there and make us our money back!"

We can never quite get our debt back down to zero. Sounds a little like the mob extorting money from a small business owner, right? Don't get me started.

Tony Ferguson talked us out of the Atlantic deal. He wasn't sour on the cash; he genuinely wanted to make sure we got on the right label. He wanted us to sign on with a company that would appreciate our style, market us appropriately, and lend us adequate support for albums and tours. It wasn't about the money; it was about who was going to commit to the band.

Tony was the best fucking manager we could have asked for. He and I were close; he kept me grounded throughout our entire ordeal. He saw through all the bullshit and helped us to understand that music was a business and not a fairy-tale. Despite his prim-and-proper British demeanor, he could get into a person's face when he needed to.

My God, we had some interesting meetings. And not in a good way.

I remember meeting with Bob Skoro, an A&R guy with Polygram Records. I walked into Bob's office with Tony Ferguson. Picture the scene: I'm heavily tatted, with long hair and a leather vest, looking like I just got paroled after killing a bunch of nuns with a hatchet.

Tony, on the other hand, was the extremely proper gent, as always. He sported a razor-sharp pleat in his pant legs and a side part in his hair. The two of us made for one hell of a Heckle and Jeckle. We sat down, and fucking Bob Skoro launched into a soliloquy. About himself.

I swear to God, he opened with, "Let me tell you about Bob Skoro."

I looked at Tony like, *The third person? Seriously? He's going to talk about himself in the fucking third person?*

Oh, yes. He certainly did.

"You see, Bob Skoro was never really into music. Bob was into sports. And Bob realized early on that he was very good at sports. He was captain of the baseball team and quarterback of the football team. But Bob's dad was big in the music business."

He paused to take a sip of water. It must have been taxing to be such a colossal asshat. I stared out the window while he resumed his monologue.

"So, Bob's dad said that Bob needed a back-up career because, you know, not many people make it as professional athletes. He got me a job at the publishing company where Bob worked his way up the ranks."

I noticed the subtle shift between first and third person. It was almost impossible to keep my mouth shut. But Bob finally got to the point.

"And today? Bob. Owns. A Porsche!"

He leaned forward in his Corinthian leather chair, "So, what do you think about that?"

I gave it about a two-Mississippi pause for effect, then met his eyes.

"This guy Bob sounds like a douchebag."

Tony was aghast; he kicked me under the table. Hard.

I turned and said to Tony out loud, "Look, why would I want to work with a guy who leads with the fact that he was never really into music?"

I wouldn't. And that was the point. Tony himself taught me that. It's not about the money. It's about who was going to be committed to the band, remember?

Another gem that came up during the meeting with Bob was that he wanted us to sound more like LA Guns, a band on the Polygram label at the time. In my mind, LA Guns was a bunch of posers who weren't very talented as musicians.

Yeah, they were selling a shit-ton of records. But, what the fuck? Again, it's the commitment, not the money. If Bob wanted us to sound more like them, then he didn't get it. Or maybe he got it, but I didn't get it. Either way, I wanted no part of Polygram and their superstar athlete, Bob Skoro.

Suffice it to say, that meeting didn't go very well. It ended very shortly thereafter.

Driving away from the Polygram offices, Tony said, "Dude, you were fucking brutal on that guy."

I told Tony I was sorry—but I wasn't.

That wasn't the end of our dealings with Bob Skoro. Revenge is a dish best served cold. We'd have our day.

Our revenge was bolstered with a story told to me by the great manager, Alan Niven of Gun's and Roses and Great White fame.

* * *

We did a huge showcase sometime in late 1988 or early 1989. It was positively insane that night. The crowd was out of their minds and the audience was littered with every A&R suit in the business. As a band, we were on fucking fire. The night turned into a label feeding frenzy.

Alan was there, alongside Tom Zutaut. They represented Geffen Records, and had already signed Great White, Tesla, and Guns n' Roses. Guns had just released *Appetite for Destruction*, but it hadn't quite caught on yet; it was on the verge of exploding. The industry was moving in that direction, and the rest of the labels knew it.

That made Geffen the major player in the industry. Many other label executives paid attention to what Alan and Tom did. They became the EF Huttons of the industry; when they talked, people listened.

I hate that I felt compelled to make that reference. Now I feel old.

Anyway, Alan listened to a few of our songs and was duly impressed. He also noticed the heat we were generating. At that point, he'd seen everything he needed to see.

He leaned over to Tom and said, "This is ridiculous. Let's fuck with people and lower the temperature in the room. Let's just leave."

They did exactly that. After three songs, Alan and Tom walked right the fuck out of the place. Their goal was for people to think they wanted nothing to do with us.

Later, after they got in their car and drove off, Alan said to Tom, "Get these Little Caesar guys on the phone. We've got to talk to them."

They liked us. They really, really liked us.

* * *

Not long after that, Bob Skoro started begging Jimmy to set up another appointment with us. We told Jimmy to set it up—but under our terms.

We agreed to meet Bob at my house, which was a tiny bungalow in Hollywood. When Bob hit the parking lot, he saw a number of Harleys parked out front.

The stage was set.

He knocked. We walked him in and sat him down on my ratty couch in the corner of the cramped living room. Me, the band, and all my Harley-riding friends loomed over him in a semi-circle, menacingly staring him down. We looked like the group you'd hire to put a hit on Satan.

If I remember, I think Fidel, our bassist, flopped down next to Bob on the couch and cleaned his fingernails with a big fucking knife.

Bob almost shit himself.

He still remained true to his douche bag self, despite looking like he was ready to piss his pants. He tried telling us that he got Bon Jovi (who was on the Polygram label) $100,000—all in—to make their *New Jersey* album.

In case you're not aware, "all-in" is the royalty paid by the label to the band. The band is then responsible for paying everything involved in the production of the album from that royalty.

All I could say was, "Dude…you're telling me that Bon Jovi pulled off that album for a hundred grand?! You're a lying sack of shit!"

There was no fucking way. A hundred grand wouldn't have covered the catering budget, much less the cost of getting the record made. Bon Jovi was larger than life after their *Slippery When Wet* album. The label probably offered to suck Jon's dick to get *New Jersey*, the follow-up album.

Bob was trying to low-ball us. He was trying to sign us for the least amount of money possible. This was fucking insane, given

70

the amount of interest we were getting from Geffen and everyone else.

I got what he was up to; he wanted to cover his ass at work. As he had admitted before, Bob was never truly serious about the band. He just wanted to make the first offer so he could look good in front of everyone else at Polygram.

We weren't falling for it.

Although he was babbling like a fucking moron, he managed to pick himself up and walk out of my house. I am not exaggerating when I tell you we made Bob cry that day. It was glorious.

We never saw him again. That was also profoundly satisfying.

* * *

We nearly signed with Arista Records, but they weren't exactly a rock and roll label. Arista's A&R guy was so passionate about the band, we knew we'd be in good hands. He wanted us really bad.

However, Geffen was the bigger dog in the pound. In the end, we signed with them.

The guy who really chased us on behalf of Geffen was a junior A&R guy named Mio Vuckovic. When we signed on, Jimmy wasn't comfortable working with Mio because he (Mio) had never had a hit record. Instead, Jimmy got us a much more powerful figure named John Kalodner to work with. John had been with Atlantic Records for years, signing Peter Gabriel and Phil Collins. He was specifically sought out by David Geffen himself in 1980 to be the first A&R guy at Geffen Records. John Kalodner knew what he was doing. He carried a big stick, and he could get shit done.

Even so, we were still hesitant to work with somebody that big. We were more concerned about big egos bumping into each other. We also didn't want to leave Mio high and dry, so we struck a balance: Mio managed the day-to-day A&R stuff for us while John hovered nearby in the background. He was ready to either take credit for our success or blame Mio for our failure.

That was probably unfair. Totally true, but unfair. Mio and

our manager Tony were our everyday, reliable guys. Mio, to his credit, was more down-to-earth and accessible than John anyway. We were good with the decision for him to deal directly with us. Jimmy Iovine and John Kalodner were called in when we needed someone with weight to throw around. Everyone played their part.

We signed the biggest contract ever offered to a new artist by Geffen Records. And when I say big, I mean that in the most literal way possible. The stack of paper the contract was written on grew to almost three inches thick after a long period of negotiation.

We signed with the implicit understanding that none of it meant anything until we started selling albums. At the moment, we were all bark and no proven bite.

We were a bunch of blue-collar kids who weren't afraid to get our hands dirty. We were eager to get down to work. We would have sold our records door-to-door if need be. We simply couldn't wait to get into the studio and start laying down some basic tracks.

We were ready to go, man!

Photo Credit: Heather Harris

I became a workaholic. I didn't think much about pursuing an avalanche of pussy or a mountain of drugs. Because of my motorcycle, I wouldn't even drink. Instead of the rock and roll lifestyle, I wanted to develop traction so I could launch our careers. I became obsessed with making the band successful.

Neither Tom nor Fidel partied too hard either at that time. They were just as focused as me on getting the band off the ground.

We did have a couple of resident alcoholics in the band. Loren was a raging alcoholic during those early days. He's been sober for over thirty years now, but make no mistake; he was a hot fucking mess back then. An absolute drunken lunatic—and proud of it! A TRUE rock and roller in every sense, with every cell of his body.

I remember Loren used to own a station wagon painted with zebra stripes all over it. You could see that thing from Google Earth when it drove down the street. He would pull up in that car and get out with a 32-ounce Big Gulp from 7-11—except it wasn't a Big Gulp from 7-11. I remember taking a swig once and yelling, "Holy shit, dude! That's pure Jack Daniels!"

He shrugged. It was more of a cocktail to him.

He stayed that way for a good six or eight months into the success of the band. When things started going sideways, he turned it around. Loren didn't want to be responsible for blowing our opportunity. He got his shit together, for the good of the band. It wasn't a smooth ride for him, but he got it done. In the beginning, though, "Drunk Loren" provided hours of endless entertainment for the rest of us.

Apache was also quite the alcoholic. If you look at pictures of him at that time, he was rail-thin for his entire run with our band. Yet, he'd put away a case of beer every night.

A full fucking case of beer. That's 24 twelve-ounce cans.

I have no idea where all the fluid went. That stuff ran right through him. Apache would then wake up the next morning and eat a handful of Tylenol. None of us knew anything about the effect of acetaminophen on the liver, or that his habits should have simply killed him outright. Yet, he was one tough hombre who always showed up for work.

Say what you will about how we looked on the outside, but every guy in this band—past and present—has been a good fucking dude on the inside.

Over time, I gave in to the power of pharmaceuticals. Not long after, I gave in to heroin, as much as it pains me to admit it. I was stressed out from seeing the writing on the wall. Our careers with Geffen deteriorated rapidly, as if we were shoved into a bus station toilet and set on fire.

But not before we had a really fun run while we were on top of the world. Some of the best, most entertaining stories of my life happened over those couple years.

In retrospect, we should have all knocked on wood. But hindsight is 20/20, right?

CHAPTER 5:
BREAKING OUT

We were preparing to travel up to Vancouver, BC, Canada to record our debut album. And although we didn't know it yet, that album would eventually get out of the starting blocks like Usain Bolt. Big things were in store for us. We were a damn good band and had gotten nothing but positive feedback every step of the way.

The first sign of anything leaning sideways had to do with the name of the band. Little Caesar is the only name we have ever carried, and it has fucking plagued us from its inception. For anyone curious, I had no fucking idea it was also the name of a national pizza chain out of the Midwest. I specifically picked that name because it checked all the boxes of a good band name.

I've mentioned before that I feel the mystique around a band is similar to the mystique around a motorcycle club. Keeping that same feel, I wanted a name for our band that was powerful, but one that was also self-aware and humble.

Smash cut to the band's formation.

One night, I was up at two in the morning watching Sundance, Turner Classic Movies, or one of those channels you only ever watch at two in the morning and can't find the remote to change it, so you're stuck watching *Leave it to Beaver* in Spanish. Maybe I was still hammered from playing a gig somewhere. Hell, it could have been all of the above.

In any case, the 1931 gangster film titled *Little Caesar* was playing. It was the breakout film for iconic actor Edward G. Robinson. If you don't recognize his name, find a clip of him on YouTube. You will immediately recognize the way he talks. His voice is one of the most unique and imitated voices in history.

I watched the movie and thought, *Holy shit! What a great name for our band!*

"Little Caesar" had the powerful street cred of the great

emperor, Julius Caesar, softened by the humility of the adjective "Little."

It was perfect.

There was exactly one pre-existing "Little Caesar" of which I was aware. To be more precise, he *made* me aware of his existance. And presumably, he was the only one we would have to deal with. When my phone rang late one night, it was time to work things out with the guy who held that name before we did.

I don't know how these people kept getting my home number. I answered on the second ring.

"Hello?"

The voice on the other end was that of an elderly black man.

"Lemme speak to Caesar."

I frowned, "Uhhhh, there's no one here by that name."

Silence.

I spoke again. "I'm in a band named Little Caesar, but my name is Ron."

I'm not sure he heard me. He sounded pretty riled up.

"Listen, Caesar, listen. You and me. We got a problem."

I sat down. "Ah, alright. What's the problem?"

"Well. I'm Little Caesar," he said. "Little Caesar and the Romans. You ever heard of them?"

"Yeah! You guys had a hit song in the early sixties!"

Their song, "Those Oldies but Goodies (Remind Me of You)" went all the way up to #9 on the US *Billboard* charts in 1961. It was a huge hit for them. Apparently, their lead singer wanted me to know exactly who I was dealing with.

"You're damn right."

I listened. He continued.

"Listen man, you're out there using my name. People gonna be coming to a show, and they're thinking I'm gonna be playing, and then see it's you and your rocker boys."

Well. That was a twist I could have never seen coming. I helped him think it through out loud.

"Oh, okay, hmm. Listen, Caesar, I don't think people are

going to the Whiskey on a Saturday night, thinking they're there to see Black 'n Blue or Bang Tango opening for an old R&B band that had a hit 30 years ago."

I paused, and then finished. "I don't really think that's going to be an issue. But look, I thought you guys had been kinda defunct."

He broke in. "Well, yeah, we haven't been doing much work lately. But still."

I nodded on my end of the phone. I got it. I heard what this guy was really saying. He was frustrated by the same music business that I was currently grappling with. His good name was all he had left, and I was completely down with knowing how important that was to him.

We got to chatting about the music business. Turned out, I was accurate in my assessment. He was angry at the way things went down for himself and his group way back in the day. It sounded like nothing had really changed since 1961.

I won't speak out of turn here, but Caesar was having some health issues and couldn't get the label to pay him the money he felt he was owed. He was worried about paying for his medical treatment —a problem I could actually help him with.

I said, "What if we did a benefit show and all the proceeds would go to you in order to help with your medical bills?"

I suggested we do that to work out the "Little Caesar" name thing in a more humane way than some sort of man-to-man combat. He was stunned.

"You'd do that?"

"Yeah! Of course I would do that. I'm a musician. You're a musician. You're getting fucked, and I know how that goes. Why don't we turn this problem into a solution?"

It was a golden opportunity for him. Because, let's face it, he would have had to hire an attorney and take us—and Geffen—to court. Then he'd have to argue it out and try to come to a financial settlement regarding the name. That is, after many years of deliberation and only if the court ruled in his favor.

I didn't think it would have ended well for Mr. Caesar. I offered him a way out; a way that would both protect his dignity and throw some immediate "settlement" money his way.

We played a benefit at Club Lingerie that raised a few thousand bucks for the guy. I gave him the check and never heard from him again.

I try to be as pragmatic as possible with people. I am a problem solver. I don't hide from issues that affect the people around me. It would have been nice if Geffen's staff had operated under the same principals. Nobody at the label ever brought up Little Caesar and the Romans when we told them how we chose the name.

* * *

Nor did they mention anything about pizza.

I secretly wonder if the founder of the pizza chain, Mike Ilich, watched the exact same Edward G. Robinson gangster movie and had the exact same thoughts when deciding upon a name for his new restaurant.

I had absolutely zero awareness of this pizza chain. Neither did anyone else in the band. We were five guys that collectively did not know such a restaurant existed. We lived in California, and the franchise had yet to set up on the West Coast. It finally scratched its way to the Pacific Coast in 1987, but didn't make a serious impact until even later than that. Either way, it all happened too late to keep us from making a bad mistake.

Nobody at Geffen told us that another famous business entity already had the same name. Maybe because the pizza chain spells their name with an "s" on the end, the dumbass corporate lawyers figured we'd be fine.

That's exactly what it came down to. We spent all of our time in SoCal or in Vancouver, Canada. These are veritable deserts of Midwestern culture, devoid of any chains that used the catchphrase "Pizza! Pizza!" About a month before the release of our debut album, which was unironically self-titled and blatantly sporting the name Little Caesar, I had a come-to-Jesus conversation while I was at the Geffen corporate offices.

One of our handlers said, "Oh, by the way, there's no problem using the name Little Caesar. Our legal department looked into it. Because it's a different form of business, our lawyers assure us that we won't catch any hell."

I was dumbfounded. "What are you talking about?"

He said, "Well, you know, the pizza chain."

It wasn't registering in my head.

"What are you talking about?!" I repeated.

Finally, he spit it out.

"Well, in certain areas of the country there's this large pizza franchise…."

I cut him off, "You're just now telling me this?! Are you fucking kidding me?!"

He backpedaled, "We…we thought you knew."

I jumped up and paced around the room. I must've looked like a madman on the verge of a three-state killing spree. Everyone pushed back from the table.

My finger flew into his face as I yelled, "Why would I name my band after a fucking pizza chain?!"

He blinked. I couldn't be stopped.

"I don't care what we call the thing, but that's just fucking stupid!"

Bloody hell! Even after we'd sat through countless marketing meetings to learn about Geffen's grand plans for the band, no one ever brought up the fact that this name was already taken by a nationally recognized business.

I wanted to shout from the rooftops, "What is wrong with you people?!"

At this point, we were already well past any hope of walking it back. The artwork had been made for the album and sent to print. Marketing materials had already been ordered and launched. Singles were being pressed and prepped to send to radio stations around the country.

The name had a momentum that could not be reversed.

Oh, and then there was this fucking gem: At one of the marketing meetings following our album launch, one of the geniuses at Geffen said he had reached out to the pizza company, which was (and still is) headquartered in Detroit, Michigan. He proposed the idea of putting discount coupons toward the purchase of our CD on the back of Little Caesars' pizza boxes.

I was like, "Whoa—do you honestly think somebody is going to order a pizza, see we have the same name as the restaurant, and then buy a fucking CD?"

It was insane. And I was rolling.

"You're telling me that if someone prefers shitty pizza, they're going to enjoy a bluesy, rock and roll CD?"

I slammed my fist on the table in front of me, "That makes sense to you?! What the fuck is wrong with you people?! You have got to be kidding me!"

We wanted to distance ourselves from the pizza chain, not embrace it. The executives at Geffen seemed clueless to that concept.

As you can guess, this bullshit has plagued us ever since. I can't tell you how many times a stoner jackass on Facebook will post "Pizza! Pizza!" on my timeline. Then they bask in their own brilliance, delighted to be the first human to ever think of that.

I try to laugh about it nowadays. But once again, I feel as if I'm the butt of the universe's jokes. After this happened over and over again so many times, I figure it has to be true. If Karma had any sense of reasonable justice whatsoever, I should be destined to hit the Powerball jackpot one of these days. But then I'll probably get hit by a bus later that afternoon.

That's the story of our name. It totally bit us in the ass as time went on. Maybe we should have called ourselves "Domino's." At least their pizza is better.

Despite all this, we have worn that name like a badge of honor. It's ours, and we'll defend it to the end.

* * *

Before our first album ever came out, we went through quite a bit of drama to get it recorded and sold.

John Kalodner was the first person to bring big-time producer, Bob Rock to us. He wanted Bob to produce our debut album. John didn't necessarily force Bob upon us, but I was hesitant about bringing yet another big name and big ego into the mix. I had a list of a few other guys I would have preferred to work with. As I've said, David Geffen, John Kalodner, and Bob Rock created a formidable triumvirate of conceit.

To be fair to Bob, I was okay with him by the time we recorded. We had a good meeting where he understood the complete vision of our band. He had strong clout in the industry, so it was all systems go.

Unfortunately, what wound up happening was another load of horse shit.

We traveled to Vancouver to record the album because Bob did not want to work in Los Angeles. Not a huge hairy deal for us, but it did add a lot of expense to the final bill. There were seven of us —five band members plus two crew guys—who had to be put up in a hotel and fed for the duration of recording. Vancouver is also famous for its strip clubs, so there was a little extra pocket change thrown in for drugs and strippers.

Because of a circus parade of ego-induced bullshit, we were up there for a full *seven months* to record the album. I had gone out of my way to keep this kind of problem from happening, but the universe persisted in pushing it forward.

For example, Bob Rock got into a spat with John Kalodner about another band on the label. Of course, John then called us and said we were no longer going to work with Bob Rock. We were thrown into limbo for several weeks before the two of them ultimately kissed and made up. But the bottom line was a costly delay.

Next, Bob had to step out of production temporarily because he was scheduled to work on someone else's record. Yet another costly and maddening delay. We went back home, since we had no idea how long Bob was going to take and there was no need to waste time and money in Vancouver.

We returned to Los Angeles and sat with our thumbs up our collective asses, until it was suggested that we get out and tour a bit. No need to unproductively burn more of our advance. We could get out there and generate both interest in the band and revenue toward our recoupable costs.

We were tired of being jerked around. So, we hit the road.

* * *

We went on tour with Jane's Addiction. One cool thing we learned from that tour was that we were able to rent a super cool tour bus from the 1950s. Rumor had it that at one point in time, both Elvis and Marilyn Monroe had used this bus. Not together, of course.

Jane's Addiction is a quirky, alternative rock band with a quirky, alternative fan base. We were a blues band that looked like a bunch of bikers. Perry Farrell, Jane's Addiction's front man, comes on stage with a nose ring and no shoes. Dave Navarro was heavily strung out on heroin in those days and was a freakshow on stage every night.

By the third or fourth show, we thought, *These people are fucking weird.* We could tell this audience didn't get us. Eventually, our goal was to just get through the tour so we could record our album and do our own tour in peace.

It was such a strange fucking run. I remember dropping acid before a show somewhere in Virginia. The whole tour was so fucking bizarre anyway, we figured *Meh. Why not?* It really couldn't get any more fucked up than it already was.

We played the show, and then piled onto the bus. During the whole drive to the next city, each mile was punctuated by all of us, tripping balls, grabbing at dust particles and watching the ceiling of the Elvis/Marilyn bus drip green monkeys.

We also did a gig in Philadelphia that saw Fidel pull his knife on a guy—who in turn, pulled a gun on Fidel. It all started with us parking the tour bus in such a way that made it inconvenient to get around us on the road.

People are so fucking nuts. And that's coming from *me*.

* * *

At some point during all the hubbub with Jane's Addiction, Winger got removed from the Kiss tour. John Kalodner pulled some strings and finagled us onto the bill in their place. This whole series was a strange mishmash of music. None of the four bands were on the same label. We were on Geffen. Jane's Addiction, who were touring for *Ritual de lo Habitual*, was on Warner Brothers. Winger, touring for *In the Heart of the Young*, was on Atlantic. And Kiss, touring for *Hot in the Shade*, was on Mercury.

Yet, somehow John pulled it off. We were a better fit with Kiss than with Jane's Addiction, to be honest. But Gene Simmons was pissed about us being on the bill. He wanted Winger back, who was easily a bigger draw than we were. Headlining bands don't invite an opening act as charity. It's more of a business decision; they want an opener who can attract more fans into the venue.

I got it. We didn't even have an album yet, so we were largely unknown outside of Los Angeles. And Winger was arguably at the height of their power.

We held no ill will toward Gene for not wanting us touring with them; it was all business, nothing personal. Gene, despite his ultimate Gene-ness, is one of my favorite people to hang around with. They don't call him The Demon for nuthin'.

We were only out with Kiss for six weeks before Gene got his wish. Winger came back and bumped us off the tour. That was fine with us; we had to get back to Vancouver. The timing worked out well.

* * *

As an aside to the Vancouver madness, and running parallel on the timeline, nothing could have prepared us for the insanity we shared with the Hells Angels motorcycle club.

Yes, *those* Hells Angels. Our relationship has made for some spectacularly demented stories. It was all part of the fun, baby!

Los Angeles was the home to several magazines that catered to the biker crowd. At the epicenter of these publications was a company called Paisano Publications. Paisano was the mother publisher of a number of tattoo magazines. They also published *Iron Horse* magazine, and *Easy Rider* magazine; good reads for a niche crowd.

The band got to be good friends with the folks at Paisano because we would play at their events and ride around town with their staff and patrons. When our album came out, they did a really nice, three-page story on the band and the record. They labeled us as the resurrection of the music and image appreciated by bikers. As you can imagine, our popularity among bikers spiked after that great press piece.

All this happened right around the time we were booked to play the 50th anniversary of the Sturgis Motorcycle Rally in Sturgis, South Dakota, back in 1988. If you don't know about Sturgis, just imagine every motorcycle ever built descending upon a small town nestled in the Black Hills. It's fun, it's wild, and it's dangerous— everything you would expect from a biker rally.

The Sturgis Rally has grown considerably since then. Except now it's populated by a lot of dentists and insurance adjusters who happen to own Harleys and are able to drop a few hundred bucks on a fancy leather outfit. These days, the music is more popular than the madness. A friendlier atmosphere is the result of a natural evolution of this really cool ten-day event, which has taken place every summer since 1938.

When we played Sturgis, it was raw, rough, and meaner than anything your imagination can conjure up.

Leading up to the event, we noticed a shift in our audience. Following the article in Paisano's magazine, motorcycle club members began to show up at our gigs. This led to tension between members of rival clubs who all attended the same shows. I remember a few times where we had to hustle onto the bus because there were guys ready to kill each other in the parking lot.

Things started to get a little crazy, but these were our people. This was our audience.

When we pulled up to Sturgis that summer, we were still aboard our 1950s slick tour bus. Our intention was to drive all the way through to the nearby Buffalo Chip Campground, but we weren't able to make it that far.

Just outside the city limits, we drove past a motel that had thousands of motorcycles clogging the parking lot and the surrounding territory. We slowed to pass the spectacle, when two guys wearing Hells Angels colors ambled out into the road and blocked our bus. We stopped and they approached the window.

"You guys Little Caesar?"

"Um, yeah."

"Good. You're staying with us."

I nodded vigorously, "Yeah, yeah, okay."

What was I supposed to say? No?

Dude. I'm not that crazy.

Like clockwork, a bunch more guys appeared and backed their bikes away from the motel entrance. At that moment, I understood what Moses saw at The Red Sea. We eased the bus into the parking lot, at which time the bikes flowed back into their blockade positions.

Just like The Red Sea when the pharaoh of Egypt pulled up.

I was instructed to park toward the end of the motel where other members pointed out our rooms. We were told that the club was holding its annual business meeting, which was tradition for clubs back then. Sturgis was more than a ten-day party for bikers and clubs. It was an opportunity for representatives from each national chapter to come together and hold face-to-face meetings.

We were to remain at the hotel for the duration of the meetings. In a sense, we were held captive for about four hours. Not that we complained. We were dumb, but not stupid.

Over the course of the next few days, we struck up friendships with members of the Hells Angels. Everyone was civil and super nice to us, like they were actually fans of ours. I don't think any of us were particularly freaked out once we got past the shock of being detained by some scary looking dudes. In all, we had a good time. And I think they did too. Members of the Hells Angels started following us around on tour.

Believe me, it's nice to have friends that have your back. It reminded me of my former college roommate who was a black belt; we always felt secure with our Hells Angels buddies hanging around the show.

However, it did lead to some awkward situations.

I remember doing a show in Cleveland. We were opening for Kiss at the time and feeling like we were a pretty big deal. After our set, two guys in Hells Angels colors came backstage and handed me a Hells Angels skull ring, t-shirt, and leather vest—with Hells Angels colors on it.

Now, slow your roll, dear reader. If it seems as if I got kissed into the mob, I have some bad news. It doesn't work that way...and I knew something was off. Something about the entire thing didn't feel right to me. The Hells Angels don't just give out these colors like they're swag at some corporate event.

In reality, it was a ridiculously, insanely inappropriate thing for those two guys to do. They were masquerading as Hells Angels members. Not a smart move on their part.

Still, I hung onto the attire.

Later in the tour, we played in New York City, home to an infamous Hells Angels chapter called The Nomads. The Nomads had their clubhouse down on Second Street, which was probably the safest block in New York City. Nobody wanted to fuck with anything The Nomads might hold sacred.

On the afternoon of the show, I was down at a thrift store looking for some cool stage clothes. The girl who ran the store was dating one of The Nomads, who came in while I was there shopping. I recognized the colors immediately and approached him.

"Umm, excuse me."

"Yeah?"

I introduced myself and said, "I had this weird thing happen to me in Cleveland."

I recounted the story about the two guys and the colors and the attire. I could see his blood start to boil as the story went on. When I finished, he drew a breath.

"Do you still have that stuff?"

"Yeah," I replied.

He followed me back to the hotel and I returned the clothing to him. A man of few words, he looked me in the eye and said, "You did the right thing. We don't give these things out. These things are earned."

I don't know how the story ended for the two guys in Cleveland, but I do know The Nomads sent a few members to look for them.

That strange incident only added to our credibility with The Club. My discretion and judgment was not lost on their membership, who in turn started following us around even more heavily. They showed up in greater numbers to our shows in support.

I have been grateful for that support ever since.

* * *

Another interesting incident happened in Boston.

I formed a relationship with a club leader named Big Al. He headed up the Salem, Massachusetts chapter of the Hells Angels. At some point, Al decided to throw a huge party and hire us and our brother band, Junkyard, to play the event.

We flew out of Los Angeles to do the show. The Hells Angels sent a couple members to escort us and Junkyard on the flight. This is before the TSA, The Patriot Act, and anything else that might have slowed us down. If there had been an Air Marshal on the flight, he or she didn't even make themselves known. We were a juggernaut in motion.

The fight was delayed several times, which meant we dispatched ourselves to the bar. We were there four hours before the plane boarded. The two Hells Angels were hammered to the point that they almost couldn't get on the plane. Our guys and crew members, as well as the Junkyard guys, were pretty lit too.

I still remember the one poor stewardess who was assigned to our section. She was young and green and completely unprepared to handle the massive clusterfuck of personalities taking up her seats. We looked like Hell opened its mouth and vomited out a slam pit of demons.

It was a long cross-country flight with a bevy of out of control people. At some point during the flight, one of our escorts grabbed the bar cart and said to the stewardess, "This is staying here."

My God. That poor girl. If she didn't quit that same day, she is far stronger than I would have been.

When we finally landed in Boston, the weather turned on us. This was in January or February, and there was a big fucking snowstorm. When we played the show, it tanked. Nobody could make it through the snow to come party.

We played the show to virtually no one. Big Al lost money on the show, thus he was forced to cancel our hotel rooms. Still the gracious host, he offered to let some of us crash at his place. Most of Little Caesar went over there.

I will never forget sitting in his den and overhearing a phone conversation Al had with Steven Tyler of Aerosmith. Aerosmith had apparently released an official t-shirt that looked an awful lot like the Hells Angels jackets. They had the white rockers in the middle, with the word "Aerosmith" across the top in the same red letters and font as the Hells Angels, with "Boston, MA" along the bottom, similar to how a Hells Angels member would designate his chapter.

In short, that was a no-no.

Because Aerosmith is a Boston based band, Big Al happened to know Steven Tyler. Ergo, he had Steven's phone number. Throughout the conversation, Al remained completely calm.

"Dude, this is not going to happen."

I leaned in, interested to hear all the heinous ways Al was about to threaten Steven Fucking Tyler. What I ended up hearing shocked me.

Al continued in his conversational tone of voice.

"Steven, that is a copyrighted image. You will have to pay us a very large royalty, if we even decide to let you use it at all. And if you do not go through proper channels, we will be sending you a cease & desist injunction and will have your property seized."

My jaw dropped. Al was an enormous, scruffy dude wearing Hells Angels colors. Yet he sounded like he was a graduate of the Wharton School of Business. The leverage he used over Steven Tyler was nothing like the leverage I expected to be used by a leader of the Hells Angels. I expected body parts getting removed via switchblades and gardening tools, not an injunction and a massive lawsuit.

He finished the Steven Tyler conversation with a statement of disappointment.

"Listen, we've had a long relationship, you and me. I would have expected you to at least have the courtesy to call before doing something like this. Maybe we could have worked something out."

All I could think was, *Wow. What a great stereotype to get crushed right now. They know how to handle their business.*

He hung up and then invited me to go to a local bar with him. He had some business to attend to, which was now extraordinarily interesting to me. I went without hesitation—but was about to bump up against a crossroad between the old school Hells Angels, and the new school.

* * *

I don't know which part of town we descended into, but we ended up in a dimly lit, sleazy little dive bar on the water. In fact, the whole bar was hanging over the channel. There was six inches of snow on the ground, and it was cold as fuck. I was in no position to complain about how anything looked.

We found spots at the bar and ordered a couple cocktails. Not long after our drinks arrived, a guy slid up behind us and hissed, "Al! Hey Al!"

"Yeah?"

His voice dropped, *"There's a ni**er sitting at the end of the bar. You want me to put one in his head and dump him over the rail into the bay?"*

I froze in place. All I could think was, *Holy shit… wait!....WHAT???!!!......did he just say what I think he said???!!!*

Al calmly paused to take a sip of his drink, and then turned to me.

"Okay, Ron. What should he do?"

90

I stammered. "No, nah…seriously, dude. Keep me out of this."

Al persisted, "Nope. You hold a man's life in your hands. Right now. What should he do?"

I had to have turned bleach-white on my barstool. I was fucking freaking out internally. I'm pretty sure I let out a nervous chuckle; nothing was funny, but I didn't know what else to do. I replied like the smartass I tend to be when I get nervous.

"No, no, no…why don't you wait 'til next week when I'm gone!?"

Al turned to the guy and flatly said, "Just leave him be."

The guy skulked away, muttering under his breath, "Aw, fuck man. Fuck this."

I looked at Al, "What the fuck, dude?! That was joke, right?"

"No. That was dead serious. The guy we were just talking to has been trying to get into the club for a very long time. He's willing to do shit like that because he thinks that's what you do to become a Hells Angel."

"Really?" I said, "So you could have—"

He stopped me. "Absolutely. If I would have told him to do it, he would have done it."

We stared at each other. Al sized me up in an instant and addressed the elephant in the room.

"Ron, really. Do you think we'd kill someone just because they're black?"

I was scared of giving the wrong answer. "I don't fucking know!"

Exasperated, he let out a long sigh and slowly shook his head. I was trying his patience.

"No, dude. We're a business organization. We don't kill people just because of the color of their skin. So get that stereotype out of your head."

I sat, dumbfounded. He continued.

"That man is down at the end of the bar, just living his life. We don't just take a life like that. We're not that indiscriminate."

I understood. Holy shit, I got it.

91

Al conducted his business and we returned to his place. That night, I was invited to a party at their club house, which was a huge honor. Non-members rarely get invited to set foot into a clubhouse, much less attend a party. In fact, there was a sign above the bar that read:

What you see here

What you hear here

Stays here.

I'll never forget that. It was written in the Hells Angels font over the bar.

I went to the party. And things actually got weirder while I was there.

* * *

I was shooting pool. The crowd of members, wives, and girlfriends faded into the background as I concentrated on my shots. It was a raucous crowd having a good time. I didn't think anything of it—until some chick came over and started rubbing me and hanging on me.

I kept playing pool. She got more aggressive.

She started rubbing up the inside of my thigh and grabbed my cock. I had no idea what to do. I was sweating, thinking, *Oh no...oh shit.*

I was positive she was the girlfriend of one of the club members. What the hell is protocol when you are getting fondled by the girlfriend of a Hells Angel?

Do I mess around with the chick and piss off the member?

Do I do nothing and let her keep fondling me and piss off the member?

Do I reject her and risk insulting her, thereby pissing off the member?

This was a lose/lose/lose situation, as far as I was concerned. Not like that slowed her down.

I finished my game and figured I had to put some distance between us two. I set down the cue and hustled into the bathroom.

She proceeded to follow me in.

Now I'm on the verge of a heart attack. She sidled up close and pressed her body against mine. I was just about to say something —fuck if I know what it might have been—when all of a sudden, the door got kicked in. All the members stood there, staring at this chick draped all over me.

In that moment, I made my peace with Death. I figured I'd had a good run. Maybe they would leave my face alone. At least I would probably make a good-looking corpse.

After an eternity of frozen seconds, the entire group busted out laughing. It was all a big set-up. They just wanted to see what I would do; how I would conduct myself. They were entertained beyond belief to watch my skin crawl for an hour.

Hardy fucking har-har.

The guy whose girlfriend had been all over me—a guy who looked like he could bend a motorcycle around my neck—said, "Dude, c'mon! Do you think we just give out our old ladies as party favors?"

I blurted out, "I don't know what the fuck you do! All I know is I need a change of underwear."

That made them laugh all the more. Apparently, I handled the situation admirably. Another little test was passed. They needed to know the kind of people they hung around with and let into their circle.

I had just gotten hazed by the scariest fraternity on Earth.

* * *

The band's kinship with the Hells Angels—and my personal friendships in particular—led the FBI to open a file on me, and another on the band as a whole. Apparently, my "known association with criminal social organizations" was quite interesting to the powers that be.

In fairness to the FBI (you'll never hear me utter those words again), club members did hang around us a lot. Back in those days, members of the Salem (MA) chapter would come by our publicist's office when they were in town, and use her phone to conduct club business. They wanted access to a phone that was both comfortable (i.e., not a pay phone outside of a gas station) and not tapped by the Feds.

Our poor publicist would call me on a different line and whisper, "The Hells Angels have taken over my office!" And then we'd laugh.

Anyway, I found out about the open file through a story that began when Marlana, my first wife, was pulled over for a traffic stop. She told me about something strange that happened between her and the police officer during the stop. He was initially very nice and cordial toward her, but when he returned from running her driver's license, he was a total dick. Very curt and rude.

For most people, it would have been neither here nor there. One cop having a bad day. But something told me to check into what he might have seen when he ran her identification. Was there a flag on her license that we didn't know about?

Working in the music industry has made me a more suspicious/cautious person. Assholes everywhere are trying to game your system. I've learned to trust when my Spidey sense starts to tingle. I decided to ask some questions.

I followed up with a friend in the Bureau, who was able to help provide some answers. I'll keep their name and position out of this by making the story simple. I was tipped off to the existence of my file. Not only were the Feds monitoring me, but also Marlana and everyone else I was in regular contact with.

"Known Associations."

Although it makes no difference to the FBI, I've repeated over and over that I had nothing to do with any instances of organized crime, or whatever the fuck they think the club had been up to. Sure, they might have tortured me near a pool table and asked me if they should kill somebody and made me shit myself in a clubhouse bathroom, but that's it!

I sing in a band. They come watch. End of story.

But not the end for the FBI.

Even considering all the background noise, the knowledge of being "looked into by the FBI" never changed the way I conducted my life. Frankly, I doubt the file is still open. I'm an old fart now and can't stay organized enough to participate in organized crime. Come to think of it, it's been at least several months since my last instance of pillaging or plundering.

I'm kidding.

It's serious stuff. The FBI was doing what they had to do. Through it all, I still value the relationship Little Caesar had with the motorcycle club. They helped launch our career and have helped to keep it going over the years. When they show up to a gig, they bring numbers.

And I'm always grateful for it.

* * *

I'm grateful for another, more special friendship that grew back in those days, too.

You see, in the beginning, Music was my mistress. I could never leave her. To keep her in my life, I married her—metaphorically, that is. Music and I remain married to this day, despite our love/hate relationship.

Of course, I have been in literal marriages, too.

I have been married twice. In fact, I've only spent seven years as a single man since I was nineteen years old. Marlana was my first love. But at that time, I was too self-absorbed to know how to truly show love to another person.

We divorced, and I got a shot at redemption. The second time around, I married my best friend.

Our publicist, Renee, traveled with the band on the trip to Boston to meet the Salem chapter of the Hells Angels. That was when we got to know each other. Incidentally, following that meeting, she also became the gal whose office was taken over by the Hells Angels when they needed to use her phone.

Renee is now my current wife, and we are in sync as a couple. We built on the friendship and working relationship we had when we were younger. I'm so fucking lucky to have rekindled and built on the foundation of our early relationship. By the time we got together for real, we were both a little older and a lot wiser about ourselves and life. We knew what we were getting into when we said, "I do."

* * *

Little Caesar's stock in the music business was at an all-time high during this era. When our album was released, it sold like gangbusters.

For two weeks.

The first two weeks following our release, our record sold 160,000 copies. Our single climbed the charts, and we made appearances on national television. We were on *The Rick Dees Show* and *The Arsenio Hall Show*, both of which you can find on YouTube.

Our appearance on *The Arsenio Hall Show* was an indication of how incredibly popular we were. And it was also an indication of how we had the uncanny ability to piss everyone off without even trying.

* * *

Jimmy Iovine got a phone call one afternoon. A booker for *The Arsenio Hall Show* needed a musical act for their taping that evening. Apparently, somebody had canceled on them; they were desperate and needed an act. I don't know how far down the list the booker had to go before she stumbled upon us, but it couldn't have been too far. We were out on tour with Kiss at the time, so we weren't exactly chopped liver.

Jimmy agreed and put us on a plane back to Los Angeles. It was extremely cool to waltz into the Paramount Studios in Hollywood, knowing we were the talent that night.

Not bad for a kid from Queens.

The first thing they told us was that "Chain of Fools" was too long. We had to cut the guitar solo so they could remain on time with the show and the commercial spots.

We replied with, "Yeah, cool. We'll figure it out."

Apache played the solo on the album, so we worked with him on the new arrangement during the show's rehearsal.

It was cold in the studio, so I wore a leather jacket during rehearsal. If you see any clips of me gigging back then, I always did concerts shirtless. Pants, boots, and a microphone, baby. Tats and abs flown loud and proud.

I had a six pack back then. I kind of miss it.

At least I still have the tats.

Again, I was fully dressed and covered up during the *Arsenio* rehearsal.

When it came time to record the show, the other guys in the band started giving me shit about the jacket.

They ragged me with, "You're not actually going to wear that thing, are you?"

I was suddenly unsure about what to do.

"Should I go out there like I do every other night?"

They replied, "Yeah! Pull that fuckin' thing off! Show America your fuckin' tattoos and let's freak everyone out!"

Done and done.

If you recall, our day-to-day manager was Tony Ferguson. He was up in the control booth with the director and the technical people. He had a front-row seat to the whole spectacle.

The curtain opened, and we walked out looking like tattooed axe murderers. Tony told us later that the director immediately freaked the fuck out. She was stammering. "Oh my God, Oh my God, Where's…where's his jacket? He's naked! He's naked! Oh my God, he's covered in tattoos!"

Nobody up top knew what to do. So they did nothing.

97

We played the song, and it was a fucking home run. The audience was into it, and the band was energized and on point. In fact, we blew right through the instruction to cut the guitar solo. Apache was feeling it, so he just launched into the solo like he did every other night. We stretched out the ending too, thanks to our rebellious streak. We took all the time we wanted.

Arsenio was super pissed about the whole thing. We ended up not doing anything we said we would do. But we were more about the music and the live audience than the production or the station break timelines.

Furthermore, we weren't concerned about our image. Yeah, we looked like a Charles Manson fan club—but we sang ballads and R&B rock tunes. We were cool before our brand of cool was a thing, which was ultimately the problem.

Our image plagued us because nobody knew how to take us. We probably did scare a few people—to the point where it didn't matter how fucking awesome we sounded. Americans had to get past what they saw before they could digest what they heard.

But from our vantage point, we were just on the fucking *Arsenio Hall Show*. We were on tour with Kiss. We were about to cut a record with Bob Rock for Geffen Records.

Our future was so bright, we had to wear shades.

Then, faster than a flash of light, shit went sideways.

We should have seen it coming. *I* should have seen it coming. All the signals were there long before we recorded the album.

CHAPTER 6:
THE GENE AND I

Please allow me to step out of the timeline for a moment. I've got tell you a few stories.

As I mentioned in the previous chapter, Gene Simmons is an amazing guy to hang around. These days, he has grown into a caricature of himself. If you wanted someone to play Gene Simmons at a costume party—but told them to go *way* over the top with their portrayal—then they might get *close* to imitating Gene himself.

I can't figure out if he is more rock star or more business tycoon, but he is definitely a healthy dose of both. Yes, he can be a bit of a tyrant. He wanted no part of Little Caesar when we toured with Kiss, and he never hesitated to remind us of that every fucking day. However, he has a self-awareness that is damned interesting. He knows exactly what he's doing, and he's very good at doing it.

He rarely drops the "Gene Façade." But every once in awhile, I would catch a devilish gleam in his eye just before he launched into another full-on, over-the-limit Gene moment.

Because I saw through a lot of his Gene bullshit, I was never intimidated by his presence. I think he respected that, although he would never tell me personally. Through it all, I grew to greatly enjoy watching, and sometimes participating in, The Gene Show whenever he was around.

So in honor of The Gene Show, I figured I'd write about some of the extreme rock star moments I have witnessed and/or lived through. Some stories involve Gene directly, some involve touring with Kiss, and some involve antics before or after the Kiss tour. But all of them are "typical" rock star stories and moments.

Sit back and pour a snifter of brandy. It's time for twelve "Tales of the Certifiable." Due to the length of this chapter, I will number each of the stories in order to break up this long run for you to read.

Story 1

I'd like to introduce you to a story that's become a running joke in my family.

I am in Jenna Jameson's 2012 book, *How to Make Love Like a Porn Star: A Cautionary Tale*. I am mentioned on the second page of Chapter One. Jenna is talking about how she and her friend, Jennifer, are on their way to a biker rally/music festival called the Laughlin River Run. She mentions that they were looking forward to seeing Little Caesar because they were both in love with the lead singer.

Did you catch that?

They were both in love with Little Caesar's lead singer.

She goes on in the book to say that she and her friend are dressed sexy in order to grab the attention of the lead singer.

Obviously, I had no idea this was going on. I was married at the time, although I can't say that having two hot nineteen-year-olds fawning all over me wouldn't have had at least a small impact on my ego.

The day Jenna released the book, my phone blew up. I don't know what it says about my friends that all of them purchased a porn star's book the day it hit the shelves, but I rarely judge them for being the filthy animals they are.

Oops. I mean, good for them for being porn-positive!

This published mention of little ol' Ron gave me some extra street cred with all my old buddies. It also gave me something to lord over Renee when I am in the mood to mess with her.

Don't cry for me, Argentina. She dishes it right back at me like a pro. I have to give her props for that.

Despite all the fuss over my "stunning good looks," I have yet to meet Jenna Jameson. I probably never will, but I figured the gentlemanly thing to do was to return the favor and mention her in my book.

I don't know that her friends will blow up her phone when this one hits the shelves, but a guy can dream. Hell, maybe her friend Jennifer will see it and at least get a nice chuckle.

Thanks for giving me the cred, Jenna! I'll take all I can get.

Story 2

Right out of the gate, the band learned how life on the road was going to be with Kiss. Not anything good or bad; it was just the way things went in their camp. Personally, I learned that it was extremely difficult to be a monitor engineer for Gene Simmons.

Not just that specific role. Kiss roadies and crew got fired left and right. We learned that touring with them was a lot like being in the front lines of a combat zone. The adage "Don't get close to anyone" was perfectly applicable. You couldn't get attached to anyone because you didn't know how long they were going to be around.

But the monitor and sound guys bore the brunt of this revolving door.

Some of this information came to me as the direct result of being tight with Gary Corbett. Gary played off-stage keyboards for Kiss during their live shows. However, his job was far more involved than that.

Gary, by virtue of being a behind-the-scenes musician, was also in control of the samples. In other words, he triggered additional vocals during the chorus by simply pushing a button on his keyboard. With only four guys on stage—and presumably out of breath at times —Kiss used a little help when it came to making the chorus sound full, or making it sound like at least four people were singing harmony. Kiss didn't play to tracks, but they did push a few samples to augment the performance.

In addition, Gary could pull samples to bulk up Paul Stanley's guitar parts. Paul was the rhythm guitar player, so his parts weren't as complex as the lead guitar player's would have been. This allowed Paul to sing and dance while strumming chords or playing support notes behind the lead. Therefore, if Paul was jumping around the stage and not playing steadily, Gary would come in underneath him and "fill in" some of the rhythm guitar parts.

Kiss was the vanguard of scaling this sort of augmentation. A lot of bands were tinkering with this technology, but Kiss was among the first stage-show bands that utilized it at a professional level.

When Kiss did their sound check, Gene would never ask to hear the vocal samples. He didn't want anyone to know that Kiss used samples, so he protected Kiss's secret by not referring directly to them. Instead, he would say, "Turn up the keyboards."

To the sound guy, this was extremely vague. Did Gene mean the guitar part? Did he mean the vocals? Was he being literal and mean to turn up the actual keyboard parts?

Whatever the poor cad chose, it always seemed to NOT be what Gene wanted. There was always contention.

Okay. So there's that.

The first sound tech to go was a guy who joined the tour on the same day Little Caesar joined the tour. Not a normal dude in regular society, but exactly the kind of oddball you tend to find in any sea of roadies. Yet, his particular brand of "oddball" was arguably odder than most.

The first time I laid eyes on the guy, he was wearing a NASCAR fire suit. And I'm not talking about a replica t-shirt of a NASCAR fire suit. Hell no. This cat wore the full-body coveralls, complete with sponsor patches and fire-retardant material. It was also bright red.

Bright. Fucking. Red.

The next day, he wore the same fire suit. He may have also donned the official ball cap that went with the fire suit. This guy was a consummate NASCAR fan. Apparently.

He still wore the same fire suit the day after that. And the day after that.

What the fuck?

About five shows in, the guys in my band had watched Kiss long enough to know how the cadence went. Gene would be on stage, yelling, pointing, and gesturing wildly to the monitor guy.

On about the fifth night, Gene stormed off the stage and got right up in the face of Fire Suit Guy. I wasn't standing close to the confrontation, but I could see Gene just fuckin' screaming at the guy, right in his face. And the guy kept giving him the "gotchya" sign. You know the one. It's sort of like giving a finger gun while winking, as if he was pantomiming, "Got it, boss!"

From my vantage point, I started thinking the guy was a sound engineering genius. Because he was working for Kiss, despite being weird as fuck.

The next night, I watched the same shit go down between this guy and Gene. Gene was on stage, yelling, blustering, and gesturing. The guy was off stage, facing Gene with his left hand in the air. Not really gesturing per se, but standing with one hand up. And he didn't move. It pissed Gene right the fuck off.

It was weirder than the night before. But it got even weirder.

Turns out, this guy truly was a genius—but not in a "sound engineer" kind of way. Rather, he was a twisted mastermind in a "James Bond Villain" kind of way.

The guy knew Gene's reputation for being hard on sound engineers. His first step was to go AutoZone and get a cardboard cutout of the actual NASCAR driver who wore the fire suit and cap this guy would wear.

He then wore the bright red fire suit every day to train Gene's eye to not look for the guy specifically. Instead, he trained Gene to look for that fire suit. After awhile, Gene's eye just found the bright red beacon. He didn't focus on the guy's face at all.

Absolutely fucking brilliant. This guy was playing the long game.

On the fateful night of Fire Suit Guy's demise, Gene just looked off stage until his eye fell upon the fire suit. Then, he did what he always did: yell and gesture at the suit.

Except during this show, the guy put the cardboard cutout where he always stood…and got the fuck out of town.

The guy walked out in the middle of the show and got in a cab headed for the airport. He just quit. Yet, he still had the whole scene planned out ahead of time. When he executed his dastardly plan, it was like watching Baryshnikov dance or van Gogh paint or Tchaikovsky compose. This guy was an artist; his medium was mayhem.

It was such a thing of beauty that it brought a tear to my eye.

When Gene finally stormed off stage to confront the guy face-to-face, it didn't take him long to see it was not a living human being at all—it was a cardboard cut-out. In a fit of rage, he grabbed it and tore it into angry bits of conniption confetti.

No one was available to replace the guy right in the middle of the tour. I believe Gene sent someone to the airport to retrieve him. They spoke and made up. From that point on, Gene was more civil to the guy.

I ran into Fire Suit Guy the following morning and said, "Dude! I thought you were weird as fuck at first. Now you're my fucking hero!"

He grinned. "Nahh, man. I'm no hero. I just came prepared."

He had been dragging the cardboard cut-out with him from city to city, waiting for the right moment to spring it on an unsuspecting rock star.

My fucking hero: Fire Suit Guy.

Story 3

Not many guys dive right in to telling salacious stories of backstage antics while on the road. But notable exceptions to this rule exist. The guys in Mötley Crüe, Guns 'n Roses, and Sammy Hagar, to name a few. Most guys were married or had girlfriends, so they didn't want to admit to some of the shit they participated in. Now, a lot of the guys are middle-aged (or older) with families and jobs. They've outgrown the desire to shock people by spinning sexually explicit yarns.

I stayed out of that mess, for the most part. I was married and stayed loyal to Marlana (the exception being the other woman, heroin). Despite not having any juicy anecdotes about personally skiing down an avalanche of pussy, I saw some shit.

For example, while we were on the Kiss tour, we played a show in Philadelphia at the Spectrum. Little Caesar had just finished our set and piled into the dressing room. In walked a very attractive pair of women: one a little older, one a little younger. They were dressed in the finest selections from the "Slutty Sexy Rock Chick" collection. The younger one could barely walk in her six-inch heels.

The older one approached me and introduced the younger one as her daughter.

I remained cool. I thought to myself, *Oh, okay. This is kinda weird.* The daughter was dressed with her tits hanging out and her skirt barely covering her. The mom was totally okay with her daughter's look. Whatever.

Mom continued. "My daughter is a big fan of the band and thinks you are so hot."

I started to back away slowly. "Ah. That's very nice. Uh-huh. It's very nice to meet you. You know, meet you both."

I quickly made my way across the room to strike up a conversation with someone else. Anyone else. Mom followed and engaged me again. Except, this time she was visibly annoyed.

"You know, today is my daughter's birthday."

"Oh. Congratulations."

Mom leaned in. "Do you like her dress?"

"Yeah, yup. Very nice. Very attractive girl."

I bid her adieu and made my way across the room to find yet *another* someone else to talk to. Mom followed and engaged again. This time, she was even more annoyed.

With hands on hips, she barked, "Don't you think my daughter is hot?"

I repeated what I had said moments earlier, "Yes. Yes, I do. Your daughter is a very attractive girl."

She frowned. "I would think you'd be hitting on her."

All I could think to say was, "Well, she's your daughter."

She waived me off. "Today is her 16th birthday. For her birthday present, I was going to let you pop her cherry."

I swear to fucking God. That is exactly what she said.

I shook my head in confusion. "Uhhhh, excuse me?"

She continued like *I* was the asshole in this equation. "And you don't seem like you care at all about her!"

I pointed out that her daughter was only sixteen. Not that I could graft any logic onto her special brand of crazy.

Mom whirled around and grabbed her daughter's hand. Mom, in a big snit, dragged her poor daughter behind her as they left the dressing room together. End of story.

At least for a couple months.

Later in the tour, we bumped into some other band on the road. I won't mention which band—I'm pretty sure those guys all have kids now. They started talking about this famous mother-daughter team from Pennsylvania that, apparently, all of them had done each time they rolled through Philly.

The mother/daughter tag-team had forged quite a legendary reputation, sleeping their way through every musician playing the city of Brotherly Love.

I swear, I cannot make this shit up. But I can out-weird the sexual depravity, even in that story.

Let me tell you about a girl in San Antonio.

Story 4

While we were out on the road with Kiss, we did some club dates on our days off. Before one of those dates, we ran into the guys from the band Junkyard. After some of the usual chitchat, they asked where we were headed next. I said we were on our way to San Antonio to do a gig with the band, Tattoo Rodeo.

Their eyes lit up. One of the members said, "Listen, there is going to be this chick waiting backstage when you get there."

I urged him on. "Okaaay?"

He continued. "The club you're playing gives the band fruit platters. They'll bring it out and put it on your bus."

Everyone in Junkyard nodded along with the story.

"This girl. She's the daughter of a politician in San Antonio. She's obviously mad at her dad and wants to get even with him."

He paused for effect. He wanted our minds to race ahead in the story. Because he knew that whatever we thought he was about to say would pale in comparison to what he actually ended up saying.

"She is going to want various fruits inserted into her."

In unison, we all exclaimed, "What?"

He held his ground. "Yup." He was backed up by the rest of the group.

We were flattered that the guys in Junkyard held us in high enough regard to give us a heads-up so we didn't miss out on this amazing opportunity. Unfortunately, we decided to pass on a chance to experience hardcore fruit insertion.

He left us with one final thought. "Believe me, it sounds weird as fuck right now. But mark my words, you're going to be sitting around bored and this is going to start sounding like the best idea you've ever heard."

Sure enough, we rolled into San Antonio for the gig—and there was a girl in our dressing room. Nice girl. Cute girl. Just like the guys in Junkyard predicted.

I pulled the band into a huddle.

"Guys, I think that's the chick."

Now, in order to protect the dignity of my brother Apache, I won't mention that it was him who said, "Hmph. She's cute and I like fruit. Bring her onto the bus!"

Like clockwork, catering came out and brought a fruit platter to the bus. Shortly thereafter, she came onto the bus and retired to the back lounge with one of my band mates that I will not admit was Apache.

When we got back to Los Angeles, we ran into the Junkyard guys again. They asked about the girl.

Apache was like, "Yeah! Yeah, I got with her."

And they were like, "Well, how many grapes did you get in her?"

Without missing a fucking beat, Apache said, "Oh, I don't know. Maybe two dozen?"

Junkyard started to applaud, "Wow, dude! That's a personal best!"

I had to ask. I couldn't stop myself. "Where…where did you insert these grapes?"

"I put 'em in her butt."

The guys in Junkyard cheered.

Apache just shrugged.

I can't make this stuff up. It was like I was having an out-of-body experience here at the rock and roll freak show.

We bumped into Tattoo Rodeo a few days later. As it turned out, they did the same damn thing. The girl was known as The Human Fruit Dispenser. From the sound of things, she was especially fond of grapes.

I suppose they were easy to pass.

I'm ashamed of myself for actually writing that.

Story 5

That last story might sound like "just another Tuesday evening" in the life of a rock star. Yet, with the whole biker motif and subsequent audience that Little Caesar drew, every one of our shows was a fucking sausage fest. We didn't ever have the girls. When I read other rocker autobiographies, or hear them on the radio or on podcasts, I think, *How does that happen?*

We used to sit around and complain about how we got cheated out of our well-deserved rock and roll lifestyle.

We gave it some thought, and it dawned on us. A group of girls might pull up to a club or theater to see one of our shows, but then see two hundred motorcycles parked out front. Do you think they're about to go in and mingle with that crowd? Fuck no. They'd be more likely to say, "I'm outta here."

Photo Credit: Ross Halfin

I might be exaggerating a little bit here, but not a hell of a lot. It was a rare occurrence. When it did happen, we learned to be suspicious.

I am reminded of an incident that happened when we played a show in Tampa. This was Florida on a warm night, and the club was packed with scary looking motorcycle guys. Just another Tuesday evening for Little Caesar.

While we were doing the show, I looked out and saw a drop-dead gorgeous girl in the crowd. Her boyfriend was with her and appeared to have her in a frightened death grip. She was facing the stage, and he had his arms wrapped around her from behind, a pose that said, "mine mine mine," like he was protecting a pirate chest of gold.

Then it got weird.

I was singing, doing my best to not stare at this girl. But she kept smiling at me, blowing kisses, and winking. Her boyfriend was behind her, clueless as to what she was doing. All he could see was that I kept looking at her.

From my side of this exchange, I was enjoying the ego stroke and the attention. I was thinking, *This sure beats having a 300-pound biker dude staring at me all night.*

After the show, we went out to mingle with the crowd, have a few drinks, and do a little public relations work on behalf of the band. Of course, she was there, waiting patiently outside of our dressing room.

Her boyfriend was there, too—with his tentacles wrapped around her like The Kracken gripping Blackbeard's ship. That didn't stop her from tearing away from his grasp and waltzing right up to me. Because this could not happen any other way, she started overtly flirting with me. Hardcore flirting.

It got real uncomfortable. I didn't want to disrespect the poor schmuck. I told her, "Honey, isn't your boyfriend right there?"

That didn't slow her down one iota. She kept the full-court press going, leaning into me and doing all the sexy flirting stuff that pretty girls do.

I'm so bad at this shit.

Her boyfriend was growing more and more visibly disturbed. He would try to hold her hand and she would push it away. He edged closer and closer until the three of us were basically sharing a phone booth. I was about to extricate myself from the situation when she leveled it up a notch.

"So, you gonna take me back to your hotel?"

Oh. Okay. So that happened.

I tried to slow her roll. "Well, first of all, I'm married. And second, we're actually loading up and preparing to drive to the next town."

It didn't even faze her. "Well, it won't take long."

I couldn't tell if I was flattered or insulted.

Her boyfriend, in the meantime, was staring me down, mouth agape and fire in his eyes. She just kept fucking going.

"No, no. Seriously. It'll be fun. Just a quick roll in the hay."

And with that, her boyfriend lost whatever tenuous sliver of sanity he had been clinging to. He backed up a step and blew a gasket.

"I'm so fucking sick of this shit! I'm done with this!"

I don't know if she even glanced in his direction. She dismissed him in the most casual way you can imagine.

"I'm done with you. You're boring."

That poured jet fuel onto his fire. He stepped around and got right up in her face. They proceeded to have a knock-down, drag-out, rock-and-roll screaming match right there in the hallway.

Actually, I made a mistake a few paragraphs ago. I didn't actually tell her I wasn't interested until after they had the fight. Hmm, I suppose that makes me partly responsible for the side show that ensued.

And they say I'm an asshole.

At one point during their screaming match, she turned to me and said, "Well? Are we going?"

I said, "Uh, no. We're not."

Now, she's pissed at *me*.

"You mean to tell me that I just broke up with my boyfriend and you're not even going to get with me?"

By this point, I had seen enough to know I wanted no part of this fucking clown circus. Not that it made her any less maniacal.

"How the fuck am I going to get back to my house?"

I scratched my head, "Wow. I don't know. Maybe you should

have thought this through before you--"

She cut me off and started losing her shit. I think I may have shoved twenty bucks in her hand for a cab. As entertaining as the whole process had been, I did feel bad for her.

The rest of the guys in the band certainly didn't feel bad for me. They started busting my balls.

"Dude, what are you doing?! She's fucking gorgeous."

I threw my arms out. "I know! I know!"

But that was the person I have always been. I'm just not a dog. Therefore, it wasn't meant to be.

Story 6

Crazy shit like that kept happening because a small subset of people lost all form of common sense when they were around us. It was like they assumed they had to play a certain role in order to fit what they perceived to be the rock and roll lifestyle. They were characters in a campy movie instead of real people interacting with other real people.

Geffen's PR people made sure that our "reputation" arrived in each town a full day or two before we did. Secretaries shut their doors. Interns backed away in fear. We felt like the most normal group of serial killers America had ever seen.

A regular day on the road for us would involve a radio appearance. We'd get up early and schlep down to the station so we could hang out with douchey morning show DJs and try to drum up interest in our show that night.

If you are a fan of morning drive-time rock radio, I hate to burst your bubble. These guys tend to be balding, middle aged dudes wearing satin jackets and sweatpants. The more they try to look cool, the sadder everyone feels when they lay eyes upon them.

These poor schlubs were consistent with all out-of-touch dudes trying too hard to be cool. Almost every time we left a morning show interview, the DJs would want to take us to the local strip club. A balding dude with a gut, wearing a ponytail and a Members Only jacket, sitting in a strip club at 10:30 in the morning, is probably the saddest human being on the planet.

Again, this wasn't our scene. Fidel would be on the phone

with his wife and daughter. I would be on the phone with Marlana. Loren was sober by this time. We would just sit there in awkward silence, trying not to yawn and look at our watch.

We were around strippers a lot. Not that there's anything wrong with that, but it got to be too much after awhile. The most uncomfortable it ever got with a stripper was one night while we were recording in Vancouver. This didn't happen while we were on the Kiss tour, but it was shortly thereafter.

Bob Rock was working with Bryan Adams toward the end of our time up there. Bryan, as a result, hung out with us in the studio a lot. I love Bryan Adams's music, and found him to be an absolute delight to hang out with.

Bruce Allen (Bryan's manager) threw a huge birthday bash for Bryan in November of that year, and we tagged along. This was right after Bryan had recorded the song, "It's Only Love" with Tina Turner.

Tina couldn't be at his birthday party, so instead she sent a huge cake that got wheeled out into the middle of the floor. As the cliché would hold true, a stripper popped out of the cake and started to dance around the room. It was exquisitely uncomfortable; our band wasn't all that into her. Bryan, the guy for whom she was there to entertain, wasn't into her, either. He seemed really creeped out by her.

I ended up feeling bad for the girl. She acted pissy, but I'm sure it was just to cover up how bad she must have felt.

Thankfully, it got better.

A couple nights later, Bryan played a show at the BC Place, a huge stadium in Vancouver. He invited us to open for him, which made us giddy. We said, "Hell, yes!" before he finished asking.

That night, Bryan called me up on stage to sing a duet with him. We chose "Stand By Me," the classic 1961 R&B tune by Ben E. King.

I'm not one to get swept off my feet by a scrawny Canadian dude, but that moment was pure magic for me.

I still carry a deep respect for Bryan and the music he has written over the years. Look up the video for "It's Only Love." It's got a real R&B, soulful feel to it. A fantastic song.

During the same hiatus from Vancouver, a few more crazy things happened. We had yet to go on the road with Kiss.

Before Bob Rock was hired to produce our record, we were looking around for someone who could capture our particular sound in the way we wanted. We called a guy named Joe Hardy, who engineered a lot of the early ZZ Top records. He was tight with Billy Gibbons and everyone in that camp. We loved the sound of those early ZZ Top records and thought Joe would be a good match.

We were right. He was fantastic! He had the exact same twisted sense of humor as our band. A match made in heaven.

Once we shook hands with Joe, we went to Ardent Studio in Memphis to cut a demo with him.

Geffen wanted us to put out an EP while we waited for John Kalodner to stop fighting with David Geffen (and for Bob Rock to get done with whatever he was doing). Their thinking was that if we released an EP on a small label, they could create a buzz and bump our street cred by saying that Geffen "discovered" us—scooped a rag-tag band of dirty, street rockers out of the underground music scene.

Photo Credit: Marty Temme

It was total fabricated bullshit, but it worked with Guns 'n Roses. Geffen had them release an EP in 1986, *Live ?!*@ Like a Suicide*, one full year ahead of *Appetite for Destruction*. The rest was history.

Whatever, dude. We were down for anything at that point.

We saddled up and flew to Memphis. Apparently, Joe wanted to get a certain "energy" from the band. On our second or third day of recording, he decided we needed to play "Porn Mag Roulette." He ambled on down to the liquor store and purchased a pre-wrapped, six-pack of porno magazines. I'm not talking high-class, polished publications like *Playboy*, *Penthouse*, or *Hustler*. I'm talking about the kind of beautifully twisted smut you buy in bundles of six at the liquor store, wrapped in plastic to protect the eyes of puritans. The kind where you have no idea about what hodgepodge raunch you're getting yourself into. The kind with colorful titles like "Pleasantly Plump," "Midget Porn," and "Stump Porn."

I wish I was kidding.

He fanned them out in a tasteful array on a table, and then waited patiently while we entered the studio and looked around. Joe was amused by the shock on our faces. His sense of humor ebbed in, as he explained that he had no idea what kind of porn we were into. So he purchased a variety pack.

One of the Magazines was titled, *Fuck Queens*. When you leafed through this fine publication, you noticed that it was filled with striking images of cross-dressing men in various stages of sexual union.

As a band, Little Caesar was given a gift. We immediately latched on to the title and started calling each other Fuck Queens.

Don't ask me why. We weren't the most sophisticated group of gentlemen.

We recorded the EP, which was called *Name Your Poison*. One song, "Down to the Wire" landed on a Metal Blade Records compilation in 1989, called *Street Survivors*. That EP represented a good start to our career.

My sister, Sandi, did all the artwork for the EP. She was working with our day-to-day manager (Tony Ferguson) to assemble the track listing and credits for the back cover. Tony called Joe Hardy to ask how he wanted his name listed in the production credits.

Joe, being Joe, responded, "Produced by Joe 'Fuck Queen' Hardy."

Tony did two or three laps with Joe regarding this decision, but Joe stood firm. To Tony's credit, he held his ground on Joe's behalf when Geffen's legal team went berserk over the wording.

Sure enough, my sister finalized the typeset with the moniker "Joe 'Fuck Queen' Hardy" on the cover. I don't remember if Geffen ultimately changed it, but it's still a good story.

Story 7

Before one of our recording sessions at Joe's studio, he called us into his office and said, "Listen. We're going to get a late start today. There's something we have to do first."

We loaded everyone into the van and allowed Joe to navigate the crew into downtown Memphis. He pulled in front of City Hall and asked us to get out.

We emerged from the van, blinking and confused. There was a podium set up on the sidewalk, and members of the press were milling about in a semi-circle in front of the staging area.

Turns out, Joe had called the mayor's office and told them he had a band of luminaries coming to his studio. He wouldn't say who they were, but assured the mayor's liaison that this band was huge. Further, it would behoove the mayor to offer them keys to the city.

My hand to God—the mayor's staff bought it. Hook, line, and sinker. I don't know how Joe pulled it off, or how he had the balls to actually follow through. But there we were.

We stepped out of the van. I was decked out in full rock star regalia—hangover, tattoos, chains, earrings, biker boots, long hair. The rest of the band looked like there was a breakout from Cell Block Six.

I could see the looks of panic on the faces of all the stiff suits, politicians, and press alike. Everyone there was in a state of baffled recoil. Except for Joe. Fucking Joe was laughing his ass off in the van.

We did it. We approached the podium and accepted the generous gift from the Mayor's Office. Each key came in a nice, powder blue, velvet-lined box with our names inscribed on them. The keys were accompanied by official documents, written in calligraphy to make them look even more official. The documents began with, "Esteemed honorary citizens of Memphis present these keys to…."

I was handed a key to Memphis by the mayor, Richard C. Hackett. I didn't hang onto it for long. It ended up in the trash somewhere when Marlana kicked me out. I pulled it out, and later, it was purged from a storage unit I kept it in.

I can't imagine the optics of that moment. It had to look like the mayor was giving the Hells Angels some kind of award for being nice to children and small animals. I hope the press was gentle with him for that disaster.

An immaculate disaster orchestrated by a madman's madman, Joe Hardy.

We even pulled Peavey, the electronic audio equipment manufacturer, into the joke.

At the time, we were sponsored by Peavey. Pretty cool for a band that hadn't yet put out a formal album. We had such a strong reputation around the club scene, Peavey wanted to sign us while we were still on the ground floor.

Peavey, at the time, had a seedy reputation of being cheap bar band equipment. We loved their gear and actually introduced Bob Rock to their stuff—and he liked it. So much so, that he purchased a good half-dozen of their amps once Little Caesar wrapped in Vancouver.

Hartley Peavey, the founder and CEO of the company, approached us to ask if they could make a Little Caesar signature model amplifier. Of course we agreed, and requested that the model be called the Peavey FQ120.

Before you ask, the answer is yes; FQ stood for "Fuck Queen." We wanted the signature model amplifier to be dubbed the "Fuck Queen 120."

I don't beam with pride over every decision I've made in my lifetime. But this one was a thing of beauty.

Hartley asked what the FQ stood for. We didn't tell him.

Joe Hardy would be proud.

Story 8

Dear readers, I'd like to bring your attention back around to Gene Simmons.

Coming out of a solid blues-rock background, I was consistently disappointed by the lack of skill demonstrated by many of the popular hair metal bands. I was not alone in this disgust; I spoke with several engineers and producers who were equally dismayed by how such schlock could sell.

I chatted with Gene about it one day.

He stated very clearly, "This business is not about music; it's about entertainment. It's not about whether you play the notes correctly; it's about whether the pyro goes off on time."

He gestured toward the arena, "If you screw up the music, don't react. Just play through. These fans out here? They'll never know the difference. They're here to see the show."

Interestingly, not two weeks after having that debate about musical integrity versus commerce and entertainment, which was more of a Gene lecture than a debate, we rolled into Poughkeepsie, New York.

We arrived a day early and checked into the hotel. The arena was across the street, and on the corner was a little bar with a stage in it.

We walked over to have a few beers and hang out. There was really nothing much to do in Poughkeepsie. Soon after, Gene walked in and saw some gear on the stage. The house band had apparently left their equipment overnight, presumably to pick it up again and entertain this evening.

He looked at us. "You guys want to jam?"

He didn't have to ask us twice.

"Fuck yeah! Let's do it!"

We played three hours if we played a minute. We jammed through Chuck Berry songs, Motown songs, classic rock songs—all the recognizable hits.

Say what you will about the utter simplicity of Kiss's music, but Gene Simmons has an amazing depth of musical knowledge. He has an entire library of songs in his head and is evidently able to pull out any of them at a moment's notice. And he can play them as if he rehearsed the night before.

He certainly played the hell out of them that night.

Story 9

Fuckin' Gene Simmons! His ultimate Gene-ness was so fun to watch when it landed on an ordinary person. Kiss fans are obviously quite taken by his presence, but when anyone else runs into a Gene wall, it cracks me the hell up.

Same hotel in Poughkeepsie. Gene arrived before we did, so when I walked into the hotel lobby, Gene was standing at the front desk, talking to (or at) the clerk.

"I would like some strawberry ice cream."

The poor schmuck behind the desk. He had no idea he was dealing with Gene.

"Uh, sir, right now room service is closed. It won't open back up until dinner time."

Gene didn't crack a smile. It is an honor and a privilege to watch his mind work. He spoke very slowly, enunciating each syllable.

"No, no, no. I'm sure that if you look in your kitchen, you will find me, Gene Simmons of Kiss, some strawberry ice cream."

The kid froze in fear, wide eyed and mouth hanging open. But Gene wasn't done. He leaned over the desk and put himself nose-to-nose with the poor schlub.

"Even if that means the kitchen is at the 7-11 down the street."

With that, he turned and saw us standing there, amused.

"Good afternoon, gentlemen."

I stepped forward, "So, Gene. Do you think you have ever eaten a meal that hasn't been spat in?"

He thought about it for a moment, and replied with a deadpan, "Probably not."

And THAT, my friend, is the very definition of self-awareness.

Story 10

I don't think it's a big secret that Gene Simmons is not his birth name. I'll give away a real secret in a moment, but the name thing shouldn't come as a shock to anyone. Gene was born Chaim Witz in Haifa, Israel. His demon persona makes him bigger than life, but he is still his mother's son.

We opened for Kiss one night at the Nassau Coliseum in Uniondale, New York, on Long Island. It was a dream come true for me because when I was a teenager, a buddy of mine's dad worked for the coliseum and could get us into concerts. I saw a ton of shows in that building, including Led Zeppelin, Black Sabbath, and, coincidentally, Kiss. To play on the very stage I worshipped as a boy was a "pinch me" kind of moment.

On this night, it was even MORE spectacular for me. I got to see the enormous Gene Simmons—in full rock-star attire—get taken to task by his four-foot, eight-inch-tall Israeli mother. She lived in New York and was proud to see her son play whenever she could.

Tonight, she was there. And she was glorious.

Before every gig, Gene would do his meet-and-greets before the show started. He shook hands and kissed babies until he'd had enough, and then he would give his road manager, Charlie Hernandez, a signal that it was time to go. Charlie would step in and extricate him, allowing Gene to retire to the dressing room and finish his pre-show preparation.

Incidentally, he liked to be completely free after the show because he would have a full buffet waiting for him in his dressing room. I'm talking full hams and complete turkeys. The guys in Little Caesar would always congregate in Gene's room after a show. He was generous with us, urging us to eat whatever we wanted. We ate like kings.

But on this particular occasion, Gene was forced to do his meet-and-greet after the show. Anyone who knows anything about Gene's personality will know immediately that this was a "no bueno" for everyone around him. He was not a happy camper, to say the least.

Another poorly kept secret was that the members of Kiss wore wigs on stage. Nobody ever talks about it—especially around

Gene or Paul—but everyone who works with them knows it to be true.

While we were on their tour, they were in the "no make-up" phase of their careers, so they were not doing the kabuki-style white face with black designs. To be honest, they wore more make-up when they were going without make-up. It took a fair amount of spackle to make them appear young and beautiful.

In Gene and Paul's respective dressing rooms, there were white Styrofoam heads waiting to hold the wigs. The musicians would sweep into their dressing rooms and toss their wig onto the head.

After the Long Island show, I was standing next to Gene during the late meet-and-greet. He was simmering quietly, cursing whoever made this egregious scheduling snafu.

Out of the crowd popped his little mother. She pushed her way through the fans and right up to Gene, who was still wearing his stage outfit. Tugging on his shirt, she said in a thick accent, "Chaim!"

Gene looked down, "Hi, Mom. What's up?"

She said, "Chaim! The orchestra is done playing now. You take off your hair piece."

You could have heard a pin drop. Gene's mom spoke the unspeakable. Out loud.

But he was Gene Simmons. He patted her gently on the head and said, "Yes, Mom. The rock helmet comes off now."

She smiled warmly, "Oh, good. I like your regular hair better."

It was hysterical and touching. Gene was so far over the top for most of the time, it was nice to see him put aside the showman and accept his mother's advice.

Story 11

I'd like to give away a trade secret.

When we replaced Winger on the Kiss tour, ticket sales spiraled down the toilet. It had been Kiss with Winger and Slaughter, and Winger and Slaughter were *big* draws. As I have already mentioned, we didn't even have an album out yet. People didn't know who we were.

That's why Gene wanted to get us the hell off his tour. He wanted Winger back because Winger filled the seats. Kiss had a legacy and a lot of fans, but legacy tours weren't yet in vogue. To be honest, most of the fans were there to support Kiss, but they really wanted to see Winger and Slaughter.

We just couldn't pull them in like Kiss wanted. I remember Gene once described us as pork chops at a bar mitzvah.

I was okay with it; I took it in the spirit from which it was intended.

Which still wasn't very good.

When ticket sales would tank, Kiss would end up cancelling the show. Their collective ego couldn't handle word getting out that a Kiss concert didn't sell out. They'd rather just cancel.

Some nights during our tour, Paul Stanley would "get into a car accident." It was announced that, "He's okay, but he just can't play tonight. Sorry, folks! We'll catch you next time we're in town."

It was the standard line, and it was doled out whenever necessary.

Paul would play those up, acting hurt that Gene didn't call or send flowers after his "car accident." They had a whole routine worked out. It reminded me of my grandparents bickering.

It was all in good fun. That whole tour might have been financially devastating for Kiss, but for us, it was a clown car of entertainment. One time in Tulsa, Oklahoma, we purchased a racing go-kart from an ad in the local *Penny Saver*, and then raced it around the arena parking lot all afternoon. When you're six inches off the ground, forty miles per hour can feel like 200.

Through the short time I spent with Gene, I learned a lot about how the business works and how a band at the top of the pyramid conducts themselves on the road. I appreciated his business acumen and his ability to deliver the show his audience wanted, night after night. For him personally, it was almost moment to moment.

We were only on their tour for about six weeks before Winger returned to the fold. Gene was happy when we finally parted ways. I've got to say, we were feeling pretty good about ourselves as well. It felt like we were living in an amazing alternate reality to be on the road with such an iconic band.

Story 12

There is no way I would ever end with eleven stories in a chapter. That feels negligent. An even dozen just feels so much better. Therefore, I am going to tell a long one to round out this chapter—but one that involves one of the most interesting things I have ever done in my career. It began musically, almost ended because of the Kiss tour, and then resurrected with a vengeance.

It's a story I've abbreviated a few times on podcasts and within other media interviews. However, I don't believe I have ever told the entire story in one chunk; at least, not in a public forum. Most interviews do not allow ample time to go down such rabbit holes. It's a good story, and one I will take some time to tell—front to back—right here.

My acclaimed career as a big-time, A-list, heart-throb Hollywood movie star began through friendships Marlana and I made while living in New York. It lasted for roughly ten seconds and ended abruptly thereafter, but I choose to look at the glass as being half full.

As I've mentioned, we lived in the artsy part of The City. Subsequently, we were friends with artists working in many different mediums, including music, photography, and film (to name a few). Through this network, I was introduced to Kathryn Bigelow, an (then) up-and-coming film director.

You may recognize her name because she has directed a few monster films, including the original *Point Break*, plus *Zero Dark Thirty*, and *The Hurt Locker*—a film for which she won the Oscar for "Best Director" in 2009 (the first woman to ever win that category). At the time we knew her in New York, she was looking for a couple songs to add to the soundtrack to her very first feature film, *The Loveless*.

In the end, Kathryn decided to go a different direction. She populated her soundtrack with established songs from the 1950s, but no worries. She and Marlana became close friends and we hung out a lot together moving forward.

In a strange twist of timing, The Kingpins were credited on the official movie poster for *The Loveless*, even though we didn't have a song on the soundtrack. It's funny how things get put into motion contractually, but then cannot be walked back if a change is made at the eleventh hour.

Anyway, years went by. We moved from New York to California and Kathryn (unrelated to our move) also moved out to California. Marlana and Kathryn remained close, and both ended up owning horses and becoming riding partners.

And, in a plot twist that ended up adding another fascinating asterisk on crazy life I've led, Kathryn ended up marrying James Cameron. James, of course, eventually directed a handful small-budget, underground indie films like *The Terminator*, *Titanic*, and *Avatar*.

Perhaps you've heard of them?

So though our connection to Kathryn, Marlana and I began hanging out with her and James Cameron.

I know, right?

Concurrent to all this going on in California, Littler Caesar was in full swing and I was totally immersed in the biker/rock star "look." Long hair, tatts, biker boots…the whole nine yards. And keep in mind, this look was *way* different than anything people were doing back then.

So Kathryn, whose career was now moving forward at light speed, asked me to play a role in the Keanu Reeves, Patrick Swayze film she was set to direct, called *Point Break*. In fact, Little Caesar landed a song, "Down to the Wire," on the soundtrack to the film.

And dude…I really wanted to do it. Unfortunately, it was 1990 and we were out on tour with Kiss. But it was all good— Anthony Kiedis (lead singer of the Red Hot Chili Peppers) ended up being cast in the role.

So that happened. I was on the radar.

One night, I got a phone call from Jim (James Cameron). He told me he was getting ready to shoot the second *Terminator* movie, and that he had a part for me. It was a small part, but he was excited to bring me on set. And then hang out afterwards and get into whatever crazy shit we could think of.

He also wanted me around so he could have a confidant with whom to share his frustrations with Arnold, who (to put it mildly) was NOT a classically trained actor.

At the time, Arnold was a huge star because of the first

Terminator movie—but he was still a bodybuilder at heart, and not an actor. Furthermore, he was Austrian, and had a thick accent. His movies prior to 1984—up to and including the two *Terminator* movies—had *very* few speaking lines. Don't think for a minute that was by accident.

Obviously, I jumped at the chance to be in the movie. And I showed up on the night we filmed my scene, ready to go.

My scene is toward the beginning of the movie. When Arnold first gets transported back to 1991, he is naked (if you've seen the franchise, you get it). He orients himself and then sets out to find clothing and transportation. To do so, he walks into a biker bar.

There, The Terminator comes face-to-face with his arch nemesis and intergalactic tireless warrior of all that is good and pure, RON YOUNG OF LITTLE CAESAR!

No. But that would have been pretty cool.

I was one of the biker-looking dudes in the bar. But not just an "extra." I had an active part in the scene.

The scene was shot at a little biker/country bar called "The Corral," situated toward the top of the San Fernando Valley. Before I drove up for the shoot, Jim asked if I could find someone who could paint my tattoos onto the arms of a stunt double. It turned out, Jim was going to have my character get thrown through a pate glass window, and California law forbade the actor from performing a stunt like that.

My buddy Gil Monte was more than happy to do it—if for no other reason, Jim paid him a crazy amount of money to do so. And Gil was committed to the job. He traced all my tatts and created a stencil, then used watercolors to paint exact replicas onto the arms of the stunt double. The whole operation took like five hours. It was insane, the level of detail to which Jim wanted this to be authentic.

Speaking of which, there was also the matter of my hair.

Jim had pulled me aside earlier and told me to go down to the production office. He said they needed a sample of my hair. Apparently, they were going to make a wig for the stunt double to wear, and wanted it to match my hair exactly.

I suggested he just throw a brown curly wig onto the double, but Jim wouldn't hear of it. A stickler for detail, he wanted everything in the movie to be as precise as possible.

From what I heard later, the wig cost somewhere around $10,000 to make. Add that to the money Gil made for doing the tatts, and the number soars even higher. And this was for a ONE SECOND SHOT (literally) of the stunt double flying through a window.

Crazy. It's no wonder the film came in over budget.

So now we go to shoot my scene. If you watch it on YouTube, I interact with Arnold on screen for four seconds. Then there is one second of the stunt double flying through the window... so five seconds in all. In actuality, my character has more screen time than that because I am in the background throughout the entirety of the bar scene.

All of it was a lot of fun. But my four-second interaction with Arnold's character took way longer to film that it should have.

Here was the setup: Arnold has a conflict with another biker in the bar. I am in the background of the scene (directly over Arnold's shoulder in the final cut of the movie), watching it happen. When Arnold puts the guy down, I step up and hit him over the head with a pool cue. He then turns, grabs me, and throws me through a window.

Easy peasy.

But not.

Incidentally, when Arnold threw me for real during the filming, I jumped (to help give him some lift) and then landed on a big air bag in front of us. That part didn't take long to film. But hitting him with the pool cue took forever.

The lighting and blocking was set, and Jim yelled, "Action!" Then the characters went through the dialogue and I stepped up and hit him with the pool cue…

…and Arnold yelled, "OW!"

Everyone stopped, stunned.

"CUT!"

Jim spoke to Arnold, "Dude…you can't say ow. You're the Terminator."

Arnold, in his Austrian accent, replied, "But that hurt."

Jim just shook his head and melted back behind the camera.

Full disclosure: the pool cue wasn't a real pool cue. It was made of balsa wood, and was designed to break easily when it hit whatever it was aimed at. Arnold was getting hit square in the back of the head, so I imagine it did smart a little. But it was light balsa wood. And furthermore, he was supposed to be deadpan when he got hit—that was the reality of his character. He was invulnerable.

So we did it again. Arnold didn't say anything, but he winced upon impact.

Jim coached him again: "You have to be completely non-reactive."

Arnold maintained his protest, "But this really hurts."

So we tried to trouble shoot and come up with a solution. We tried sawing through a pool cue, just enough so that it shattered more easily upon impact. Unfortunately, balsa wood is so fragile in the first place, marring it just made the cue break from the force/momentum of my swing. In other words, it flew apart *prior* to impact.

Then we tried putting a steel pole behind Arnold so I would ostensibly hit the pole instead of his head. That arrangement never looked right.

Then we tried having me hit Arnold's stunt double instead of Arnold. But because the scene is shot so close-up, there was no way to pull it off without being obvious that it wasn't Arnold.

In all, I must have hit Arnold twelve times. A couple times I hit him in the neck, and that wasn't going to work. It's difficult to hit the exact same spot every single time when you're swinging a balsa wood pool cue like a baseball bat.

I actually left some welts on the poor guy. Jim kept urging me on.

"Ron…really wallop him! You have to put everything you've got into that swing."

He wanted the scene to look as authentic as possible. Much to Arnold's chagrin, of course.

As you watch the scene, pay attention to how it's edited. When I hit Arnold with the pool cue, the scene cuts away quickly—you cannot see Arnold's reaction. This is because we ran out of balsa wood pool cues, so Jim had to go with the footage we were able to get. He cuts away before the audience can see Arnold wince and cry out in pain.

As a strange footnote to this story, on the night we filmed my scene, we ran long. Not only because of the pool cue fiasco, but also because we kept getting interrupted by police sirens blaring in the background. We would begin to shoot, and the sound guy had to keep cutting because of ambient noise.

Finally, Jim asked one of the security guys (who were all retired cops) what was going on. They told him there was a big thing going on about two blocks away. A guy was in a car chase and they were trying to stop and subdue the driver.

Turns out, it was Rodney King.

We were filming the bar scene in *Terminator 2* at the same time as Rodney King was getting hauled out of his car and having the shit kicked out of him by members of the LAPD. Apparently, in order to pull him over, they sent like, thirty or forty cop cars. The blaring and the sirens kept going and going and going…

It was nuts.

By three or four in the morning, my scene was wrapped. However, Jim wasn't done. He had to fuck with me a little before I was allowed to go home.

As another piece of context, I was also filmed for the scene where Arnold drives off with a "procured" motorcycle. You can't see me in the final cut of the movie, but we shot footage of me *after* being thrown through plate glass. I was lying on a car outside of the window. And, true to the story, I was covered with broken glass and blood.

I took my position on the hood of the car, and Jim

approached with a giant, quart-sized bottle of fake blood. The base of this shit is a sugar-based glycerin, so it's sticky and gooey, and ends up hardening over time.

Jim poured that shit and mashed it into my hair, all over my face, and everywhere he could. And he was laughing like a hyena while doing it.

I was like, "Dude...fuck you!" (which made him laugh all the more).

Meanwhile, Arnold has to say his fucking lines—but he can't say his fucking lines to save his life. He has to peel out on a motorcycle, but he can't figure out how the fuck to do that either. So someone is sent to rustle up the motorcycle stunt double—who, incidentally, is different from the regular stunt double. The double steps in and peels out...but his look doesn't match Arnold's look well enough to satisfy Jim.

By now, it's gotten to be freezing cold outside, and I'm lying there in a hardening pool of sticky shit that I'm NEVER going to get out of my hair. And I had ridden my motorcycle up to the location, so also had to think about how I was going to drive home with all this shit stuck to me.

And James Cameron loved every minute of it. Probably danced and fiddled while he cut my bloody scene from the final version of the movie.

But let me tell you this: it was all worth it. Not only was the experience extremely cool, but I wound up getting my SAG (Screen Actors Guild) card out of it. SAG is like a union for working actors, and is very difficult to get into. You have to log a certain number of hours on a union set in order to qualify—and you have to be active every year in order to re-up.

Jim was nice enough to give me a "credit" for my work in the movie. In other words, I am not listed as an "extra;" I was a member of the official cast. I have my name in the credits at the end of the movie.

Directors have a few slots available to gift union credit for "specialty actors." I was fortunate enough to get one of those slots, thanks to James Cameron's generosity.

Oh—and the long night paid off financially for me, too. My first check for residuals showed up in the mail some months later...

and it was (if memory serves) about $13,000. Six months later I got another check for $8,000. Thank you, SAG!

I continued to get some pretty good checks for the next four or five years. Still do, in fact—although these days, they are only for eight or nine dollars. But what the Hell…it was all a unique experience for me.

CHAPTER 7:
BIRTH OF AN ALBUM,
DEATH OF A MOTHER

Back to the timeline.

Somehow, in a mere matter of months, we went from being hailed as the second coming of Led Zeppelin (it's my book; I can write whatever I want) to being on everyone's shit list. It happened so stunningly fast that I frankly don't know if we could have done anything to stop it.

I'll tell you about the exact moment I got on John Kalodner's shit list. It happened just before we headed up to record with Bob Rock in Vancouver. We were pulled off our "pre-album" Kiss tour, necessitated by Bob Rock's commitment to another band in the meantime, and were getting prepped by Geffen.

I was floating around their offices one day when John pulled me into his office. He had just received the mix of Blue Murder's debut CD. Geffen, and John in particular, was extremely high on Blue Murder. They were also extremely high on Little Caesar, of course, and John wanted to prepare me for recording our debut album. We hadn't yet gone to work with Bob Rock, so the Blue Murder CD was a nice portal into understanding Bob's style, since he had produced that CD as well.

Blue Murder was a super group, put together to feature its founder, John Sykes, who had recently left Whitesnake. The other two members of the trio were Tony "The Fretless Monster" Franklin, fresh off his stint with Paul Rogers and Jimmy Page in The Firm, and Carmine Appice, one half of the Appice Brothers, who, with his brother, Vinny, were drumming royalty in rock music.

I joined a few promotional staff and radio people in John's office. He popped in the CD and went directly to the first single, "Jelly Roll."

All the suits were bobbing their heads out of time, trying to look like they knew what the fuck they were doing. I just grew annoyed.

When the song ended, they created a weird group circle jerk —saying how amazing the song was, and how amazing each other was for noticing how amazing the song was. They praised the tones and the echo of the snare drum and the production of the song ad nauseum.

I watched with the same disgust I feel for idiots on social media who do their best to sound smart. The harder they try, the dumber they come across. When the din died down and they shot their asinine loads, I chimed in.

"Kids don't buy sounds, or tones, or production. They buy songs. They buy hooks. If there is no hook, there is no song."

They stared at me in confusion.

I challenged any of them to sing the chorus of the song.

Crickets.

That was the point. Jelly Roll is a cool song. I like it well enough. But there is no hook, no identifiable chorus. When you hear Zeppelin sing "Whole Lotta Love" for the very first time, I guarantee you walk away singing, "Wanna whole lotta love," and then you make the soaring guitar sound that follows.

Jelly Roll might make you play along with the drums on your steering wheel, but it has nothing for you to grab onto and take with you.

One idiot in the room replied, "Yeah, but did you hear the tom-toms during th—"

I interrupted him, "Kids don't care about the fucking tom-toms! You're listening like an industry guy, not like a consumer."

That was it. The defining moment. From then on, John Kalodner hated me. I shamed him in public. History will back me up on this: the other aspect of this event, the one he hated the worst, was that I was right. The single did nothing and Blue Murder is not a household name. Blue Murder could have been a great band, but they were mismanaged out of existence.

Hold on to that. You'll recognize this tune again later on.

In hindsight, I should have kept my fucking mouth shut. Politically, that moment fucked Little Caesar going forward because I was in his permanent doghouse.

Granted, I was in there with good company. From what I understand, the guys in AC/DC wanted nothing to do with Kalodner —and Steven Tyler wouldn't let him into the room.

Still, it was a valuable lesson to be learned. Maybe pick and choose your spots. Not every battle needs to be fought; sometimes, you win a war by keeping your sword in its scabbard.

I think Confucius said that. Apparently, Confucius had to deal with his own John Kalodner.

Even working with the great Bob Rock turned into a six-month nightmare for the band. I've already mentioned that we had to go to Vancouver, only to have Bob immediately step away to do a project with another band.

As I've mentioned, we went out with Kiss while Bob was gone. Things still had upside potential, but they started to seem a little fishy to us. Upon Bob's return to our project, things got incredibly worse.

* * *

Finally, we were set to record. I was looking forward to being in Vancouver, one of the most beautiful cities in North America. I brought my Harley with me, as well as a vintage car, a 1971 Challenger. Driving around the city and the wooded Canadian countryside sounded awesome.

When we arrived, things were weird from square one.

The first task was to meet Bruce Allen. Bruce was the godfather of the Canadian music scene. He managed Bob, as well as Bryan Adams and Loverboy, to name a few. He was the guy, and he was obviously interested to sit down with a hot new band rolling into his town.

The entire band was road weary, but we dutifully drove to Bruce's office building in downtown Vancouver. We entered the lobby and rang the buzzer. And waited.

And waited.

And waited.

After awhile, we were like, "Well, this is weird."

Finally, we got buzzed in. But as we turned the corner from the security doors leading from the lobby, we could hear office doors slamming shut all along the hallway.

Bruce's office was at the far end of the hall. We filed in and noticed that he had a baseball bat lying across his lap. Like he had chosen a weapon before entering the battlefield.

What the fuck?

He opened the conversation with, "Listen. Just letting you know. We don't put up with any bullshit up here."

None of us knew what he was talking about. Thankfully, he clarified.

"There will be no beating up women. There will be no shooting up heroin. No bullshit."

We looked at each other, puzzled. I stepped forward.

"What are you talking about?"

He met my gaze, "I got the lowdown on you guys."

That was it for me. I understood that we looked like a bunch of guys you'd steer away from at a county fair, but we were all good dudes. I have known a number of truly bad guys in my life, and would not stand for my band getting lumped into that same category.

"Listen, I don't know where you got your lowdown, but I have never lifted a finger—none of us have ever lifted a finger—against a woman. I don't know what you're talking about."

Also, none of us did heroin at the time. Later on, that would change, of course. But the whole accusation was appalling to me.

I gestured toward the band, "This guy here, Fidel; he's got a wife and a daughter. Tom is a choir boy, for God's sake. Loren is a total fucking character, but he's a really good guy. Apache—well, I gotta be honest; he actually is pretty crazy. But he he's a really good dude, too. I'm married. All of us are good guys."

By the end of the conversation, Bruce realized I was telling the truth. What we came to piece together was that Bryn Bridenthal, Senior VP and head of publicity at Geffen, had put out a metric ton of bullshit in order to raise our "street cred." It was the same approach taken by the publicist working for Guns n' Roses. Although, Bryn was elevating our scare-o-meter to the point that we made GnR look like a bunch of girl scouts.

We used that persona to our advantage once we learned how to navigate people's initial perceptions of us. We'd hit radio stations and magazine interviews, winning everyone over by being the exact opposite of what they expected.

Face-to-face, we changed people's perception of us so drastically, they ended up liking us even more than if they had anticipated liking us in the first place.

Keep that last sentence in mind before you move on. It'll make sense in a couple minutes.

The way we looked physically would ultimately come around to bite us in the ass. Our appearance did not match the music we played...and especially the way we were produced. People had a hard time reconciling what they saw with what they heard. When you listen to music, your mind's eye pictures the band performing the song. When the average music fan tried to do that with us, it created cognitive dissonance for them. It just didn't work.

Photo Credit: Heather Harris

It hurt us on a business level. People couldn't square the circle.

I have looked like me for my entire adult life. I completely understand what people see at first. But I have lived my life knowing that anyone can look like a train wreck and still ride for the brand, so to speak. My dad taught me that integrity is the one thing that cannot be taken away—it can only be given away. Everything else in life can be taken away from you, but not integrity. So, treat it as such.

Dad urged me to know what's important in life; that your word is your bond, and a handshake is your contract. I took these lessons very seriously, and I have continuously adjusted my moral compass accordingly. I want to like the guy that looks back at me in the mirror each morning. If you're a scoundrel, you know you're a scoundrel. And if you're a scoundrel, you expect everyone around you to be a scoundrel, as well. Because that's who you are internally.

That was the great thing about Little Caesar. We were all honorable men.

It didn't take long to win over Bruce Allen and his staff. In no time, he put the bat away and was laughing and carrying on with us like we were old chums.

Even his secretary melted when Fidel asked to use her phone so he could touch base with his wife and little girl. I heard her voice from the reception area, "Oh, that's so cute!"

We pulled that one out of the fire. But we didn't stay that lucky for very long.

* * *

The band fell almost immediately into a raging rock and roll party scene. Bob Rock's Little Mountain Sound studio was quite active during this era.

I've already commented on how Vancouver is well known for its strip clubs. The prettiest girls on the continent perform around town, entertaining the throng of rock stars and their followers. Aerosmith, Mötley Crüe, Poison…a Who's Who of 80s hair metal all blew through Bob's studio, and therefore through Vancouver proper.

Once we landed in town, word got out quickly that Little Caesar was the new project being undertaken by Bob Rock. That status gave us a blank check in the local party scene. We walked to the front of every line and never paid for a drink.

Sounds good, right?

Hell to the no. That spelled danger for our guys.

In the strip clubs, it was like tossing meat to a carnivore. The

136

strippers might not have recognized us as famous rock stars—yet—but they figured we were well on our way. As we came to find out, that meant special attention from the girls.

The dots many of them tried to connect were strange ones. I'm fairly certain those women thought they'd get with one of us or marry one of us. Either way, we would be their ticket to going to Los Angeles and partying with Slash and Tommy Lee.

That part of our existence was cool; it was one non-stop party. To defend my honor, strip clubs and strippers were never my thing. I always feel lecherous when I'm in a place like that. I don't like seeing the girls demean themselves and honestly don't get into it. Everyone in that place is a victim. The girls are being victimized by the guys who reduce them down to their tits and asses. And the guys are being victimized by girls who are doing everything they can to remove guys from their money.

All parties involved are there voluntarily, of course. But I hated it.

I can hear you calling bullshit on me. I'm really not trying to be an asshole on this; I'm just telling you what I've seen. I've been to many strip clubs in my career. Every time I go, I end up milking an over-priced beer and watching baseball on one of the televisions in the back of the bar.

Two of our crew guys ended up hooking up with strippers. A lot of crazy went down in those relationships. Our drum tech got together with a stripper who was amazingly intelligent. She had a five-year retirement plan. Being drop dead gorgeous and knowing how to play the game, she had amassed almost $1,000,000 working at the strip club and investing her earnings.

She blew my mind when I learned more about her. The relationship with our drum tech eventually ended—but not because she went psycho on him. Rather, they didn't work out on a human level. And that's the way things should end if they have to.

I just sat back, drank my beer, and watched it all happen.

At the restaurant in our hotel, one of the cooks was a drug dealer on the side. We could order coke or heroin or whatever we wanted. Loren, who was at the height of his addiction during these days, was like a kid in a candy store.

I remember walking past his room one morning, on my way

to the studio. His door was wide open, and his room filled with ten strangers. They'd been up all night doing eight-balls and drinking. Loren had his guitars lying all around, not a care in the world.

I told him to put that shit away because he was going to get ripped off, but it never happened. He never put them away, and he never got ripped off.

Canadians are very polite people. Lucky bastard.

The Hells Angels were all over Vancouver as well. They hit the strip clubs and bars with us as our own personal security force. All that shit was starting over again.

It turned into a three-ring circus.

The reason we were up there in the first place was not going very well, either. Bob Rock turned into a perfectionist who could take a nice, gritty, raw piece of musical art and overproduce it into a bland, washed out, generic piece of garbage.

We never did see eye-to-eye when it came to how the album was supposed to sound. To make matters worse, the disagreements took forever to resolve because he had us do things over and over and over and over. It was fucking exhausting.

It wasn't like all the takes made the music better. It got down to the molecular level. Bob was not able to disengage and say the magic words: "That sounds good enough." But Bob didn't understand "good enough." All he knew was "Let's do that again."

You want to know how to spend six months and 1.1 million dollars making a record? Hire Bob Rock to produce it. There's your answer.

It was a merciless grinding process. We worked on drum tones for a full week. Not the basic tracks or fills—just tones. Capturing the tones. Recording the tones. Tuning the drums. Doing things to the drums that I can't remember because I was losing my fucking mind.

As a band, we had nothing to do for weeks at a time. Bob would be in with Apache for a week or in with Loren for a week. We weren't making music; we were masturbating our instruments while Bob watched and shook his head and told us we were doing it wrong.

Worse yet, none of us had any idea what "doing it right" was actually *supposed* to sound like. Obviously, Bob had no regard for what we thought was good. I'm partly convinced that Bob didn't know what exactly he wanted to hear half the time, either. He just kept telling us our instruments were out of tune and having us do things differently, assuming something would sound good eventually.

In any case, it was absolutely maddening.

Bob remained disconnected and cold. You'd think a person would warm up after working with a band for six months, but that wasn't his process. In fact, instead of getting better over time, the process got worse.

* * *

About three-quarters of the way into making the record, Bob became even more rigid and anal retentive in his approach. The record he stepped away to make—the one that caused us to go out on the road for six months without a record to promote—was Mötley Crüe's *Dr. Feelgood*.

A fun album, but definitely different from any other record put out by Mötley Crüe. Also, it was their most successful by a long shot.

About four and a half months into making our record, *Dr. Feelgood* hit #1 on the album charts, propelling Bob Rock into a whole different orbit. I hate to say this, but the success really went to his head. Mio Vuckovic was with us in Vancouver, and Bob took all of us out to celebrate. If memory serves, I believe we ran up a $3,200 tab that night.

Hang on a minute. Bob didn't exactly "take us out." Little Caesar ultimately paid for the whole thing. The dinner and drinks went on our tab back at Geffen.

Bob had a little more strut in his step, and we paid the price. We went from Bob Rock making a Little Caesar album, to Little Caesar making a Bob Rock album.

And the new formula for a Bob Rock album was to follow the template created by *Dr. Feelgood*. Unfortunately, we were not Mötley Crüe. In fact, we weren't metal or glam or hair metal or whatever the fuck you want to call it. We were a blues-rock band.

I wish he could have understood that.

Adding insult to injury, we also heard that Bob was spending some time on a side hustle, helping Bryan Adams finish off his *Waking Up the Neighbors* album. That album was produced by Robert "Mutt" Lange, whose attention to detail made Bob Rock look like a hippie on a camping trip. Bryan and Mutt worked that album for almost three years before Bryan asked Bob to lend a hand.

I don't think Bob's name is listed in the album's liner notes. However, my understanding is that he did pitch in to facilitate moving the album along. That's what we were told, anyway.

That relationship affected us and our first album. One new phenomenon in the recording industry in 1989 was the 64-track digital overdub machines. Using these, producers and engineers were able to create a multi-layered sound to the songs. A five-piece band could record a song that sounded like it was performed by a 64-piece band. Or a 40-piece band with 22 background singers.

Bryan owned one of these machines because he was using it to record tracks for his album. When Bob went to Bryan's home studio to help him, he was introduced to its capabilities. Bob rented Bryan's 64-track machine and used it on Little Caesar's debut album.

I don't think I need to remind you that we are a gritty, edgy, guitar-driven rock band. I would compare our sound style to a band like Bad Company, rather than to an electro-synth band like A Flock of Seagulls. Or Mötley Crüe's *Dr. Feelgood*, for that matter.

We're stripped down to just the basics. If we can't play the song just the way it sounds on the album while we're live in concert, then it has no place on the record.

That alone should tell you how far apart Bob was from the way we wanted to do the album. He wanted six, seven, or eight guitar tracks, laid over keyboards, background singers, effects, reverbs, and a shit-ton of other fuckery.

I was on the phone daily, trying to get John Kalodner or Jimmy Iovine to intervene. One of them needed to get his ass up to Vancouver and stop this madness before our album was ruined beyond repair.

This crazy, over-produced, anal-retentive bullshit was nothing like what we had discussed during the pre-production meetings. Geffen knew we had a pop/hook sensibility to our songs. And they knew I had the ability to sing R&B ballads like an old blues singer. Combining those factors together, they saw a biker band with the potential to have huge crossover success. They knew we could become a much larger music entity than Raging Slab or Nashville Pussy or Circus of Power.

But they lost track of an extremely important element: You've got to make the sound match the fucking picture on the album cover. You can't go with a crazy, polar-opposite dichotomy like this.

The massive egos carried by these powerful label execs ended up being the death of a very good album. John Kalodner was a pop music guy who was in the middle of generating enormous success by ushering Aerosmith, formerly a gritty guitar-driven bluesy rock band, into the more heavily produced and pop-sounding Desmond Child/Diane Warren era of their career.

Aerosmith pulled it off because they were an established band with an established fan base. Plus, they were not pulled too far off center from their original trajectory. We were brand new and didn't want to fuck up our debut album by confusing the fans.

I knew our sound and our style, but nobody wanted to listen to me. To them, I was just a tattooed long-haired singer who has never sold a record in his life. How could I know fuck about shit?

You couldn't tell Kalodner, Iovine, or Rock anything. They each had their own personal idea of what sells a million records, and they weren't open to anything else.

Making matters worse, we were on an island in Vancouver. All of our support was in Los Angeles. I am confident to this day that, had Jimmy Iovine set foot in the studio while Bob Rock was warping our sound, he would have shrieked, "What is this shit?" and changed our direction.

But it was not to be. It was just me, sticking up for my band, screaming at the sky.

In the end, Kalodner gave in to Rock. He couldn't fight with Bob anymore. Plus, Bob Rock had swagger because he had a #1 record on the charts. It was decided by the brass at Geffen that they were just going to let Bob do his thing and have his way with us.

Two months later, when the mixing process began, the shit really hit the fan. I was bound and determined to make this fucking record sound like Bad Company or Zeppelin. None of this overdub bullshit was going to slide through on my watch.

Bob Rock did treat me well as a singer. When I went into the studio to record the vocal tracks, I was nervous as hell. I had heard a lot of stories where Bob had been absolute Hell on Vince Neil when the *Dr. Feelgood* lead vocals were cut. Even before Vince, Bob's reputation as a "slayer of singers" was legendary.

In fact, I heard that every time Vince did a pass with a verse or a chorus, Bob would sit in the control room with a lyric sheet and scrutinize every syllable coming out of Vince's mouth.

Not every word. Every *syllable*.

Poor Vince would have to sing and re-sing, sometimes making 50 or 60 passes per line.

Then Bob would go back and edit syllables together until the words had a sound he felt was proper for the vocal take.

Fuck.

I was getting really nervous. I knew that an OCD-like attention to syllables wasn't my style. I would rather have a solid vocal track that includes a few bumps and bruises than go to the extreme lengths of examining every syllable.

Bumps and bruises make a song sound more organic. Think about the difference between a band like Chicago versus a band like Blood, Sweat, and Tears. Two bands that play a similar style of music, but on opposite ends of the spectrum when it comes to production and "polish." Chicago has a sound that feels like they're from the mean streets, while Blood, Sweat, and Tears has a sound that feels like they have perfectly straight teeth and wear spit-shined boots.

Neither sound is better or worse; both bands found enormous success with the path they chose. But the sound has to be right for the band. And that was my problem.

The first vocal I cut was "Chain of Fools". I heard the voice of Randy, our engineer, come over the talk-back monitor, "Okay, Ron, you ready? Here we go!"

I looked through the glass partition. I could barely make out Bob in there with Randy and Chris, another engineer. My balls were tight as fuck, but I thought, *Okay, here I go.*

I did a pass through the song and waited.

Bob leaned forward and spoke through the monitor, "Yeah. Let's do another one."

My heart sank. Oh my God. How many of these are we going to do?

I did a second pass.

Same result.

I did a third pass.

When the music faded out, I took the tiger by the tail.

"Okay. What're we doing?"

Silence in my headphones.

"Hellooooooo?"

I couldn't tell what was going on in the control room. After a few moments, a voice crackled to life in my ears.

"Hang on, give us a minute."

I threw my head back and winced. Oh fuuuuck.

I felt like an asshole, wearing my little headphones and waiting for more words to come down from the mouth of God. I don't know how long I stood there, stewing in the dark. It felt like an eternity.

Finally, I tore off the headphones. Fuck this. I'm going in there. I'm going to be a part of this conversation because I know they're talking about me.

When I entered the control room, the only person sitting there was Randy. Bob wasn't even there anymore.

My first thought was, Oh no. He was so fucking pissed, he left.

"Where's Bob?"

Randy looked up. "Oh, he went home."

"He went home? Jesus, did I ju—"

Randy held up a hand. "No, no, no. Bob listened to your three passes and said you sound great. He said you got better with each pass."

I exhaled. "No shit?"

"Yeah. He said to just let you do your thing. He'll be back in the morning, and we'll get some good comps."

I stood there, blinking.

"And then we'll be done?"

Randy chuckled and got back to work, "Yup."

Oh, thank God. I was giddy.

I have no idea why, but Bob wasn't a tyrant with my vocals. He was really cool with me. But good lord, with the drum parts and the guitar parts, he created total fucking misery.

* * *

Ultimately, the record we cut was the result of massive compromise on both sides of the war. And honestly, nobody liked it. The label wasn't happy, Bob wasn't happy, we weren't happy. It was a mess.

I'm not talking about the songs. I stand by our ability to write and play music. But the way we sound on that record is absolutely unacceptable to me. Somehow, Bob Rock was able to take fantastic music and wring the ever-loving life out of it.

However, after all that time and all that money, Geffen finally said "Let's go!"

With that, our record was pressed and sent into distribution and fulfillment. Obviously, that all broke down and went straight to hell for us. I'm sure you expect nothing less by now.

I'll tell you about that in a few minutes. For now, let me add that in the midst of all the madness, my mother died.

I would like to share with you three important points about my family: (1) my siblings and I share a sick and twisted sense of humor, (2) Dad would go down the same sick and twisted rabbit hole with us, and (3) Mom was so remarkably evil, she even terrified the shit out of the Grim Reaper—to the point that he *sent her back*. I'm sure she did that just to torture us a little bit more before she finally kicked off for good.

* * *

Mom's final days were a nightmare. She developed a condition called myelodysplastic syndrome, or myelodysplasia. Think of it as a subset of leukemia, or cancer of the blood. Some blood cancers kill you quick, others take years to fully develop and overtake the body.

Mom's was a terminal diagnosis, but it ended up taking about ten years to take her out. I was in Los Angeles and my folks lived in the Bay area. When I got the call that Mom was in the final stretch and wouldn't last much longer, I traveled up to northern California to meet my family.

When I arrived at the hospital, Dad, Sandi, and Michael were already assembled. The word from the doctors was that Mom would pass away within mere hours, so we set up vigil in the waiting room. Surrounding us were the bereaved families of other folks in the intensive care unit. Car accidents, heart attacks, cancers—they represented maladies that placed their loved ones at Death's door.

It was a somber atmosphere. For the Young family, we handled our grief in a vastly different manner than anyone else on Earth.

At least, different from anyone else in the waiting room.

We shared stories of my Mom's life. Even though three of the four family members were her children, nobody referred to her as "Mom." Instead, we all called her by her name, Margie.

145

We took turns telling stories and adding to each other's stories. The other people in the waiting room were mortified. After all, Mom was not a pillar in the community. Our stories reflected the life she lived, but not in a mean-spirited way. We didn't highlight how awful of a person she was.

Well, maybe we did. But it wasn't from a position of bitterness or resentment. Instead, we were all in a giddy, nervous headspace. Mom was about to go and none of us were emotionally equipped to handle the weight of that news with any sort of dignity whatsoever. We're all dark, comedic people. We laugh at the darkness.

The other families were aghast. We told insane horrible stories about my insane horrible mother, who was about to die. Yet, we giggled through the stories, sometimes laughing too hard to finish a sentence or a thought.

It wasn't all gallows humor, though. We weren't necessarily sad. Shit, we weren't sad at all. We were celebrating that we were finally going to be free of all the bullshit.

Even my father was a part of it. I'm not even kidding. Mom was an enormous burden to everyone in her inner circle. Yet, there we all were.

Despite all she put us through, every one of her family members was present and accounted for during her final moments.

It was a bizarre show of loyalty.

Finally, the doctor came out to the waiting room and informed us of Mom's passing. Per hospital policy, he suggested each of us go in and make our peace with Mom.

We did. Each of us went in, one by one, and spent a little time with her to say a few words.

I can't remember what exactly I said. I think it was something along the lines of, "Well, you know, you gave it your best shot."

What the fuck was I supposed to say in that situation? I didn't have a speech prepared or a few notes jotted down on a napkin. I had me and my fucked-up sense of humor. The sense of humor that *she* created. It only seemed fitting.

I walked out and met the family. We were quiet, which was a rare moment. We decided it would be good for everyone to stay together for awhile. Thus, we went to get a bite to eat.

For most people with normal mothers who were not drama queens or the epitome of pure evil, that would be the end of the story. We would have eaten dinner, made funeral arrangements, and eventually laid her to rest.

But, no; that ain't the way my mom rolled. Because my mom was who she was, I have to add this one more time: But wait! There's more!

The meal we shared that night was healing for us. We vacillated between dark humor and serious conversation, but we processed our feelings rather well. We were relieved that Mom had passed. We needed to speak those words out loud in a way that was sincere.

They were spoken, and we felt cleansed.

The four of us left the restaurant and went back to Dad's house. I think we all planned to stay there for a few days to help him get Mom's affairs in order. But about two hours later, the phone rang. It was the hospital.

Dad answered and listened for a few beats, and then went pale. He hung up the phone and addressed his children.

"She's alive."

"What?!" The three of us yelled in unison.

Mom had flat-lined and the physician pronounced her dead. Dad had signed a DNR order (Do Not Resuscitate) in case Mom was diagnosed terminal. In other words, the doctors were not to do anything to extend her life if she started slipping away naturally.

His thinking was that if she is knocking on Heaven's door, why the fuck would he want to put her—or any of us—through the nonsense of resuscitating her? Let her go.

But not this time, apparently.

I learned that as the doctor was calling Mom's time of death, there was a code blue down the hallway. Somebody went into cardiac arrest or something. When the doctor and nursing staff got back to Mom's room, there were vital signs again.

We were stunned. And not in a good way.

Dad added that she would not live for more than a few hours. Holy shit.

That's Mom in a nutshell. This was Margie Fucking Young

having just one more drama queen moment. This. Was. Perfect. It put a fitting punctuation mark onto the end of her life.

I could just hear her saying, "Hold on, people! I'm not done with you yet!"

Sure enough, a couple hours later she passed away again.

Again.

Did I mention "again"? It bears repeating.

You couldn't have written a better script for the end of Mom's life. If she was going to go, it couldn't be simple. Why do anything the easy way? The way most people in most families do things? The way that made it so much easier for the family around her?

Not my mom. Not Margie Young.

In fairness to Mom, she came by her quirks honestly. Her own mother was a piece of work, too. Dad told us stories of some of the insane things our maternal grandmother would try to pull. She also loved attention and wanted people to feel sorry for her.

I get it. I have a sliver of empathy for Mom, but that's as far as I let myself go. My preference is to hide my feelings behind my sense of humor. It's the only way I know how to operate. And cope.

* * *

The very first time my wife, Renee, met my dad, it was after Mom had already passed. Renee and I rented a house by the beach and Dad came down for a visit. He arrived reasonably late one night and went almost immediately to bed. The next morning, we all gathered in the living room.

Bear in mind, Renee hadn't yet spoken much to my dad. They were still strangers at this point.

Out of the blue, my dad turned to me and said, "Ronnie, I had a terrible nightmare last night."

"Really, Dad? What's up?"

He gazed out at the surf.

"I heard the waves down by the beach, you know?"

148

I nodded, "Yeah."

He turned toward me and leaned forward, eyes beaming with a glint of mischief.

"I dreamt that your mom's ashes came together, and then she rose out of the water and went looking for us!"

We busted out laughing. It was glorious. I turned to catch Renee's eye, and she had a look that I'd seen many, many times before. It was the look people would give us whenever our dark humor came out in polite company. For Renee, I'm sure she was thinking, *What kind of family did I just marry into?*

It was a shortcut to helping Renee understand that I wasn't kidding when I told her we didn't like our mother. I'm not sure if people from normal families can relate to that sentiment, regardless of how earnest the story sounds.

Well, Renee got a good taste of it that day in the beach house.

* * *

Mom's death was only one component of a gale-force shit-storm that my life turned into. Everything that happened to me and the band seemed to be the absolute worst thing that could have happened. It was like we kept rolling snake eyes on the craps table. We kept hitting green "00" on the roulette wheel.

It didn't matter how many times we rolled the dice or spun the wheel—it was snake-eyes and double zeroes over and over and over, ad infinitum. It was like flipping a coin a thousand times and calling heads, only to have it come up tails, 100% of the time.

Some of the issues occurred because of our, or my, own doing. We were young, brash, and outspoken back then. But many of the things that happened to us were completely out of our control. Once we started sliding down Shit Mountain, we couldn't stop until we hit the bottom. Then we'd get hit with a Shit Avalanche.

Murphy's Law was the only law we followed religiously: Anything that can go wrong will go wrong.

CHAPTER 8:
BREAKING DOWN

We survived Bob Rock. Thank God.

With the recording behind us, the band returned to Los Angeles to begin the next phase of our ascent into rock and roll stardom.

At this point, I didn't have a clear idea how our accounting worked with Geffen. I knew the label was spending money while we were in Vancouver, but I had no idea how much was pushed up front and out the door. I had a vague notion that we had to pay some of it back, but didn't have my arms around exactly how that end of the financials worked either.

In fact, we didn't find out the precise numbers until we started the second record.

The label doesn't tell you this shit, and with good reason. If an artist or a band knew how much money they were in debt before selling a single record, the label would have a mutiny on its hands. Even idiots with no concept of how money works would be shocked that they would not be getting paid for the next thousand years or so because they had to work off the debt they accrued from the start.

That last sentence isn't completely true. Each band member will still receive a weekly stipend or allowance (more like a pittance) while their album and tour dates are selling and paying the label. Unfortunately, even that pittance will have to get paid back in the long run. From an artist's standpoint, there is almost no way to break even, much less get rich. The songwriter will have an advantage over the other players, but even they have a rough time in the business trying to survive long-term.

The artist gets famous, but the label gets rich. I can't repeat those words often enough.

Things have definitely swung toward the favor of the artist since about 2010. The internet and the ability to self-promote have changed the rules of the game for our industry. But I'm still talking about 1990 here.

We got home from Vancouver and renewed our excitement in the process. For me personally, I found the whole Vancouver experience to be depressing. The bloom was definitely off the music industry rose, and with Geffen records specifically.

Whatever. I looked forward to selling some albums, playing some gigs, and finally making some money.

It was at this time when we found out that our name was shared with the pizza chain I mentioned back in Chapter Five. That bullshit chased us home from Canada.

Despite all that stress, all the egos, the agony, and the wailing and gnashing of teeth, we arrived at a release date: May 15, 1990. Talk about five kids wetting their pants waiting for Christmas! We couldn't wait to storm the Bastille with our new album. The record got out of the gate like gangbusters. We were even primed to have the full support of MTV.

One of the decision makers at MTV, Abbey Konowich, caught one of our shows while we were in New York. He got in touch with John Kalodner and basically told him to throw a video together. Abbey wanted to put us into heavy rotation on the station. He loved our music and told John this was his kind of band.

He didn't care for the proliferation of hair metal on his beloved MTV. In the end, he got his wish. The more stripped-down and organic music genre, Grunge, took over for the glitzy and glammy hair metal. Unfortunately, we got leap-frogged en route.

Kalodner told me about his conversation with Abbey and about the MTV opportunity. Also, he was arranging for a video to be shot in support of the first single, which Geffen had decided, unbeknownst to the band, to be "Chain of Fools."

Another big battle ensued. Because it couldn't have happened any other way for us.

It might surprise some readers that I didn't want "Chain of Fools" to even be included on the album. I'm not kidding; I didn't care much for the song itself. Don't get me wrong, Aretha's version was an incredible version, but the incredible factor was there because of Aretha, not the song. Honestly, it wasn't all that great of a song. It was a great performance.

To me, our version of the song was intended to be a B-side album track designed to introduce people to rhythm and blues. Little Caesar bridged that gap; the least we could do was give a little historical context for our fans. I felt obligated to turn 1990s kids onto that old style of music. Make connections and create a new generation of music lovers who appreciate the classics.

Unfortunately, I saw early on that Geffen was fixated on that song. Their logic was at least reasonable. They said that Van Halen broke big in 1978 with a cover of the Kinks' song, "You Really Got Me." It should stand to reason that we could follow the same path they cut twelve years earlier and break out behind a cover song.

To me, the Van Halen argument was absolutely irrelevant. I couldn't understand how something they did over a decade earlier had anything to do with anything. I wanted to establish Little Caesar as a new band, so thought we should lead with a song that we wrote.

I lost the argument. Again.

Geffen came up with a grand plan for a music video to be shot for "Chain of Fools." The director, Tamra Davis, gave us a grand total of zero input while we were shooting the individual scenes that would get mashed together to form the finished product. We figured she was just mailing it in. Later, I learned that she was so intimidated by the way we looked, she was afraid to approach us. Because of her fear, the band had no fucking idea how any part of our performance was going to link together, or how the finished product was supposed to look. We were flying blind.

When the final edit came out, I wasn't happy with it. In my mind, we looked stiff and awkward. I got over it quick, since I couldn't do anything about it anyway. I still don't like it to this day, but it is what it is. We had a product to give to MTV.

* * *

In 1990, David Geffen decided he was going to start a secondary label under his Geffen umbrella. At the time, Geffen had over 260 artists on their label. Most of these artists may be unfamiliar to anyone because they never saw the light of day. The late 1980s was a feeding frenzy in Hollywood, with labels signing hair metal acts left and right. A lot of shallow schlock made it to the radio during that era. That garbage came from only ten (or so) of the 260 artists Geffen had! The other 250 artists were absolute bottom feeders.

Still, David Geffen wanted to start a label that focused on new bands. So he started DGC Records, where the letters stood for David Geffen Company. DGC was earmarked as the home for new bands and newly signed artists. At the helm of DGC was a man named Marko Babineau.

We got shifted onto the new label, which meant we no longer worked with the marketing and promotional people over at Geffen. We got moved to a brand-new label with our brand new General Manager, Babineau, and a group of fresh-faced, brand new promotional people.

To say I had some concerns would have been an understatement. Those concerns hit a crescendo when I met with Marko for the first time.

I remember sitting in his office, trying to formulate a game plan for our album. I asked him about other artists on the fledgling DGC, and Marko was quick to respond.

"Yeah, it's going to be you and a couple other bands to kick things off. We have a fun, poppy kind of metal band called Nelson, and a little indie college band that'll probably sell about 30,000 records. We signed them because we wanted to have an eclectic list of artists. The indie band is called Nirvana."

He gave me copies of their music, and I listened to it on the way home. Nelson didn't strike me as anything special. More of the same old, same old. But Nirvana? Holy fuck! Their stuff was unique and cool. This was the sound I had been trying to capture while knocking my head against the wall for the past four years.

In my head, I thought, *This shit is going to change music. This shit is about to blow up and there isn't anything that anyone can do to stop it.*

Marko assured me we were in the hopper to begin a marketing and promotion blitz. He said he was doing everything he could with Nelson, but he just couldn't get their music on the radio.

I was like, "Radio? Why are you trying to get these guys onto the radio? Nobody can see what these guys look like on the radio. You've got to get them on MTV."

To this day, I still remember his answer.

"Yeah, no. The head of marketing, this guy we just brought on board, he doesn't want to spend the money on a video."

What a fucking idiot. This is the kind of moron I was dealing with, day in and day out.

Nelson ended up going out of pocket to shoot and produce their own video. Sure enough, once it finally broke through and got shown on late night MTV, it blew up. Radio naturally followed suit. Nelson created an audience, and then capitalized on that audience.

Their music is cute and poppy, but you've got to let the girls see what the guys look like. The Nelson brothers can play their instruments and put out decent music, but the girls will flock to them and buy their product because of the way they look.

It takes a big man to admit when he's right.

Once again, it was illuminating for me to get slapped in the face with the reality of how tone deaf the label suits could be. I had a better feel for what would work and what wouldn't work. And I gave them my advice for free!

Not that anyone listened. I would have been better off printing my advice onto tri-fold pamphlets and then passing them out on a freeway off-ramp.

Our turn came up at DGC. Abbey did exactly what he said he was going to do. "Chain of Fools" went into rotation on MTV. We also got 128 radio adds during the first week, which is huge. I think we ended up with 140 total. All the "Z-Rock" stations, which is the generic name for stations that played rock and hair metal back then, picked it up. Then, when people saw the band's photo, all the heavy metal stations picked up the track.

The song did pretty well. It got up to #17 on the US charts, which was super fucking awesome to us. As a result, the album started selling. We sold about 160,000 units within the first two weeks of its release.

For the first two or three weeks, we were shot out of a medieval catapult, hurling toward every dream we had ever dreamt.

But.

Yeah, There's always a "but" for us when things seem to be going well.

But Geffen was disappointed.

I think the execs at the label were expecting us to go platinum in a week. I'm not joking.

I remember talking with them, saying, "Guys, we're a new band. The fans don't know who Bob Rock is. They don't care who Jimmy Iovine is. Give them a minute to fall in love with the music. So far, we're doing great."

Then came the phone call. It was one of our promotions people at DGC. "Hi, Ron. Umm, there's been a bit of drama at the label."

"What do you mean?"

"You remember Marko? The head of the label?" he said slowly, like he was choosing his words carefully.

"Yeah."

I braced for impact. Leading with a stupid fucking question meant this was probably going to be bad news.

"Well, it turns out, he walked into his secretary's office with his dick in his hand. Uh, she was sitting there. At her desk. And he had an erection and jerked off onto her desk."

My eyebrows shot up. He continued.

"Yeah, well, he blew his load onto her desk and onto a magazine she was looking at," he paused, collecting his thoughts, "She scooped up some of…um, some of it…for evidence. Now

Marko is gone."

I was slow to show up to the party. "What the fuck?"

"Well, they're looking for someone to replace him and run the label. But don't worry, we'll have everything right back on track in no time."

A couple days later, I found out that David Geffen sold the entire Geffen label, including DGC, to MCA Music Entertainment Group. Apparently, a bunch of people knew this was coming because there were a bunch of records that had their release date held up in the pipeline, ahead of the transition.

Once MCA had their people look over the full roster of Geffen's label, they were immediately struck by how many bands he had control over. So rather than bleed money while trying to keep these bands happy and remain afloat, they brought in their own marketing guy. This was to be the hatchet man, charged with the responsibility of cutting ties with most of the artists. They wanted to cut the budget and make the numbers work.

We survived the initial cut, but a good old-fashioned screwing wasn't about to let us off the hook that easily. The final nail was about to be driven into Little Caesar's coffin. We were on the road when it happened, so we had no way to stop the impending train wreck.

This one change may not seem like a big deal, but it created a huge crack we slipped right through.

Geffen, like all labels, has an outsourced manufacturer that will make hundreds of thousands of music recordings and send them to the distributor. Out of that mountain of tapes, CDs, and records, the distributor fulfills the orders made by Best Buy, Walmart, Sam Goody, and all other music retail stores.

That's the entirety of what a distributor does. But this one thing they do has a huge impact on the artist.

Normally, a label wants to make damn sure that if a consumer wants to purchase a CD, then a CD will be on a shelf waiting for them. The label makes a shit ton of records, tapes, and CDs; that way, they're never left without product to ship.

As they sit in the warehouse, those records, tapes, and CDs are worthless. Sitting on a shelf at Best Buy or Tower Records, that record, tape, or CD can be turned into a cash sale. The distributor's *only* job is to make sure all the recorded music gets sent from the warehouse to the store.

An important change that came with MCA was that they wanted to use their own distributor. Geffen/DGC used WEA (Warner-Elektra-Atlantic) as their distributor. MCA used BMG (Bertelsmann Music Group).

Since we sold 160,000 units in only two weeks, Geffen had thousands more copies of our records, tapes, and CDs manufactured and sent to the WEA warehouse, ready to go.

Of course, WEA stopped shipping our stuff to record stores. Since they were no longer getting paid by Geffen, they were not willing to ship our records to BMG's warehouse, either. Tens of thousands of our albums, tapes, and CDs sat languishing in WEA's distribution facility.

Not that anybody at DGC bothered to notice or take care of the problem.

Little Caesar was in heavy rotation on MTV and riding a wave of 140-plus adds on radio stations across the country. We were in demand. Yet, we were stuck; nobody could buy our music.

We had no product in stores because nobody worked this shit out between Geffen/DGC and BMG. Either of the distributors or labels could have rented a few U-Haul trucks and some day laborers from the Home Depot Parking lot to schlep these things across town to BMG's warehouse. But that would have solved the problem instead of ignoring it.

Which, looking back, was probably their M.O., anyway.

These were the early days of Sound Scan, a part of the Neilson ratings company now owned by MRC Data. It's a service that tracked sales figures and reported them to record companies. Our data showed that Little Caesar's record sales fell to somewhere between the memorable recordings of "The Grunting Tribesmen of Papua New Guinea" and the self-recorded demo tape of a middle-school garage band from Des Moines, Iowa.

I still remember the insane phone call I got from a marketing genius at Geffen. "Ron, your sales numbers don't look especially strong at this point."

I abruptly cut him off. "No shit, Sherlock! Nobody can get their hands on our fucking record!" The conversation deteriorated from there.

And then—you may want to sit down for this—things actually got worse.

A day or two later, I received yet another phone call. I was at the emotional point where I thought about crying whenever the phone rang. This time, as with every time, I made the mistake of answering. It was yet another representative from Geffen. I don't even remember who the fuck it was exactly, but the news was dire.

"Hey, um, David Geffen and Jimmy Iovine had a pretty heated argument. They're not talking to each other anymore."

I snarled. "What are you talking about?"

"Well, Jimmy announced that he's going to start his own label called Interscope Records. He's doing his own thing."

My understanding is that David got wind of Jimmy's new toy and asked Jimmy if he wanted to bring Interscope under the Geffen umbrella. Geffen wanted control over the Interscope artists and publishing. Jimmy's mom didn't raise a fool, so he told Geffen to fuck off. This made David really mad at Jimmy.

I was also told by the rep that David Geffen was really mad at Little Caesar…and specifically, at me.

Why, you may ask? Welp, Ron Young has a charming quirk that pissed the ever-living fuck out of David Geffen.

Ron Young tells the truth.

Even when our records were available, our sales numbers disappointed the Geffen brass. When our sales started to slow down, I provided a reasonable and convincing explanation. To me, it made no sense for listeners to think that a band who looked like Motorhead would do a ballad like "In Your Arms." The public were already confused by Geffen releasing our cover of "Chain of Fools" first. We had much better songs on our album that went with our look, like "Down-N-Dirty" or "Wrong Side of the Tracks."

Geffen's marketing of Little Caesar sucked.

And it spit, too.

Unfortunately, David cherry-picked the one off-hand thing I said, took it out of context, then twisted the conversation against me when our sales completely tanked. He used our look as an excuse. Rather than admit his company fucked up and dropped the ball with marketing and distribution, he claimed he couldn't sell our records because our look scared the kids who would have purchased the albums in the first place. I can't remember if this is an exact quote, but he told me we were too ugly to be a platinum-selling rock band, particularly in the era of MTV.

I know. Extremely flattering.

Of course, it was obvious what happened. The owner of the record label—the person who makes every decision regarding the success or failure of the signed artists—wants to blame the band for poor sales. It had nothing to do with illogical promotion, bringing in a new head of marketing, selling the label, changing distributors, or having no inventory on hand for record stores.

Nope. It was the band. And their ambiance of evil.

I must be missing a gene that allows me to spin a story or bend the truth or obscure relevant facts. Thus, I told the truth some more. We were still on the road, and opportunities to tell the truth materialized at every turn.

The band did promotional work while on tour. We did morning radio interviews, met fans at in-store record signings, sat with magazine columnists, did phone interviews with media outlets, and made appearances on MTV. Over and over again we were asked, "Hey! How come we can't find your records anywhere?"

I thought about lying or spinning to cover for the label. I am a loyal guy, almost to a fault. But my loyalty only goes as far as it gets returned to me. As long as David Geffen blamed us for his own mistakes, I told the truth to anyone who asked.

I was not about to tow the company line. I pulled the curtain back and elegantly presented Geffen's behind-the-scenes bullshit and in-fighting. I didn't pull a single punch.

If you want to know the truth, just ask me. I may not answer every question, but when I do, I guarantee you it will be the truth as I see it.

Word of my truth reveal got back to David. This made David hate me even more. Along with Jimmy Iovine. And Santa Claus, for all I knew.

He probably hated the Philadelphia Phillies too, but that's normal and to be expected.

Sorry, Philly fans.

(Not really)

One last factor that killed our chances of survival was perpetrated at the hands of whoever succeeded Marko Babineau. Geffen/DGC was a rudderless ship after he was shown to the curb, so I think decisions were made either by committee or by the seat of someone's pants.

Right after Marko got fired, Geffen hired a hatchet man to start cutting budgets left and right. After Geffen was sold, the new parent company needed us to try ANYTHING they could think of to right the ship that was Little Caesar.

Our band had so much positive buzz, we were the Great White Hope. Thus, the label made the mistake of trying to push us up the sales ladder way too fast.

The Geffen/DGC idiot sent copies of "In Your Arms" to every Top 40 radio station across the country, but did not include a photo of the band on the jacket of the single. The hope was that a grungy-sounding band would fill a void in current music, and that we would change the paradigm.

Unfortunately, we never got the chance. When all the Z-Rock and Metal stations heard we were being peddled as a Top 40 band, they dropped us like a rock from rotation. We fell off the radio before we had a chance to catch on within a new genre.

The bitch of it all: Geffen/DGC's instincts were spot on. There was a void in current music that needed a grungy-sounding band to fill it. Nirvana had not started their meteoric rise yet. Never had Top 40 radio ever pushed the likes of a band like us or Nirvana —but times were about to change.

We obviously failed at our attempt; we never pierced the veil of Top 40 stations. But when Nirvana started taking off, Top 40 broke their own rules and started playing a band that scared their previously safe rules. When Nirvana was pushed toward Top 40, they were welcomed with open arms.

They changed music forever.

We sat with our dicks in our hands. Just like Marko.

No offense to Marko.

When we failed at Top 40 radio and got knocked off Z-Rock stations, David took that as proof that we were unattractive to the average music buyer. To him, we were a dead horse.

A fugly dead horse.

Our reviews remained great, but Geffen wanted to torpedo the SS Little Caesar.

I remember hanging up the phone from one of the shitty conversations with Geffen, turning to the band, and saying, "Boys, we're fucked."

We were being thrown around in a pit of monstrously huge egos, millions of dollars, enormous decisions, and high-end corporate shuffling. It was the perfect storm.

The final insult came when I was forced to fire Jimmy Iovine. When he struck out on his own, he could no longer legally manage us. Even if there would have been a way, he would have still dropped us. He had new talent with a new sound signed to Interscope: Dr. Dre, Tupac Shakur, and Marky Mark. With thoroughbreds like that kicking in his stall, he didn't have a need to support a donkey like Little Caesar.

We parted ways.

Our world changed quite a bit in late 1990 and early 1991. We didn't have a manager, the new head of marketing was slashing the budget left and right, we were $1.1 million in the hole, we had no records in any record store, and we were getting hit with a deluge of bad press that claimed our "look" was responsible for our failure, thanks to David Geffen's subversive maneuvers.

In our defense, we were not ugly. Sure, we sported a gritty, edgy, non-traditional look, but take a gander at Guns n' Roses back then. Those skanky, scrawny dudes weren't exactly ready for the red carpet. Hell, look at The Rolling Stones! Those poor gomers are so ugly they make their blind fans cry.

But strippers liked us. Or at least they danced to our music every time a radio DJ took us to a club after every radio interview we did.

So we've got that going for us.

* * *

Geffen assigned us a temporary liaison, who was just as frustrating as anyone else we had dealt with there. I remember the

162

first phone call we had. The label's position baffled me.

I asked, "Okay. What do we do from here?"

"Ron, we need to start thinking about the second album."

My jaw dropped. "Wait a minute—we just released this first one. You're talking like we have four or five singles waiting to piggyback us into another record."

He continued, "This one went so bad so quick, and we have so much ground to make up. We're under new management now."

"Yeah?" I nudged him along. I wanted to get to the point.

"Tell you what. Let's just bury this one and we'll move to record number two."

I couldn't believe it. This was years of our fucking lives they were flushing down the toilet. And they didn't give a flying fuck. That was the real pisser for me. It really demonstrated how they thought nothing of us, our time, or our careers.

I fired back. "All of your great fucking plans! I told you they would never work out. When that came true, you decide you're going to just write the whole thing off?"

The actual truth was that John Kalodner didn't want the reputation of having a failure on his hands. David Geffen didn't want that, either. They just wanted us to go away.

I knew it. We were fucked.

In the middle of all this, Apache stormed out and left the band. The last thing he said to me was, "This is bullshit. It's not what I signed up for."

Never fear, dear reader. Apache will resurface later. At the time however, I honestly didn't know if I would ever see him again. He was one of our brothers for sure, but he was also a real quirky cat.

As for the rest of us, we decided to stick together and tough it out. We fell back and licked our wounds for about a year, then got Earl Slick to join the band. We needed a lead guitar player, and Earl came with an amazing pedigree. He had recorded and played with David Bowie (*Young Americans*; *Station to Station*) and John Lennon (*Double Fantasy*; *Milk and Honey*). He was talented, had the right look to blend in with our band, and was eager to get something going with us.

We got to work on the second album. How could anything go

wrong?

HA!

The cruel hand of fate stepped in and said, "Hold my beer."

CHAPTER 9:
HELLO, HEROIN

At this point, we were a riled bunch of distinguished gentlemen.

Or, as some would say, a bunch of pissed off motherfuckers.

We were extremely bitter and living off $100 per week stipends. We had burned through our entire first advance and were starting to run on fumes with regard to the more modest second album advance. Geffen claimed we owed them over a million dollars. I'm not exaggerating; that was the amount. I don't know if we ever thought that debt would be paid off. But at that time, we were pinned against the ropes and punching.

As for me personally, this was when I really started getting high.

One bit of good news was that we found a new manager. Having almost no money and no real possibility of clearing the debt with our label, we were not a hot commodity when it came to finding someone willing to manage us.

In no time at all, we not only found someone willing to take a shot on us, but he was one of the top managers in all of music: Herbie Herbert.

Herbie was an old-school manager. He cut his teeth in the early 1970s managing Santana; later he went on to manage what was arguably the biggest band in the world at the time: Journey. Rumor has it that Steve Perry didn't get along with Herbie and asked that he be replaced in 1993. Irving Azoff took over, but Herbie had a great run with the band. He took Journey from being a Bay-area darling in 1973, to a world-wide phenomenon throughout the 1980s.

He wasn't a one-trick pony, though. He also managed The Steve Miller Band, Europe, Mr. Big, Enuff Z'Nuff, Hardline, The Storm, and other bands fighting for airplay in the crowded field of the 1980s and early 1990s.

We caught him just as he transitioned out of Journey. Although he was still technically employed by the band, the writing was on the wall. Herbie was looking for other opportunities.

From our perspective, Herbie was the perfect guy for the job. He had vision, he knew the business, and he was connected with all the right people and venues to get us the attention we needed. I couldn't gauge how tainted we actually were; I was too close to see the forest for the trees. But I knew we were going to need some calculated guidance to steer us out of the mess we were in, and then get us back on track.

To Herbie's credit, he infused hope back into our situation. He met with the band and gave us a good, hard look. After we finished weaving the tale of woe that had become our career, he pushed back from the table and said, "I think I can put a light at the end of this tunnel."

That got our attention.

"You still have great reviews and everyone who hears you loves your sound. Face it, you're a solid, tight band who's well-respected by critics. The best way to make everyone forget the last record is to make another one. Let's just fuckin' do it."

Herbie wasn't the type of manager who sits back and waits for opportunities to come to him. Instead, he's proactive; he picks up the phone and starts making things happen. He arranged for a meeting with the label, and we were off to the races.

However, the band was in a dark place. Actually, let me own that one: *I* was in a dark place. Heroin was ebbing into my daily routine. As a group, we were not in a good position to make a strong album.

I don't know how many of you picked up a copy of our 1992 album, *Influence*. If you can, call it up on YouTube if you don't have access to the CD. My vocals and their delivery are fucking angry. The lyrics sound like they were written by a rebellious teenager, and the music is more aggressive than our typical style.

As the lyricist for the band, I found immense catharsis in the writing process—I purged my pain. I wrote not-so-cryptic jabs at David Geffen, thinly veiled complaints about our failures, and words that generally led the listener to understand how big of a miserable fuck I was.

The song "Ballad of Johnny" in particular was a poignant ballad about how I sat alone some nights, wanting to kill myself because my career was in the fucking toilet. I was such a delight to be around back then!

I honestly didn't realize how autobiographical that song was to me when I wrote it. That's a part of the addiction—I didn't realize I wrote about my own feelings, or that I pulled emotion from my own experiences. Only years later, as a part of my spiritual journey, did I understand it.

Howard Benson produced the album. His career was just on the rise in 1992, and we caught him on the upswing. Since then, he has been absolutely spectacular. Howard has been nominated for sixteen Grammys, winning two of them. I don't know how he got saddled with our lame horse, but he did a good job for us.

I probably owe him an apology letter. Or a nice Bundt cake.

Despite all that Howard did, the album was dead on arrival. Nobody wanted to touch the band. We were a dog in the road with fresh tire tracks running the length of its mashed body.

I'm sure that last remark painted quite a picture for you. It's difficult for me to remember much these days, much less write about those memories. My life was about to enter an extremely dark chapter.

From a mental health standpoint, I struggled to keep my head above water. My lust for life really dimmed during my next meeting with Herbie Herbert.

The meeting with Herbie wasn't anything monumental with regard to earth-shattering news. Instead, it was like most things regarding the band. Our career seemed to fail like a falling tree instead of an exploding bomb. Slowly at first, but then gathering momentum as we crashed to the earth with a loud boom.

Influence was finishing up, so I did the math. We recorded the tracks on a shoestring budget with no money available to market or promote the album.

I said to Herbie, "Man, I'm not getting the vibe that the label is behind us anymore. They really want us to just go away."

Working with the label was an exercise in futility. That futile feeling soaked into the rest of my existence. My life was an exercise in futility.

I started to get high on heroin.

Music had been my drug. Then success was my drug. Those two forces combined to keep me swimming forward and looking ahead to brighter days. With both of them gone, I had nothing to fall back on and stop my descent into madness.

Nothing except for the warm, tingly escape of heroin.

I began to self-medicate. Whenever I assumed I could not cope with whatever was in front of me, I felt completely helpless. I did not believe I had the agency to change the course of my own life. Instead of pushing a boulder uphill for the rest of eternity, I chose to numb out and not give a fuck.

Even the great Herbie Herbert had to admit his optimism was misplaced.

Herbie met with the label and played the *Influence* record for them. He told me they liked it, but refused to put anything behind it. In other words, it was dead to them.

Herbie said to me, "Remember that light I saw at the end of the tunnel?"

"Yeah." I was depressed.

"Well, I still see it—except now it's a freight train and it's headed right for you guys."

Herbie, being the go-getter and the planner that he is, came up with an alternate game plan. He still wanted to manage us…only we needed to pivot. He called a band meeting and addressed all five of us.

The plan was to release *Influence* and let it do whatever organic sales it could muster. Herbie voiced his position. "Who knows? Maybe we can pick up some steam and do a tour over in Europe."

We had a legion of fans in Europe and the reviews over there were stellar. Geffen Europe was a completely separate entity from Geffen North America. Working with Herbie, we could have probably swung some deals across the pond and made some money on the down-low.

Herbie's idea held some promise.

At that very moment, we needed something positive to hang our hats on.

* * *

None of those good things actually happened. Without distribution, radio play, or a budget for promotions, I'm fairly certain that my dad and my high school gym teacher bought the only two copies we ever sold.

However, sales weren't the most important thing to Herbie. At least, not yet. Obviously, some cash flow would have been nice, but he had a bigger vision for the future of the band. The most important step was to get the hell away from David Geffen.

That's how he laid it out to the band. Our contract with Geffen was for two albums, with an option to pick us up for a third. Herbie was convinced, like everyone else on Earth, that Geffen would not pick up our option. That would leave us as free agents. No longer under contract, we would be able to sign with any label we wanted and choose our destiny.

It would be perfect. We could get back to doing what we loved, in the way we wanted to do it—a new lease on life.

That is, if it only worked out the way we planned.

As with everything else that our band touched, it didn't go the way we wanted. We had the anti-Midas touch—nothing we touched turned to gold. It all turned to shit.

The whole contract situation went in a direction I didn't even see coming. It was still shit; don't get me wrong. But the new ways that the universe fucked with me was almost impressive in its creativity and originality.

* * *

We were able to book some shows in Europe.

We booked a gig at the Marquee Club in London and another at the Markthalle Theater in Hamburg, Germany. We also added ourselves to the music roster at the Bulldog Bash, a Hells Angels-run music festival. It's an extremely cool weekend at the Shakespeare County Raceway grounds in Stratford-upon-Avon, England. Don't let the pretentious name fool you; the event is as down to earth and fun as any I have ever been a part of.

We went over the Atlantic to do the tour and I was in abject misery the entire time. It never occurred to me that when a person does heroin every day for six months, they are physically dependent on the drug and will suffer through gnarly withdrawal symptoms when the drug is taken away.

That story defined my experience in Europe. I obviously couldn't bring any drugs onto an international flight. These were the days prior to 9-11 and the subsequent Patriot Act, but airlines still weren't stupid. No weapons or drugs would be tolerated, even back in the day.

Without my "medicine," I became "dope sick."

And it was bad. Like, bad bad.

Like, I was shaking-and-shitting-my-pants bad.

Cold turkey is a motherfucker, and it hit me like a sledgehammer. It turned my insides into quivering jelly.

Wanna know how fucking ignorant I was about drug abuse and addiction? I thought I had the flu. After all, I didn't shoot heroin, I smoked it. Only junkies shoot heroin. Only losers do that shit. Obviously, I wasn't going down that dark path. I was a casual user, not a dirty addict.

When it comes to smoking versus shooting heroin, it is a self-delusion to draw that dumbass line in the sand. Thinking pragmatically, I might as well have shot heroin. It would have been a hell of a lot cheaper.

Welcome to the "terminal uniqueness" of being an addict. I was so screwed up during this phase.

I shit you not (pardon the pun): I knew nothing about addiction or withdrawal. Therefore, the only explanation that fit my data was the flu.

I didn't have a lot of context for what was happening. In all my years of popping Quaaludes and guzzling alcohol, I never became an addict. I had never found a drug I liked or obsessed over doing every day. When I did too much, I pared back for awhile until I felt stable again.

Not heroin, man. Heroin was fucking perfect. I did it every day, rain or shine. Yet, despite all the shit I smoked off tin foil, I remained naïve and arrogant about the cycle of addiction. I went over to Europe assuming I could put it down temporarily and pick it back up once we returned stateside.

Despite not feeling 100%, Europe was exactly what we needed to regain some self-respect. When we pulled up to The Marquee, a long line of fans wound around the block. They were so happy to come out and see our show; they arrived early and created a buzz around the venue. Our European fans are so fucking awesome —still are to this day.

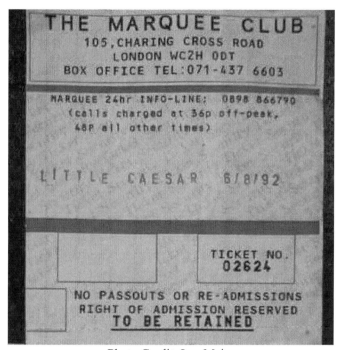

Photo Credit: Lee Mairs

For all the energy crackling outside, the Marquee Club was a high voltage Tesla Coil inside. We went in through the back door, completely unaware of the sight that would slam our eyeballs when we took the stage. The place was fuckin' packed! Kids were jammed into the place, nuts to butts. People hung from the rafters, doing whatever they could to catch a glimpse of the

Mark Danzeisen was playing drums with the band. Tom had decided to leave the band because at time, he had a deadly fear of flying—and going to Europe meant getting on a plane. Mark laid down a backbeat to introduce our opening number, and the place exploded. The Marquee Club isn't exactly Yankee Stadium; it held roughly 1,000 people on a good night. But the fans generated a roar that drowned out our equipment.

It was the greatest thing I had ever heard. Music to my ears. They gave a cacophony of love to a group of weary musicians they heard on the radio. So fuckin' awesome.

All of a sudden, our spirits lifted into the great frontier of freedom. The band looked at each other, and we knew what everyone was thinking.

This is it! This is what we signed up for!

When I prepare backstage, I feel like an airplane idling on a runway. I'm never completely calm; its all like jet engines churning and turbines twisting their powerful blades. As the clock ticks toward show time, my inner pilot pushes forward on the accelerator, and my heart pumps faster. Nervous energy takes over. I am both placid and giddy; running through the show in my mind's eye.

As we gather around the stage door, every man is called upon to live the dichotomy of being in a band. Our task is to bring our individuality onto the stage, but act as a single organism while we're up there. The whole is greater than the sum of its parts.

Inside, my head is hitting maximum amplitude as the plane screams toward lift-off.

That's how it feels. From the moment we hit the first note of the first song, until the moment we bow and run back to the dressing room, it feels like I am in flight. All of my earthly problems and stresses and demons are 35,000 feet below me. I am soaring, at peace and away from it all.

I'm not saying that I ease my proverbial seat back and take a nap up there. One the contrary; I give it all I've got. My overall energy has changed over the years. I had a rain barrel of energy when I was 30, and cling to a shot glass of energy in my 60s…but I give 100% of what I've got 100% of the time. There is no high like the feeling I get when I am on stage. It's the "high" I have chased since the first time I held a microphone in my hands.

On that night, in The Marquee Club, I was above the clouds.

These people got it. The Europeans were more dialed in to blues-based rock and roll. It was no longer a mystery why Jimi

Hendrix and Brian Setzer went across the pond to establish themselves. This is where it was at.

Yeah. This is definitely what we signed up for.

Photo Credit: Lee Mairs

That night at The Marquee wasn't just food for our souls. Sure, it was pure psychic manna from Heaven, but it was also good for the business side of the band. Representatives from Geffen Europe attended our show that evening. They saw the reaction of the crowd and evaluated the talent level of Little Caesar.

After the show, they put their heads together. They were as excited as we were. I took a call from one of the suits, who was both sincere and urgent when he spoke.

"We can break this band. What we saw tonight was something we haven't seen from a band in the last fifteen years. The fans…the crowd…you guys fuckin' exploded!"

That got my attention.

Yet, a little darkness crept into my heart. My mindset shifted from being a rock star to being a fallen hero. I was living for the opportunity to return to the scene of the crime and exact revenge for my mistreatment. I fantasized about making it big in Europe so we could return to the states and shove it in David Geffen's face.

I wanted to spike his ugly head like a football.

Figuratively speaking, of course.

Of course.

"Great! We're totally down for that!" I replied, elated.

With that, a little sunshine peeked out from behind the storm.

We traveled to Hamburg and the same thing happened. The place was fuckin' packed and the fans were better, louder, and more bat-shit crazy than anything we had experienced in the United States.

The band was euphoric. The three original members had never been able to feel "at home" on our home label, so this was invigorating. Earl's career as a sideman was such a roller coaster prior to joining our band, he was happy to feel like he was a part of a family instead of being another outsider looking in.

* * *

In the early 1990s, the biggest band in the UK was Thunder. Luke Morley and company were at the peak of their success when we arrived. They were enjoying five straight Top 10 albums, one of which hit the #1 spot. Later, they passed the "Biggest Band in the UK" torch to Oasis, but our mini tour was still a couple years ahead of the Gallagher Brothers releasing *Definitely Maybe*.

When we were there, Thunder was the big dog in the kennel.

Our tour coincided with Thunder's tour. They had recently released *Laughing on Judgment Day*, an album that would hit #2 on the UK album charts. They were hot that summer, touring the big venues around Europe. The guys in Thunder caught one of our shows —and loved us.

Photo Credit: Paul Harnes

I cannot for the life of me remember the guy's name, but one of the guys in Thunder rang me at the hotel and asked if we were interested in joining them on tour. They were touring with that year's incarnation of The Monsters of Rock, culminating in a huge festival at The Castle Donington. He mentioned that their average audience size was 57,000 people, and that they took care of their opening bands.

To let you know what a big deal The Monsters of Rock was, Iron Maiden's album, *Live at Donington*, was recorded at the festival that year, 1992. That pretty much sums up how enormous this tour was.

I either shouted "Yeah!" or "Fuck yeah!" The details escape me. I do remember this: all the fun and excitement I had felt before Geffen fucked us over had returned with a fury. I felt like the little kid running down the stairs on Christmas morning. The glowing tree and all the colorful packages underneath…the world was our fuckin' oyster again!

For about a minute.

Check out the line-up for the 1992 Monsters of Rock show at Castle Donington. You'll see Thunder, of course. Also on the bill were Iron Maiden, Skid Row, Slayer, W.A.S.P., Pantera, and The Almighty.

Can you see where I'm headed with this?

No Little Caesar.

Why?

Because we're cursed. As fuck.

Here's what happened. Herbie Herbert sent his day-to-day guy, Bill Thompson, to Europe with us. His job was to fill the manager role while Herbie took care of his affairs in the states. Unfortunately for us, Bill Thompson was no Herbie Herbert. In fact, he was the exact opposite. Bill represented everything we hated in a manager.

The head of Geffen Europe at the time was a woman. I wish I could remember her name, but I couldn't even find it on Google. Nice lady. Very professional. And she came out to see us play The Marquee on our first night in the United Kingdom.

However, when she approached us after the show, it became quite clear that she had heard some rumors about the band. Similar to our experience with Bruce Allen's staff in Vancouver, she had received word that we exploited women and did drugs.

I don't know that I had much to say about the drug rumor by that point. But once again, I was put on the defensive regarding rumors that we assaulted women. Or being unkind to women. Or anything of the sort. That rumor was so far from the truth, it had to be shut down fast.

I told her, "Look. Watch the videos we have on MTV. Watch the tapes of our appearances or interviews. Have you ever seen a naked woman? Have you ever seen me grope a woman? Have you ever seen a hint of any of us doing anything unbecoming toward a woman?"

"No," she replied, arms folded.

I continued. "We don't do anything of the sort. We're not a tits-and-ass band. So please don't mistake us for one. I've been fighting this shit for two and a half years. Our publicist put that shit out there without our knowledge."

She relaxed a little. I put the finishing touches on my plea.

"So, if you do business with us, it won't be with a scummy biker band. We like to ride motorcycles and we look rough around the edges. But we are just as professional as you are."

That did the trick. She warmed up to us and was ready to sign on the dotted line.

"Thanks, Ron. That's really nice to hear."

"You won't be embarrassed by anything we do," I assured her. "Everything we say and present to you on behalf of the band will be top shelf."

It was going so well. Until Bill Thompson walked up and opened his fucking pie hole.

"So, Honey, you coming up to the Hells Angels fest?"

She leaned back, trying to figure out if he was being ironic.

He wasn't.

"Those bikers! I'll bet they'd dig a hot chick like you."

Her face soured. But he wasn't done chewing on his foot after he stuck it in his mouth.

"You might get raped—but you might like it!"

Then he laughed like a teenage douche bag.

Yup. I swear I'm not making this up. He was kidding in his own, sophomoric asshole way. But this is not shit you joke about. The fact that he thought he was being funny says a lot about who he was as a person. Dude...*particularly* in this situation. He was approaching her as the on-site manager of a band she was interested in representing. If he were a random shithead, she would have doused him with pepper spray and been done with him. And me and the band would have given her a standing ovation.

This incident happened so freaking fast. Asshole + complete inability to read the room = another shitshow for Little Caesar.

I stepped between them and fired Bill on the spot. I told him to go to Heathrow in the morning and get his ass on a plane back to Los Angeles.

The Geffen executive thanked me. I wish I could remember her name. I told her she will never have to go through a manager like him again; she should deal with me directly. I had been fucked by this kind of shitty judgment on behalf of the suits from Day One.

Her and my working relationship was pulled out of the fire, but Bill created a smudge. The smudge would have turned out fine had it not been for the actual insanity of the Hells Angels Bulldog Bash.

* * *

Fifty thousand people attended the Bulldog Bash that year. It was a sea of bikes, bikers, bikers' "old ladies," tents, and food trucks. We pulled up in our bus and were escorted behind the gate. Parked toward the rear of the stage, we got out and surveyed the landscape.

The stage was massive, of course—the kind of open-air stage you see at big festivals like this. There was also a huge chain-link fence that surrounded an area roughly the size of a football field. It was meant to separate the music area from the rest of the grounds, which were littered with tents and campers. Thousands of people cordoned off their little fiefdoms for a full weekend of live music and partying. Obviously, the fence also created an opportunity to bottleneck, and then charge, people to enter the show.

Surrounding the chain-link fence was an army of food trucks and wagons. They were serving a veritable ton of fish and chips, from what I could see and smell. They were lined up tight, nose to tailpipe, to create a visual blockade. Event organizers wanted people to pay for admission to the football field, not watch the show from their tents and campers for free.

To us, the whole scene was very cool. Great vibe; grounds covered with people who were eager to see the band and have a good time.

Further heightening our mood and our expectations for a fantastic (and possibly career-reviving) show, the Hells Angels paraded us into a trailer behind the stage. There, they presented Little Caesar with a commemorative manhole-cover-sized plaque with our name, the date, and "Bulldog Bash" inscribed on it.

We were on Cloud 9! Our career was about to take off *for real* this time. Little Caesar had finally broken the curse and there were calm seas and smooth sailing ahead!

By this point in the book, I can't even lie to you anymore. The whole thing ended in a fucking catastrophe.

Here's what happened.

Leading up to the Bulldog Bash, Geffen had arranged for a VJ (the video version of a disc jockey) from MTV Europe to tag along with us. I wish I could remember her name; they were all interchangeable as far as I was concerned. Her job was to break in at various points during the Bash to join members of Little Caesar on stage and introduce different videos from artists being promoted by Geffen.

MTV Europe filmed the whole event. The plan was for them to air clips and concert footage from the Bash. Also, the new Little Caesar video would get launched to significant fanfare, Geffen could promote its stable of artists, and MTV could gain a toehold with the type of consumers who were attending a Hells Angels bash.

Win/win/win.

Whatever. She (the VJ) arrived to start her promotions during our concert. It was a good way to introduce her to the crowd and to demonstrate what the audience could expect for the rest of the event.

So far, so good.

She rolled into the festival on a big, double-decker bus. Tagging along was her fourteen-year-old brother, for reasons that were never made clear to me.

This poor girl. As you can probably guess, she was young and pretty. I'm sure she had been a model before MTV came along and gave her a cushy job. I'm not saying she was pampered, but I am saying that she was not pleased with her current assignment—getting dropped into the middle of 50,000 scummy bikers.

As a result, she adopted a nasty, condescending attitude all day. I don't know if it was a put-on because she was scared, or if she really did feel a sense of entitlement over the rest of us. To my eye, she sure as shit seemed to think she was better than everyone around her.

We just put up with it. We had a job to do, and a shitty 23-year-old former model with a microphone wasn't going to harsh our buzz.

Throughout the day, she interacted with the band. We recorded a bunch of vignettes while setting up our gear, walking around backstage, doing sound checks, and introducing videos by Bon Jovi, Boyz II Men, 4 Non Blondes, and whoever the fuck else was popular back then.

All in all, it was a good day. It felt like we were at home with our people, eager to re-break the band.

As the sun was setting on the western horizon and we were getting close to show time, a fire broke out in one of the food wagons. Not a big deal. Each wagon was required to carry equipment capable of extinguishing a grease fire. Fires like this weren't a common thing, but they were not unheard of, either. Food wagons aren't exactly the Taj Mahal.

However, this grease fire proved to be extremely problematic. It spread from one wagon to the next because they were tucked in so close to each other. Just as one crew would seem to get their fire under control, it would jump to the wagons surrounding it. Then it would jump to the wagons surrounding those, and so on and so forth.

I climbed onto the stage in time to see frenzied people running around, flames licking the air in every direction, and panicked shouting rising above the din. A propane tank exploded, and the hysterical cacophony rose an octave.

It was fucking bedlam.

The next thing I knew, our tour manager, Steve Waite—who I'm still friends with today—grabbed my shoulder and yelled, "Get on the fucking bus!"

The fire was about to make its way to the side of the stage, and our bus was directly in the crosshairs.

He whirled me around and looked me in the eye. "We need to get the fuck out of here!"

We grabbed the VJ and carted her off the stage with us. For all the attitude she exuded earlier that afternoon, she seemed grateful as fuck to have me pull her along to safety.

Before I could evacuate the area, another explosion rocked the night air. A piece of timber (Christ knows where it came from) hurled through the air and then fucking exploded against the chain link fence a mere ten or fifteen feet from us. A giant plume of burning sparks detonated in all directions, causing us to cry out and leap toward the bus.

I skidded to a halt. The sparks were threatening to ignite parts of the stage. Our equipment was still up there—potential kindling for a hungry inferno.

Our gear wasn't insured, of course. We were all fucking broke. All I could think was, *Fuck! I have to get our gear into the bus before the whole thing burns to the ground.*

Meanwhile, The Hells Angels were running around barking, "People! Hey! Calm the fuck down!"

Whoever decided to defy that order got their face beat in. It was like a giant ballet of violence, breaking out in the seventh ring of Hell.

For those of you not familiar with Dante's Inferno, the Seventh Circle represents Violence. For those of you familiar with this work, I'll let you figure out which of the three Rings this whole scene should sit in.

The Hells Angels were trying to restore order while the entire place was on fire. There were no fire trucks on the scene since the motorcycle club wanted no part of any type of governmental authority on the premises. They wanted to handle security, and all of the shit that went along with it, on their own.

Cops, fire trucks, and paramedics were all stopped a good mile up the road.

As if we didn't have enough to deal with already, the fourteen-year-old brother of the VJ was nowhere to be found. She was walking in circles, screaming and freaking the fuck out. She wanted to break loose from us and go look for her brother.

Thank God, she finally found the kid, not that we had time to deal with that unnecessary headache. I don't know who thought it would be a good idea to bring a kid to a Hells Angels event in the first place. But we fucking can't help being good dudes. We abandoned our priceless gear to help her until he was found.

Once the fire was fully extinguished, ambulances were allowed onto the scene. Real, qualified help was there about two hours after the mayhem began. Better late than never, I suppose.

Behind the stage, we were soot-covered and totally spent. It was one hell of a fucking night.

However, a few members of the Hells Angels' leadership made their way toward our bus. They stood before the band and said quite seriously, "Okay—we've got to turn this thing back into a fucking party. You guys ready to play?"

It was more of an order than a question, to be honest. I don't think they allowed for an option other than, "Hell, yeah!"

Not to mention, we wanted to get paid.

As we walked onto the stage, a sea of traumatized faces stared back at us. You could hear a pin drop—the entire crowd was in shock.

Fidel swears he did not say this, but I remember it clear as day. He walked up to his microphone and said, "Boy, you people really know how to throw a barbeque!"

Needless to say, it wasn't the icebreaker he hoped it would be.

We played the show and piled back onto the bus. It was a disaster.

For the next several days, the press tried their damndest to get a hold of us for the legit story, since bullshit stories started leaking into the papers. I read somewhere that six or seven people died during the fires, which was completely false. I think a handful of people had to get rushed to the hospital, but nobody died.

You've got to love the English tabloids.

Our name got associated with the headline "Hells Angels bedlam!" Not that we had a stellar reputation in the first place, but this kind of PR didn't help our case with Geffen Europe.

But we kept our heads up. We boarded the bus doggedly, but with a sense of optimism. We had a new plan to free ourselves from David Geffen's clutches.

* * *

We dragged ourselves back to our London hotel. Time to get serious about the Monsters of Rock.

I had called Geffen Europe right after the guy in Thunder invited us to tour with them. I spoke to one of the financial people, telling them we needed tour support if we were going to be able to pull this off. Remaining in Europe required money—the label had it; we did not.

After some hemming and hawing, they referred us to the label's U.S. headquarters.

Back in Los Angeles, Geffen's executives weren't exactly doing cartwheels during the conversation.

"Well, how much do you need?"

"Ten grand a week," I answered, knowing they would get a significant return on this investment.

"Hmm. We'll get back to you."

Those five little words. *We'll get back to you.* They're never a harbinger of great things to come.

Several hours later, they called back.

"Nah. It's too much money."

"Too much money!?" I couldn't believe my ears, "We're about to go play in front of 70,000 people! We only need 10,000 for the entire WEEK."

"No."

Fuck that. I'd heard of bands offering to *pay* $20,000 to get onto the tour. They didn't want to get paid, they wanted to PAY. These were successful bands you have absolutely heard of, not small-time hustlers. That's how big of a deal Monsters of Rock was.

But no.

I don't even remember hanging up the phone. It was too surreal to think about. I'm not prone to feeling despondent. I am much more likely to reconfigure a plan rather than bow to defeat.

But this was too much.

I called a band meeting in my room. The guys of Little Caesar are so fucking fantastic. They worked with me to cut corners so we could make ends meet. We put together a completely re-tooled budget.

I called Geffen back.

"Listen. We're all willing to take less draw money and sleep on floors if we have to. All we need is $5,000 per week. Can you do five grand per week?"

"No."

What the actual living cinnamon toast fuck?

No explanation. No remorse. Just, No.

That's when I knew. It all came like a tidal wave and hit me.

This.

Is.

Over.

Even the "new" plan was over. Geffen in Europe wasn't going to go up against Geffen in the United States. Therefore, they wouldn't want to revive the band. They wouldn't want to support Little Caesar. We were always seen as more trouble than we're worth.

They wanted us to go away.

This. Is. Over.

We flew back to the US, and my downward spiral picked up right where it left off. Only this time, I was going to ride it all the way to the bottom.

There was still an outside chance that Herbie Herbert could come through for us. Still a chance that a different label would sign us once we escaped from David Geffen's dungeon. Still a chance we could *be*.

But there wasn't a chance. Not for Little Caesar.

Before I even drove home from the airport and to the apartment where Marlana was waiting for me, I called my dope dealer.

I bought a giant chunk of tar heroin.

I sucked that shit into my lungs for the next five years.

CHAPTER 10:
NUMB

I am an addict.

Those words, and the meaning behind them, were completely lost on me for many years. Not that I didn't understand them. It's just that I had no intention of believing them.

The darkness enveloped me in late 1992. I don't know what provided the light that kept me going, but something kept the darkness from taking me away for good. One little ember kept the fire alive while misery and addiction poured down from the heavens.

* * *

I sat in my truck, fresh warmth spreading through my arms, legs, belly, and brain. The lighter was still in my hand, wasn't it?

Yeah, there it is.

At some point, I must have tossed the foil onto the passenger seat. I saw it lying there, winking at me. One dark eyelid closed over the silver sclera. It was blackened with heroin residue. The remains of my current fix.

I leaned my head back and let my thoughts float; clouds passing the midday sun.

I wasn't an addict. I was a talented guy who was supposed to be making music for the rest of my life. Everyone said so. Everyone knew so.

Fuck rich. I wanted my music to be famous. I wanted to write songs everybody knew. A household name; a poster on the wall; lyrics kids would recite when they sang into hairbrushes in front of bedroom mirrors.

Fuck famous. I don't give a shit about any of that. I'm too ugly for posters anyway. I just wanted to feel like somebody important.

Fuck important. I wanted to have purpose. I needed purpose.

Fuck purpose. I had no reason to be. It all got taken away from me. I got shit on by the music industry.

They did this to me.

Fuck them.

I closed my eyes and rode the magic carpet into oblivion. Somewhere along the way, I thought about the very last meeting I had with David Geffen. The meeting where the final screw got twisted into the lid of my career's coffin. The meeting where I learned of the phrase, "Key Man Clause."

But before I got there, I thought about my family. Mom was dead. She died before ever revealing if I was truly a sinner or saint, hero or villain. She alone knew The Answer. And she left me not knowing for myself.

Who the fuck *am* I?

I might have cried if I could. But the drug coursing through my body kept a tight rein on feelings. I was in an emotional coma.

My brother and sister were still alive, but they didn't have much of a relationship with me. Probably because they didn't understand me. I didn't understand me. Probably because they didn't know me. I didn't know me.

Or maybe because they did.

* * *

I've spent decades trying to get my brother and my sister to know who I am. They didn't have much of anything to do with me, frankly—but it wasn't their fault. For way too long, they didn't know me, because I didn't allow them. It was my choice. I didn't know myself, and therefore hid behind my career and geographical distance from them.

We were so far apart in age; one would think that we grew up in entirely different families. In fact, we did not...much to the surprise of my brother.

Michael is far more volatile than I am. He and my mother had an explosive relationship, interacting more like MMA fighters than true mother and son. From his point of view, I was walking on sunshine with Mom.

When I got a shit ton of tattoos and grew my hair long and played biker music, neither Michael nor Sandi could figure out where "that guy" came from. They had no idea how somebody who had it so easy could wind up looking like a death row inmate.

As they got to know me in our adulthood, the veil was lifted from their eyes. Michael's in particular. Michael thought he was unique in feeling Mom's wrath. Sandi was the only girl, and she was extremely smart. She pulled the ripcord and got out of our home at fifteen years of age. I was Mom's favorite; he figured Mom gave me a pass and might have treated me with dignity and respect.

And that left only him to be smacked around and hated by our mother.

Funny how a kid's perspective can be so distorted when they are constantly in a state of distress. The survival instinct is weird that way.

187

In fairness to my brother, Mom was extraordinarily doting on me at times. I think it was done in a last-ditch effort to finally have a kid who loved her. Add to that her weakened physical state, and she clearly needed me to take care of her. She would sling-shot from screaming and beating the hell out of Michael and/or Dad, to getting all kissy-faced with her sweet little baby boy, Ron.

I never fought with Mom. Michael taught me one very important lesson growing up: fighting back means you're either going to get the living shit beat out of you or else live in constant chaos. Being a total ass-kisser didn't keep me out of harm's way 100% of the time, but it gave me better odds than Michael's way. I tried my best to keep Mom in doting mode. As a result, she went through spells of loving me in front of the others.

It was all bullshit, of course. But my brother probably took offense to it. He got called a piece of shit and I got called a little angel. I wouldn't blame the guy for thinking I got an easy ride. He saw the side of her that cooed and gushed all over me. He didn't see the dark side, when the Mr. Hyde side of Mom's personality would screech out of the sky like a drunken Valkyrie.

Publicly, I was the Golden Child. Privately, I was just like everyone else in her wake.

Michael gets it now. But I swear it took decades for it to completely sink in. Honestly, I'm not sure if he has completely bought into the reality of the situation.

And hell, from my perspective, I might have actually had it a little worse than Michael did. He had Sandi to commiserate with; a sibling who knew exactly what he was going through. Misery loves miserable company, right?

I had nobody. Not even Dad. I was the soldier that got left behind.

Now the three of us are pretty close. The glue that binds us together is the knowledge that we all survived Mom's fucking insanity. Each of us has his or her own experience and perspective regarding our younger days, but none of us was spared psychological damage from the war we fought.

It was a war we didn't ask for and didn't deserve. But that and fifty cents will get you a shitty cup of coffee. It was the hand we got dealt, and that was that.

We all seem to share a similar demented sense of humor. I'm sure we got it from Dad, which proves the old adage "the apple doesn't fall far from the tree." We have turned the pain and the anxiety into a morose sense of self-deprecation and awful, poorly-timed jokes.

Humor continues to be my superpower. But when humor wasn't enough to completely mollify the pain, I turned to drugs.

* * *

My eyes fluttered open. I shifted in the driver's seat, wincing from the bright sunlight microwaving the interior. My ass was falling asleep. So was my right leg. I couldn't feel either one, but I knew they were there. And the pins and needles. Far, far away.

Thinking about my family made me sad. And angry. But mostly sad. For today, at least. Most of the time, I didn't think about them at all.

Instead, I thought about my career. Attached to that was an overwhelming feeling of fear. Music was my only sense of purpose; it was everything. Even that got taken away.

And when you take away your everything, you're left with nothing.

I thought about music. And how I was nothing. And David Geffen. And how he made me into nothing. And the Key Man Clause.

A teenager was staring at me through the glass. I thought the park was deserted this time of day. I wonder if he's going to rob me.

The thought almost made me laugh. If I could laugh. The emotional coma held me in carbonite. My dopamine and serotonin were frozen like Han Solo.

The teenager was gone. He didn't rob me.

Good for you, kid. I've got nothing.

Because of the fucking Key Man Clause.

* * *

Herbie Herbert's voice was confident.

"We're about a month away from your contract expiring. I've spoken to at least six other labels, and they all said they'd sign you in a minute."

I nodded along, "So we just have to wait it out?"

"Yup. Just get out of the Geffen deal. Everyone in the industry sees potential in this band."

I was about to bring up The Curse, but Herbie hit it head on.

"The other labels know the behind-the-scenes stories. They know what the deal is."

I nodded again. He took a gulp of coffee and finished his thought.

"They would all love to start fresh with you."

Sounded great to me. Maybe another light at the end of the tunnel.

About a week ahead of our contract expiring, we arranged for a meeting at Geffen. I was there with Herbie. So was Tony Ferguson, David Geffen (who popped in several minutes late), Eddie Rosenblatt, and a couple other lower-level people.

I don't remember who spoke up first, but the bottom line will haunt my dreams forever.

"Okay. So your contract is up. We're not going to be picking up your option."

Inside, I was thinking, *Great. Okay, great. Just make this go away.*

Right about then David showed up. He unbuttoned his suit coat and took a seat at the head of the table. Without pausing to see where the conversation was at, he jumped right in.

As best as I can recall, and my memory is affected by the utter rage and despair I felt in the moment, David told me that he can't have Little Caesar go to another label and be successful. Because then everyone would know that what I had been saying in the press was true.

190

He didn't want anyone to know that it wasn't about the music or the band. It was about the business.

I waited him out. As long as he got to the part where he was releasing us from our contract, I was fine listening to whatever nonsense he had to say. Unfortunately, the path he cut started to circle around.

He went on to mention that he had a whole label he was still in bed with for the next two years. During that time, he couldn't make himself look bad.

My back stiffened. What was he talking about?

Then he got to a part that seemed to be precisely calculated to intimidate. He said he'd been in this situation before. And as a result, he'd gotten into a bit of a tussle with one of his artists. It happened with Don Henley, who ended up not putting out a record for about ten years.

He leaned across the table, gaze intent. His implication was that he had prevented Don from producing any more original content on the Geffen Label.

I will never forget what he said next.

"I collect artists like I collect artwork. And if I want to put you on a shelf or store you in a warehouse, I will do so if it is for the betterment of my business."

I couldn't move. I didn't want to hear the words that came next, but they could not be stopped. David Geffen folded his hands on the table in front of him and finished me off.

"So what I'm going to do is this: I'm going to hold you, Ron. I'm optioning the Key Man Clause in your contract. I'm letting the band go, but I am going to hold *you*."

He didn't even crack a wry smile. Instead, his tone was flat, like he was reading box scores out of the sports section in the *Daily News*.

"Now, if you want to write something or work on a new project, then bring me the demo. If it's good, we'll talk. But as far as Little Caesar goes, it ain't gonna happen."

And with that, he was out the door and gone.

I left the meeting feeling like I had just shot-gunned a bottle

191

of NyQuil. I had been vaguely aware of the Key Man Clause. I hadn't researched it in depth because I didn't think anything of it at the time we signed with Geffen.

The clause states that the label can cut ties with a band if a designated key member of said band (hence, the "Key Man" or "Key Person") leaves. The clause is put in place to protect the label. If the lead singer leaves, the band is basically useless as a marketable entity, so the label can drop them without recourse.

Imagine if Jon Bon Jovi had left his band after the *Slippery When Wet* record. Mercury Records would have been left to pay for a band that would have been DOA in the marketplace. Without Jon at the helm, they would have never been able to sell over 7,000,000 copies of their follow up record, *New Jersey*.

The clause can be written to the advantage of a band, should the band have leverage entering the negotiations. For example, The Foo Fighters had some muscle when they signed with Capitol Records in 1997. Dave Grohl was coming out of the band Nirvana following the death of Kurt Cobain. With him, Dave brought Nirvana's tremendous legion of fans. When he signed with Capitol, he inserted a Key Man clause and designated his friend, Capitol Records President Gary Gersh.

When Gersh was forced out of the label in 1999, Grohl enacted the Key Man option and left the label. The Foo Fighters subsequently signed with RCA, who put out the *There Is Nothing Left to Lose* album. It subsequently went platinum for RCA.

In my case, the clause was written to partial me out, should the band implode. David Geffen had a whole separate deal when it came to me specifically. I don't know if he didn't trust the rest of the band to keep their noses clean, or if he saw something in me he wanted to pursue beyond Little Caesar.

Whatever the case, he had me in a death grip. He owned any future creative endeavors in which I decided to engage, as long as they weren't Little Caesar.

None of that meant shit as far as I was concerned. David didn't seem to want anything creative out of me. He didn't seem to want to do anything with me other than keep me from showing him up on a different label. And if that meant killing my career, then so be it. I'm sure he slept like a baby that night.

I looked into Don Henley's situation. I don't know what exactly, if anything, happened between him and David Geffen, but David's story checked out. Don released *End of the Innocence* on Geffen's label in 1989. The album went 6x platinum, meaning it sold over 6,000,000 copies in the United States alone.

At that point in his career, Don could have released an album of him singing the A-B-Cs and it would have gone platinum. The follow up was destined for high sales, regardless. However—and this is baffling if you're not looking for it—Don took the next ten years off. When he returned to record *Inside Job* in 2000, eleven years had passed, and he was now on the Warner Brothers label.

Did David Geffen have something to do with the long hiatus? Maybe. Don certainly didn't need the money, but artists create and entertainers entertain. Don had to be itching to write and record music during that time. Yes, he rejoined the Eagles for several tours during that stretch, but his solo career mysteriously disappeared.

And now David owned my ass indefinitely…or at least, for my "prime years".

I called my dealer. And I got high.

* * *

The teenager was back, looking at me.

Or was he really there? Hard to tell what's real and what's not real when you're messed up. Not that you care. You hardly notice anyway.

I flopped an arm onto my face. My nose itched.

Fuck it. I'll get it later.

For now, I just want to feel high. It won't last forever. Sooner or later, I'll start coming down, and that will suck worse than living. When the high strayed too far away, I'd call my dealer and score some more tar.

My eyes blinked shut, and the teenager was gone again. Slowly…slowly…I unplugged my internal switchboard and descended into the abyss.

It all felt like darkness. I didn't see any light.

I was numb again.

CHAPTER 11:
ALMOSTS

I'd like to step out of the timeline for a short moment to recall two other times I almost became famous. Coming "oh, so close" seems like a recurring theme in my life. Which bolsters the theory that I'm cursed.

Honestly, I've felt that way a lot.

However, I also know that I reached a level in my career that few musicians ever achieve. I had a recording contract. I played for a band that people loved—and still do, to this day. I have played in front of millions of people in my career. I was on MTV and had a record on the *Billboard* charts.

For every one of the dozens of musicians who hit that level of moderate success, there are thousands who work their asses off and never get there. In all, I am absolutely grateful for all I have and all I've done.

But that's the mature, 62-year-old me. Back then, I was filled with spit and venom—not toward others, but toward myself...which fueled my self-pity.

Despite all that, there were still two other times I stepped up to the plate. I thought I hit home runs both times, but I only managed to foul out.

* * *

I was the lead singer of The Red Hot Chili Peppers for a minute in 1986. Close your eyes and picture that for three or four Mississippis. Weird, I know, but 100% true.

At the time, they had only released two records on EMI and were still considered a local LA band with some serious promise.

Their singer, Anthony Keidis, had left the band. At the time, I didn't know why; I had never even heard of the Chili Peppers. I later learned that he was in rehab for a drug problem, so the band was unclear about his future as their vocalist. All I knew was that I was told to go audition.

I showed up. We were in the basement of the Capitol Records building. When I walked in, I was greeted by bassist Flea, who was there with guitarist Hillel Slovak and drummer Jack Irons. All super nice guys who liked what I had to offer. They wanted a singer who could help them expand their repertoire into a melody-based musical vibe. Anthony had been more of a rapper than a true singer. The band wanted to push into a mainstream-friendly direction. It was all good with me.

They gave me some raw demos for the album they were working on, *The Uplift Mofo Party Plan*. I took it home and worked on lyrics and melodies. It was all very cool and pretty legit.

When I came back to the band, they loved what I had written. Flea approached me with a litmus test question.

Before I reveal the question, I want to assure you: this is *exactly* what went down.

Flea said, "I've only got two questions for you, Ron."

"Fire away," I offered.

"Would you be okay going out to perform on stage, wearing nothing but a sock over your dick?"

Not exactly the question I was expecting. In fact, it wasn't a question I could have *ever* expected. Anywhere. From anyone. In any universe, parallel or otherwise.

Still, I am never one to spoil an opportunity. I replied, "Yeah! I could do that. Fuck it!"

We laughed for a minute, and I heard myself say, "Really? Really? That was the first question you wanted to ask me?"

"Yeah," he chuckled, "That was the deal-breaker question."

Then he said something that has stuck with me ever since. It was the most powerful thing I think I have ever been told by another player.

He looked down at his guitar and said, "I've got to let you

196

know, Ron, that when we play, even if it's in rehearsal, we play every note like it might be the last note we ever play."

He paused, and then continued. "We don't put a governor on it. We play every note and savor every note. One hundred per cent, full tilt."

All I could say was, "Dude, I totally respect that."

Flea is really an amazing player and person.

Michael Beinhorn produced that record. He listened to what I had written and loved it. It was a different direction for the band, but they were on board and ready to roll out Ron Young as their new singer and collaborator.

I had a couple cassettes of demos I cut with the Chili Peppers. When Marlana split, she took the box of cassettes with her, including the Chili Peppers demos. I don't think she knew they were in there, but I never had the heart to ask her for them back.

Unfortunately (are you sitting down?), I got bumped. Anthony got out of rehab and had a heart-to-heart with the rest of the band. They decided to take him back, which I completely understood. Flea called me personally to apologize. He said he had known Anthony since they were kids, and he couldn't turn his back on him.

Oddly enough, Anthony has stayed pretty much sober since then, but Hillel died of an overdose soon thereafter, in 1988. I don't think they even knew he had that big of a problem when I was hanging around.

It's a weird world we musicians live in, man.

* * *

In 1994 I received a phone call from Mike Clink, Guns 'n Roses' producer. How he got my number, I'll never know. Mike produced the 30x platinum (which is over *30 million* units sold) *Appetite for Destruction*, and the follow-up albums, *Use Your Illusion, Vols. I and II*, both of which went 7x platinum. To say he was a big deal in the world of music would be a gross understatement. Mike was currently working with Slash on his side project, Slash's Snakepit.

If you don't know who Slash is, please just put this book down and slowly back away. Then do yourself a favor and look him up on both Wikipedia and YouTube.

You're welcome.

To give you a good idea of how rock and roll Slash was, I'll tell you about The Swimming Pool.

I went to a 4th of July party at his house. Slash had lost his primary house earlier that year to the January, 1994 Northridge Earthquake. So he was renting a nice house with a pool somewhere in The Hills.

Incidentally, he also lost his snake collection when his house broke and fell apart in the quake. I think he lost close to 100 snakes, which included live samples of some of the deadliest snakes in the world—such as black mambas, king cobras, and a few others. I don't know where the snakes went after they escaped, but I like to fantasize that they showed up at David Geffen's house.

Anyway, Slash was deep into his run with alcoholism during this period. When you opened his refrigerator, there was wall-to-wall cranberry juice. And then when you opened the freezer, it was wall-to-wall vodka. The dude was a serious drinker.

Lenny Kravitz showed up to the party carrying a bottle of a rare Asian-Indian alcohol. Christ knows what it was exactly, but the bottle had cobra heads floating in it like worms in tequila. The liquor was rumored to be infused with real cobra venom.

We did shots of that shit. Fucking rock stars.

I mentioned the pool because Slash decided to make a subtle (ha!) renovation to the house when he rented it. He drained the pool, installed a chain-link fence around the pit, and purchased a mountain lion, which he kept as a pet. The lion's pen was the empty pool.

Later on, I heard that one of Slash's workers got attacked by the mountain lion and had to have a whole bunch of stitches. So, Slash had to give up his pet puma.

Fear not, dear reader. He still had his other pet: his solo band, Slash's Snakepit.

GnR hadn't put out a record in a few years, and the tension

between Axl Rose and Slash was palpable. In fact, that's probably why they hadn't put out a record. The primary songwriting team couldn't get together and get anything done. Hence, Slash decided he'd had enough of that shit and set out to put together a solo project.

From what I understand, Slash was excited about the project and eager to record and release some new music. Evidently he had tried out dozens of lead singers but couldn't find the vibe he was seeking. So, Mike Clink called me.

"Are you willing to go up to Slash's house in the Hollywood Hills?"

I said what I say every time, "Hell, yeah!"

"Okay," he instructed, "The way Slash auditions guys is that he starts playing stuff and you write melodies and lyrics right there on the spot. You sing them into a mic."

He paused. "Does that freak you out?"

Always the pragmatist, I replied, "Nah, dude. If that's what everyone else does, then sure. It's a level playing field."

I showed up. Slash started noodling on his Les Paul and I stepped up to the mic to do my thing. I've gotta say, despite being fucked up on heroin, I did okay. I started riffing and spitting out some shit, and Slash was like, "Wow! That's pretty good."

We finished a few tunes and he said, very simply, "Do you want the gig?"

Pfft. Did I want the gig? FUCK YEAH, I wanted the gig! Financially, I was a hair's breadth away from turning tricks behind the Exxon station. Join a band with one of the biggest rock stars of my era? Holy crap, yes!

I said, "Yeah. That would be great."

I started singing as a member of Slash's Snakepit. Mike Inez of Ozzy Osbourne was on bass, and fellow GnR refugees, rhythm guitarist, Gilby Clark and drummer, Matt Sorum rounded out our crew.

It was all going so well. At least, that's what I thought.

There came a point where, suddenly, Slash wasn't returning my calls. Mike Clink also ghosted me. I didn't know what was going on, but I knew it was something.

That was when Mike Inez called me.

"Look, Ron, I was asking around and nobody seems to be talking to you about this, so I'm just going to give you the lowdown."

My heart sank. This wasn't going to go well for me.

He said, "The reality is, the only other guy that Slash was even considering for vocals was Eric Dover, from the band Jellyfish."

I silently nodded into the phone.

"So, the deal is, Eric can sing Guns 'n Roses. Your vocal register is too low to do Axl's stuff."

I didn't interrupt him. He finished, "Slash loves your unique style, but he realized that when he goes out on tour, everyone is going to want to hear all those Guns 'n Roses songs."

Mike went on to assure me that he liked my style and thought I fit the project better than Eric. But Slash couldn't give up his bread and butter.

When Slash finally called me a couple days later, I was gracious in accepting my defeat. What else could I do? It was purely a business decision, and I got that. Once again, I came so close. As Don Adams said in his iconic *Get Smart* television series, "Missed it…by *that much*."

Another grand opportunity fell apart, pushing me deeper into my depressive, heroin-laced funk.

That, kiddies, is rock and roll.

CHAPTER 12: BREAKING THE CYCLE

Prior to doing our second record, I had only done heroin a few times in my life. My typical pattern was to use too much of it, get sick as a dog, and then stay away from it for awhile. That all changed, of course, when I did some with a good friend of mine, Gary Corbett.

For those of you who knew him, Gary died on July 14, 2021. It was just a few months prior to me starting on this book. He lost his battle with cancer on the same day that his Cinderella band mate, Jeff LeBar, died.

Weird coincidence.

Gary played keyboards for quite a few other high-level acts, including Molly Hatchett, Lou Gramm, and (as I have already written about) Kiss. I first met Gary while we were on the Kiss tour, prior to recording Little Caesar's first album. He was playing keys off stage for their live shows at the time. Both of us were smart-assed New Yorkers who formed an immediate friendship.

A couple years later, I invited him to play some stuff with us on the second album. He was happy to do so.

That was when my love affair with heroin really took off.

Gary pulled me aside in the studio one afternoon and mentioned he had brought some heroin. Being the cool New Yorker that he was, he asked if I wanted to do it with him.

I said, "Fuck, yeah!" I was down for anything during those days.

We did some, and it was pretty good. Gary knew his way around the drug; he helped me to figure out the right amount to maximize the high and minimize the sick.

I liked it. So I did it again with Gary the next day.

And the next day.

And the next day and the day after that.

At some point, he ran out. I made a few phone calls and replenished our stock. I hooked up with my "guy" at the 7-11 and got some more.

I didn't realize I was already well down the road to addiction. I just thought I liked heroin, so I wanted to do a little more. Kinda like ice cream: when you run out, you make a quick trip to the market and pick up another quart.

Only instead of getting fat, you get addicted.

When Gary returned to New York, I kept calling my "guy." Every day or every couple days, I needed to fill my freezer with more ice cream.

Wait—heroin. I needed fill my brain with heroin.

This went on for six months before we went over to Europe where I got dope sick. I presented that story earlier. When we got back, I started to consider the possibility that I might have a problem. Because I *did* call my guy and I *did* pick right back up where I had left off.

Heroin became a daily ritual. I am serious when I say I wasn't convinced I had an addiction. I knew I had just stopped doing it for two weeks in Europe, so obviously I wasn't hooked on the stuff. Every addict in the history of addiction is convinced they can stop any time they want to.

Except I couldn't.

Denial is a powerful tool used by a drug when it hijacks the thinking part of an addict's brain. Whenever I started to wonder if I was in trouble, the heroin would whisper, "Shhhh…everything is going to be okay."

I was good at being an addict, even if I do say so myself. I kept it completely hidden from Marlana. I know every addict and alcoholic thinks they are hiding it from the rest of the world—but I really did

Marlana hated heroin. She had seen what it did to several of our friends back in New York. Heroin had the power to royally fuck a person's total existence. She would have probably fared better if I had developed a porn or gambling addiction. Heroin was the worst of the worst, and she made no bones about her opinion that way.

I hid my shame. I was clandestine in my purchases behind the 7-11. I somewhat controlled my intake. Part of that was financially based, but another part was to maintain a degree of awareness so I could keep my usage hidden. In other words, I never got fucked up to the point of nodding out at home. I tried to do just enough to maintain the low-level warm buzz and numbness.

Then David Geffen dumped the band, kept me under the Key Man clause, and rolled his dick in kitty litter to fuck me like there was no tomorrow.

As for my music career, there was no tomorrow. So I kept doing drugs like there was no tomorrow. Seize the day because you only live once and all that happy horse shit.

I fell into a deep depression during the next few months. It was easily the lowest I have ever been. Emotionally, I was out of gas. I wallowed in self-loathing and self-pity; the poor little rock star that never got to fulfill his dream.

My drug usage ramped up, but my daily use was still intended to keep me off of Marlana's radar. I kept getting loaded, but I also kept trying to gain some traction in music. David Geffen could dry hump a Minotaur, for all I cared. I was a musician and I wanted to make music.

A few cool projects came up along the way. For example, in 1993, I received a phone call from Adrian Vandenberg. He and a few refugees from the band Whitesnake had formed a side project called Manic Eden. Adrian explained they had just fired their lead singer, James Christian, and wanted to know if I would be interested in stepping in and taking over his gig. James is more of a "melodic metal" singer, and they wanted it to take a more bluesy, edgy turn.

At the time, I didn't know much about the guys personally. I knew they were seasoned musicians who were accustomed to making high quality metal. Tommy Aldridge was on drums and Rudy Sarzo was on bass.

I liked and had a lot of respect for Whitesnake; they were a better band than 90% of the artists in the hair metal scene. I also knew their style of music wouldn't be well received in our current, grunge-dominated era. When I expressed this concern to Adrian, he explained that this project was formed so they could make a throwback, bluesier sounding brand of rock and roll. Think Jimi Hendrix mixing it up with Paul Rodgers, who led Free and Bad Company.

That was totally my cup of tea. I said yes immediately. I recorded an amazing album with them, the 1994 self-titled *Manic Eden*. I know I keep telling you to go find stuff on YouTube, but seriously—find this album. It is an extremely good album, and one for which I am extremely proud.

Truth be told, two songs on that album are among my most favorite I have ever written and performed. The song "Dark Shade of Grey" is about the break-up of my first marriage. I wrote it early in 1994, which was the beginning of Marlana getting sick of my miserable, drugged-out personality.

I remember running out to my car between takes while we recorded that song in the studio. I would take a few hits of tar heroin off a foil I kept stashed in there. What a fucking nightmare.

The song "Do Angels Die" is the other of my favorites. Like "Dark Shade," it is a ballad, and a fucking good one at that. You can find a professionally-shot music video online for "Do Angels Die."

We shot the video in Paris. Exactly like the time I went over to Europe with Little Caesar a couple years prior, I was dope sick out of my fucking mind. I was a hurting unit while we filmed the footage for the video. I don't know if a casual observer would be able to tell in the video itself, but dude, it was some gut-twisting shit.

I loved working with those guys, but there was no money available for marketing and promotion. The record was funded by a company called JVC (Japan Victor Company). Yes, it is under the umbrella of the same company that makes JVC stereos, VCRs, and speakers.

They were expecting a Whitesnake-esque record, not a Jimi Hendrix/Free/Bad Company record. When we didn't present them with a heavily produced 1980s-type of album, they were disappointed. Yet, the album still did very well in Japan. I think it almost went gold despite the label not putting anything behind it.

Adrian decided to fold up his tent and leave the project after our sales were slow to take off. His initial plan was to give Japanese rights to JVC, but keep the rest of the world-wide rights for himself. That way, JVC would pay to produce the record and put it out in Japan. Once it kicked some ass in East Asia, Adrian would take the record and pitch it to American labels, then do the same thing in Europe.

However, when we got back to the states, we couldn't *buy* a meeting with any American A&R guys. Nobody wanted to touch the album. Grunge had such a strangle hold on music at the time, there wasn't any room for other genres to breathe—including an album recorded by four guys from the 1980s hair metal scene.

We tried to explain how our sound was an evergreen; we defied genre-specific stereotypes. We were a guitar-driven rock band.

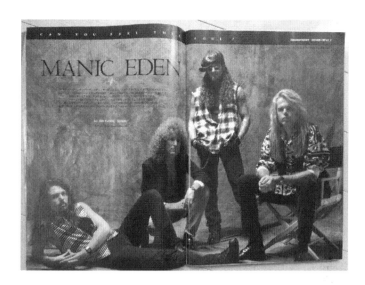

But our words fell on deaf ears. Nobody would listen to it.

One executive tried to tell us that our type of music was "dead." Who was I to argue? The other three guys had sold over 20 million records with their various projects over the years. I had sold about 75 records, mostly to friends and family.

Although, to be fair, I probably purchased 30 of those records myself, to give as a gift to the Poor Handmaidens of Christ Elementary School in upstate New York.

That was a joke.

There was no way Little Caesar could have sold 75 records.

Kidding. Again.

In all seriousness, I think Little Caesar had sold about 180,000 albums by that point.

Adrian told the guy to fuck off. With that, Manic Eden was pretty much done. We did some acoustic dates over in Europe to promote the record. But when we got back home, everyone had to go back to work. Nobody had been paid for almost a year and the wolves were at the door.

Adrian returned to Whitesnake and began work on their *Restless Heart* album. Tommy hit the road with various bands, including reuniting with James Christian in House of Lords, and working with former Whitesnake and Blue Murder guitarist, John Sykes. I think Rudy got back together with Quiet Riot for awhile, although he has always been in high demand. He's worked with many, many bands and artists over the years.

As for me, I was fucked.

* * *

Marlana was basically supporting our household during these years. She had a decent enough job, but money was always tight. Every dollar I could surreptitiously get my hands on was spent behind the 7-11. In 1994, I was up to about 40 dollars per day for dope. That may not sound like a lot of money in the grand scheme of things, but dude, I was just scraping by.

And I was such a conniving shit back then. When Manic Eden was in Japan, JVC gave us an advance to do the album. Mine came out to about USD $12,000. I took $9,999 in cash so I didn't have to declare it when returning through customs, and had JVC send the rest in the form of a check.

I took all the cash and squirreled it away. I didn't shove it under my mattress per se, but I might as well have. I didn't want Marlana to know about the money because I needed it to maintain my drug habit.

It's probably an understatement, but I was deep into addiction by that point. I was a complete slave to the drug—physically, spiritually, and emotionally. It was everything to me.

Internally, I was scared shitless. I lived a life steeped in a state of constant fear. I knew that if Marlana ever found out, it would be the end of our marriage. Paranoia mixed in with depression; the cycle of numbing highs and detoxing lows pushed a hurricane of distress.

Like every addiction story, I couldn't keep my secret forever. Marlana did find out. My memory is a little fuzzy with the details, but I think she found a foil in my truck.

For anyone who isn't familiar with tar heroin, it is sold in hard, sticky chunks that resemble black tar. In order to get it into the body, a user has to break it down into a liquid form to inject it, or else inhale the smoke fumes coming off the burning product. Either method requires you to heat it up.

The most cost efficient and controlled way to burn it is to place the heroin onto a piece of aluminum foil and hit it from underneath with a lighter. Once liquefied, the user will take either a glass tube, or the hull of a hollowed-out ball point pen, and use it to inhale the smoke coming from the burn.

Of course, for those I felt were TRULY addicted, the liquid heroin can be pulled into a syringe/needle and injected into the vein of an arm.

When you hear about drug paraphernalia, this is what they are talking about. Pills are so much easier than crack cocaine, crank/methamphetamine, or heroin. You don't need to change the physical structure of pills in order to get high. You pop them in your mouth and they go to work.

No matter how you slice it, I was a dope addict. That meant leaving a trail of paraphernalia in my wake.

Marlana found out, but she didn't leave me. She found some grace in her heart and sent me to a three-day detox center. Her goal was for me to get my shit together. My goal was to get through it so I could get back out and get high.

Honestly, I think I did want to get clean. But I was like every addict; I tried to control the narrative in everything and everyone around me. Do whatever I had to do to keep my friend (heroin) in my life. I wanted to stay married to Marlana, and that required her to be happy. I also knew I was in serious trouble with regard to heroin— but fear gives way to craving. Your need for the drug outweighs all rational thought.

Hell, I wasn't even dope sick until the second day of my stay in detox. By the time I really started coming down and going into withdrawals, they kicked me out. I think they threw a twelve-step book at me as well as a list of Alcoholics Anonymous (AA) and Narcotics Anonymous (NA) meetings in my area.

I did read the book. It was comical to me. I was like, *Pfft. You've got to be fucking kidding me. "God?" What is God going to do?*

I was completely unaware of the psychological make-up of an addict. I didn't know how damaged I was. I had never thought about the battle raging within many artists, especially the sense of grandiosity coupled with crippling self-doubt. The dichotomy of creativity. My broken sense of self had no means of navigating it.

I remember reading a particular article by an American psychiatrist, Harry Tiebout. It was *Ego Factors in Surrender in Alcoholism*, written in 1954. He was a big proponent of AA and sat on their Board of Trustees for ten years, from 1957 to 1966. Dr. Tiebout wrote a lot about the psychological components of addiction, and how addicts and alcoholics have the same behaviors.

The component that speaks to the dual nature of creativity is Tiebout's notion of "His Majesty, the Baby," which is a term he borrowed from Sigmund Freud (Tiebout, 1954). This addresses the sense of entitlement addicts have. But emotionally, they operate as children.

According to Tiebout, children act like little monarchs who are the born rulers of all they survey. This little ruler must never be questioned! As Tiebout notices, they are no different from any insufferable autocrat. And like an autocrat, they show three distinct behaviors: Impatience, Entitlement, and Intolerance (Tiebout, 1954).

Tiebout explains *impatience* as a tendency to do everything in a hurry. The child has big goals and big desires that must be immediately met. They run anywhere they go, and cannot stick with any one activity for any length of time. They are eternally restless, and may think that they are getting nowhere if they don't get there now (Tiebout, 1954).

Entitlement refers to the self-centered nature of the child. They were the sole occupiers of the womb they came from. They believe they are special, better than anyone else, and they wield an exceptional right to dominate over those they think of as lower. Humility and failure give them a great deal of distress (Tiebout, 1954).

Intolerance deals with the inability to accept frustration. They must do what they want to do with no interruptions. They take waiting as a personal insult. Because of this, they cannot let things organically evolve; they must create a plan set in stone in order to navigate through life's difficulties (Tiebout, 1954).

Normally, as the child becomes an adult, this selfishness gives way to the patience, tolerance, and self-awareness of lived experience. The addict may revert back to these infantile behaviors to offset the approval and admiration denied to them in their childhood.

Thus, they become His Majesty, the Baby.

That concept described me to a T.

When the trauma of losing the record deal started picking at the scab of the trauma created by my crazy mother, I felt out of control and unable to cope with the pain. Like most addicts, I felt that normal people could neither understand nor relate to what I was going through.

As a consequence, I felt totally justified in doing whatever it took to maintain my sense of self.

Noboooody knows…the trouble I've seen.

Noboooody knows…my sorrow.

All the justifications a drug whispers sweetly into our ears are nothing but pure bullshit. But bullshit will always stink, no matter how pretty the package it comes in.

When I got out of the three-day detox, I didn't get well. Instead, I doubled down on my efforts to hide it.

And that worked. Temporarily.

* * *

After Manic Eden fell apart, I spent the next couple years hustling in the industry. I sang on any number of bullshit records and projects; anything I could do to make money and push the ball forward. I worked on tribute records, demos, anything thrown at me. I never said no—that would mean financial suicide.

Privately, I had become a miserable human being. I was using up Marlana, squeezing every ounce of forgiveness, comfort, and emotional energy she had to give. My addiction had reached its height of excess. I bought dope, hid dope, used dope. My entire existence revolved around dope.

I was having an affair with heroin. I completely neglected my marriage. My personality vacillated between numb disconnection, wallowing in misery, and demanding comfort. When I would run out of money, I would be dope sick and absolutely terrible to be around. I would try to explain it away by telling Marlana I was depressed. It was like living with a rage-filled Eeyore.

Dope was the centerpiece of my life.

In the end, I used her up. Marlana had nothing left to give.

She was not stupid. She knew something was going on throughout those few years. I was totally disconnected. I wanted nothing to do with anything that didn't involve getting high.

In 1997, she was done with me. She stumbled upon my paraphernalia once again. With that, she could no longer live in denial.

I still remember the conversation. She was at work (at the same place I worked), and called me at home.

"Found your dope. Get your shit and get out of the house. You don't have a job anymore. I'm getting you fired. I don't give a fuck what you do. Be gone by the time I get home."

With that, I knew. All the balls I was juggling hit the floor. I knew it was over.

She was done with me. I had used up every ounce of love, empathy or care she had for me.

* * *

I was in therapy by this point, which was probably a good thing. At least I had somewhere to turn when the marriage ended.

I called my therapist as soon as I hung up with Marlana.

"I've destroyed my career. I've destroyed my marriage. There's no point in living."

Of course, once a therapist hears those magic words, they have to act. Mine did. She put me on hold for a couple of minutes

212

and called the police. Not out of fear or punishment, but to save my life.

When she returned to the line, we continued chatting. A few minutes later, there was a knock on my door. Four LAPD officers stood on my porch, ready to intervene.

I yelled through the door, "Who is it?"

"It's LAPD. We heard you're trying to hurt yourself."

"Hurt myself?! I've been hurting myself for years. I'm trying to KILL myself!"

Ah, that Young sense of humor shines through.

But that quip broke the tension. They laughed but continued to assess the situation.

"Do you have any weapons?"

I thought about it for a moment.

"No. I'm such a fucking pussy, I don't even have a weapon. I can't even do this right."

More laughter.

"Can we come in and talk to you?"

At this point, I was out of fight. I was introduced to rock bottom.

"Yeah," I swung the door open. "Come on in."

They entered and explained that I had to be transported to Olive View Psychiatric Hospital at UCLA. I had to be committed, which is called a 5150 in the legal parlance. It meant that I would be held—whether I liked it or not—in the hospital for treatment and observation.

It was for my own good. I was not stable.

They handcuffed me. They did it gently, but I was walked out to the squad car in cuffs. It was for my protection. More importantly, it was for their protection.

Listen man, cops have a tough job. They come rolling up to a scene and don't ever know what to expect. Sure, we were joking around, but business is business. They don't know me or what was going on in my head.

At the end of the day, they each wanted to make sure they could go home in one piece. I got it. No problem on this end. I have a deep respect for the job they do.

When I was taken into the hospital, I was initially strapped to a bed. I am claustrophobic to the point that I lost my shit. The staff took pity on me and pulled me out of the bed. They cuffed me to a chair, which was fine. Then I had nothing to focus on except my fucked-up life.

I was in a dark, dark place. I kept thinking, *Ah, man, I can't even kill myself right.*

After what felt like an eternity, a psychiatrist walked in. He was cordial, and said, "Let's go down to my office for a chat."

We ended up talking for three or four hours. It must have been a slow day at Olive View, but I was grateful to have the conversation. We talked about my family history in general, and my mother in particular.

One tidbit that came out of me during the talk was that my mother had been committed to a mental institution when I was three years old. She underwent shock therapy at the time. That is some crazy stuff. Prior to this moment with the UCLA psychiatrist, I had buried that memory.

My sister was on medication at the time, and my brother was diagnosed with bipolar disorder many years ago. A whole lot of shit fertilized my family tree.

The psychiatrist listened and thought for a moment. And then he said, "I think you have something called dysthymia, which is a mild chronic depression. Along with the addiction, it's what is referred to as a dual diagnosis."

He explained that everyone's moods fluctuate from day to day. If a 0 is contentment, a +10 is like you're shot up on an eight ball of cocaine, and a -10 is depression to the point that you can't get out of bed. Most people operate somewhere between a -2 and a +2 on any given day.

He said that I never really hit a -7 or -8; that might signify a clinically depressive episode. Instead, I had been hovering at around a -3 or -4 for years and years.

He added, "And then you became a drug addict because you couldn't handle certain events in your life."

I bowed my head. He was spot on.

He continued. "You found something that worked, and you began to self-medicate."

He leaned back in his desk chair and folded his hands over his belly. He had kind eyes.

"After awhile, you became physically dependent. Thus, you have what we refer to as a 'dual diagnosis;' a mental health issue and an addiction to heroin. Unless you treat both, you'll never get over either."

All I could say was, "Well, that makes perfect sense to me, but I don't know how to do that."

"There are programs." He smiled, "A three-day detox isn't going to do anything for you in the long term. You'll need to go in for at least a month. Maybe three. Maybe six. We won't know until you begin. After that, the professionals on site will assess your recovery progress and make sure you are prepared for sobriety once you leave."

I explained that I didn't have a pot to piss in. He whirled his chair around and picked a brochure off the credenza behind his desk. Laying it in front of me, he addressed my concern.

"There is a program called MAP, the Musician's Assistance Program. It was founded by a guy named Buddy Arnold. He's a recovering addict and helps musicians secure the money to go through treatment."

I was definitely interested. I might have been slogging through life using a drug-addled brain, but I was still smart enough to know that I couldn't do this on my own. Furthermore, there was nowhere to go but down if I continued on my current path. Death or jail. Those were the only two end points.

I called Loren to come get me out of the hospital. By this time in his life, Loren was a savvy practitioner of sobriety—so he proceeded to yell at me the entire way home. He also informed me that Marlana, probably with his help, had moved all my shit into a storage locker. He handed me the key.

I turned the key over in my hand. The sun glinted off its shiny silver coating and put a flash of brilliance in my darkened mind. The key represented everything I had fucked up. However, it also represented a chance to "unlock" the door leading into a new life.

"Take me to this MAP place," I said.

Loren did. I set up an appointment. A few days later, I did an intake with them. I qualified for financial assistance, which allowed me to enter treatment and rehabilitation at a facility called Cry Help.

It was September 23, 1997. I have been clean and sober since that very day. In the parlance of recovery, that date is my new birthday.

* * *

I won't say a lot about the treatment program. Addicts and alcoholics, who are really one in the same, like to have a modicum of dignity and privacy as they walk their path of recovery. Therefore, I will honor that tradition. I'll just give some broad strokes, in case anyone is curious about how they treat addiction.

A lot of work was done to help me handle emotions in a healthier way, to identify cues and triggers in my life that might make me want to use again, and to learn strategies to manage tough moments when an addict will begin to teeter toward relapse. Make no mistake; most days are pretty solid, but every addict and alcoholic will have a handful of days when their continued sobriety becomes an act of sheer determination.

They also introduce the residents to AA (or NA or CA, cocaine anonymous). Through these organizations, you become connected to a network of other folks in recovery; folks who can relate to your struggles and concerns. You will also choose a "sponsor." This is a member who is further along in recovery than you, and who will provide guidance, mentoring, and a voice at the other end of the phone on days you are grappling with that act of determination.

As a full disclosure, I will add that I had been attending meetings for about two years before I entered Cry Help. I even tried to titrate down (slow my usage), thinking I could eventually coast to a stop.

Obviously, addiction does not work that way. But what did I know? I wanted to be clean and sober, but I didn't want to stop using heroin.

I know; it sounds crazy. Hence, the addicted brain.

Because Marlana was sickened by the thought of me using heroin, she wanted nothing to do with meetings, my recovery, or anything that had to do with the process. She thought I was staying clean. So, in order to keep my addiction hidden, I would grab any opportunity I could find to either meet with my dealer or cook some heroin.

When I would attend AA or NA meetings, I would arrange to meet my dealer during the bathroom break. He would come out to the church, or wherever the meeting was, and get together with me in my truck. I'd hand him a wad of cash, he'd hand me a wad of tar, and we would go our separate ways.

How's that for fucked up?

I wasn't listening while I was at the meetings. I was doing a lot of judging at the meetings. It was my Majesty-Baby thing. I kept thinking, *I don't belong here—just look at yourselves. You people are FUCKED UP!*

I wasn't fucked up. I was…complicated.

I mean, Jesus Christ, did any of *them* used to be a rock star?

NO!

Did any of *them* lose a record deal?

Hmmm?

NO!

These people have no idea what I'm coping with! I'm an incredibly talented, dynamic, creative human being. These people are just fuckin' drunks!

A bunch of fucking losers.

That was my attitude. Not exactly an ideal mindset to face the challenge of sober living.

Meanwhile, I was selling CDs out of my car in order to afford dope. But that isn't being a loser. Nope…that's being *special*.

I knew I needed to get sober. But I couldn't bear the thought of sitting through any more of these drab meetings and droning tales of woe spun by people whose lives were far inferior to my own.

If only I had worked as hard to get sober as I worked to score drugs.

I needed a shot of humility. That storage locker key provided the shock. It became the exact moment everything snapped into focus for me. That key represented my rock bottom. Everything I owned had been tossed into a 10x10 space and locked away from the rest of civilization.

I had no career. I had no wife. I had no stuff.

I had nothing. Except my dignity—and I was giving that away, hand over fist.

Cry Help broke through my strange bed fellows of arrogance and self-loathing. They helped me realize that the fear of continuing to live the way I had been living was greater than the fear of the unknown—of doing something different. Of facing my inner demons instead of running away from them.

I'm not going to say it was easy. It wasn't. When I walked out of Cry Help six weeks later, I was a different person than when I had entered. My sobriety was still young and fragile, like a newborn colt rising onto wobbly legs.

But I was ready for the challenge.

* * *

My first stop was straight into a sober living facility. Sometimes called a "halfway house," these facilities dot the Los Angeles landscape. Their intent is to provide a transitional living experience for people coming out of treatment. When you live there, you are required to do chores and keep a steady job. As long as you obey these and other rules, you are welcome to be part of the community. Leaders are on site to provide guidance and support, as well as monitor the residents and enforce the rules.

In all, it was good for me. I shared new sobriety with

everyone from incredibly wealthy and powerful record industry executives, to children of rock stars, to guys who were struggling to pay the rent. It taught me that we all have a different bottom…and that we all hit it.

During the six months I was there, I became more self-aware than ever before. I worked very hard to recognize when I was struggling emotionally. Then I would apply some of the simple techniques I had been taught at Cry Help, in an effort to self-heal.

That's the whole goal of clean living, right? Recognize when you are struggling and then either pluck the strings of your social network or heal yourself from within. Normal people learn this stuff while growing up. I had to walk through fire as an adult before I was able to learn it.

And, urgh…I'll tell you how hard I had to work to remain clean. When I left the sober living facility, I found out that Marlana had already moved in with another guy.

What the actual fuck, right?

Well, not "what the fuck." It was her life. I had to let it go. Frankly, I had made her miserable for years prior to finally getting my act together. She needed to find her own path toward happiness.

Honestly, more power to her.

Not going to lie, it hurt like a motherfucker…but I dealt with the pain. Marlana's entire situation was my creation. This is what I did.

It was *my* fault.

I can't say the thought of heroin never crossed my mind, but I will say that I did not succumb. I worked my program and talked through the experience with my therapist. I had to arrive at a place where I could own my decisions and my past mistakes. I had to stop blaming everyone else and the world around me. I had to stop blaming God or fate or Karma or the universe or whatever else I could point the finger at.

The only person I can control is myself. The only decisions I control are my own. I had to accept my responsibility in the mess that my life had been and for the glory that my life could be.

Dude. Those first couple years were fucking rough, but I got through them. I had to accept that there might come a day where I would want to blow my fucking brains out. But it was not going to be today. I can get through one more day.

One day at a time.

Not just an idiom. It's the way I live my life.

* * *

I read my ass off during those first two years of sobriety. I learned about spirituality and the diseased mind of an addict and any recovery literature I could get my hands on. I also attended meetings; daily at first, sometimes multiple times per day. I eventually tapered down once I had my yearling legs under me.

I was doing better. But I still had a whole lot of walking to do.

CHAPTER 13:
CUBA

I met Fidel Castro.

I bet you want a few more details. I got you.

In 1997, I was sober and working as the production manager at The Key Club in Hollywood. One evening, Peavey sponsored a big event at the club. Their rep, a fellow named Ladd (I can't remember his last name), came in and we introduced ourselves. Little Caesar had been on hiatus for a full five years by this point, but I had to tell the rep about my history with Peavey, including the FQ 120 story.

We had a good laugh. Ladd was cool.

Ladd told me that President Clinton was planning to open up relations with Cuba. Bill Clinton's administration was planning two events to punctuate the new US/Cuba relationship. First, they were going to send the Baltimore Orioles down to play the Cuban National baseball team. Then, they'd have a huge music festival.

The wanted to send Bonnie Raitt, Meshell Ndegeocello, Montell Jordan, Mick Fleetwood, Gladys Knight, and Lisa Loeb, among others. Further, they had arranged for the sound guy from The Rolling Stones to show up and work front of house (FOH) to mix the event.

Apparently, I made quite the impression on Ladd that night. He asked if I would accompany the envoy and mix the monitors at recording sessions leading up to the event.

The plan was to send me down to Havana, where I would stay at the Hotel Nacional. Then, I was to build six small recording studios, where our artists would write songs with Cuban artists, culminating in the big music festival at the Karl Marx Theater.

Oh—Fidel Castro would be there, as well.

I agreed on the spot. We had to begin quickly because, for the first time since 1959, the US was about to issue travel Visas to Cuba. The process would push through some red tape.

I had to pass a security check, which led to another discussion with a US government official about my involvement with the Hells Angels.

It was exhausting.

I guess I passed muster because, before I knew it, I was flying to Miami so I could catch a plane to fucking Havana. We were briefed by two US government officials regarding protocol. Both looked like Hunter S. Thompson, right down to their cheese-ball Hawaiian shirts and bad hair.

The plane we took out of Miami was a huge jumbo jet; yet, the only passengers on the entire thing were me, three crew guys, and the two government agents. Later, I learned they were from the CIA.

I'm sure I got another file opened on me that day.

One of them handed me a business card. It claimed his name was John Smith and that he was an aluminum siding salesman. On the bottom was a phone number.

I am NOT kidding about this.

John Smith told us to behave while we were down there, and not to fuck anything up for the United States. You know, the usual blah, blah, blah.

He also mentioned that we should stay away from Cuban prostitutes. With a lecherous glint in his eye, he talked about how stunningly beautiful they are. Then he got serious, warning us of the mandatory four-year prison sentence if we got busted visiting one. John Smith got even more serious when he brought up the US Intersection.

The US Intersection is a group of highly trained Green Berets. If we got in trouble—which is effortless for me—we call the number on the card. One of the Green Berets would show up and get us out of it and clean up our mess.

I'm not kidding about this, either.

John Smith also made damn sure we understood that the Cuban government watched everything we did. We'd be followed by the Cuban secret police 24/7, so we shouldn't freak out when we see them lurking around. Again, the CIA guys emphasized that we shouldn't do anything to embarrass the United States.

Yeah, we got it: we're going into the only Communist country in North America. But it was still surreal, man.

I got to Cuba and hauled my luggage to the hotel. I was told ahead of time to bring as many batteries, flashlights, and rolls of toilet paper I could cram into my suitcase. Cuba is notably lacking in these products, so I should make sure to have my own supply.

This advice came in handy. Not only for my own personal use, but I also handed them out as gifts to locals, who gushed with appreciation.

The Cubans are such an amazing group of people, man. I hate that their country is in such financial disarray. Communism as a concept is fucking beautiful, with the idea that everyone shares everything they do or make without money, poverty, or a greedy government. Unfortunately, it only works on paper, not in practice. Look at history. Straight-up Communism never works; it quickly corrupts leaders, no matter how good their intentions may be.

We settled in and got to work. My job was to set up equipment in the recording rooms and in the Karl Marx Theater. I got the recording studios up and running first. The American artists began their writing/recording sessions with the Cuban artists. Next, I set up and tested the equipment in the theater.

That damn building hadn't been touched since 1959. Old speakers hung from the ceiling. Only twenty percent of them worked. Copper wire connected everything, and some of it looked hand-wound. Only one monitor was functional. The mixing console only had three working channels on it. It was a mess; no way it could support the show we planned. At one point in our show, twenty people would be on stage—each needing a microphone.

I returned to the hotel and called Ladd. I didn't know what could be done but I was intent on solving this problem before show time. Frankly, if I didn't solve the problem, there would be no show time.

Ladd called Hartley Peavey and explained the situation. Hartley was a man of action.

When Ladd called me back, he told me to show up at the Hemingway Marina in a few days. Hartley was going to sail his 50-foot yacht into the marina, and the yacht would be stacked with Peavey cabinets, mixers, cables, microphones, and everything else we would need. Hartley wanted to donate all of it; he thought it would look good for his company and a be nice diplomatic move for the United States.

Ladd let us know that when the boat arrived, the Cuban Customs officials would all "go to lunch." We would then unload the gear into trucks (without any hassle) and drive it to the theater.

I'll be damned! That's exactly what happened. Hartley pulled all the furniture out of his yacht, then filled the boat from stem to stern with as much equipment as he could jam in without sinking the entire vessel.

We got to work building out the theater. It was an exercise in creativity. We duct-taped the cables and cords to the floor, the walls, and anything else that wouldn't move.

As we worked, something interesting caught my eye. The production staff working with me was all Cuban. And when we pulled up a piece of equipment or had it moved, the Cubans carefully took up the duct tape and folded it neatly. They saved all that shit, because they didn't have duct tape in Cuba. Okay, they probably had some duct tape—but it was either rare or expensive. They grew accustomed to using and re-using stuff until it couldn't be used anymore.

It was a noble undertaking to figure out how to re-use duct tape. It was also an incredibly sad commentary on how awful the poverty is in Cuba.

Example number two:

At my beautifully amazing hotel, I received a little note from my maid. She wrote,

Sir, I see you have all these batteries and flashlights. I have not had power in my house for the last three weeks. My kids cannot do their schoolwork. In lieu of a tip, could you please leave some batteries and a flashlight?

She wasn't trying to shake me down or panhandle. She sincerely needed these items. I left her a few flashlights and some batteries. The following day, she found me, hugged me, and sobbed into my shoulder.

She didn't have power and couldn't get a flashlight.

Fuck.

We got the theater up and running and all was good. At one point during the process, a Cuban production guy looked at me like he had a glimmer of recognition. He asked for my name, and I told him, "I'm Ron."

He persisted, "Young?"

"Yeah."

"Of Little Caesar?"

"Yeah."

He leapt to his feet in excitement. Apparently, our band was very popular in Cuba.

Who knew?

The next day, he showed up with a bunch of kids who wanted my autograph. From that day forward, more and more people showed up to get autographs. It got to the point that I had to put some of them off until the next day because I had to get to work.

As popular as I was with the locals, the celebrities didn't know me at all.

For example, I spent an entire day running around Havana with Lisa Loeb. Lisa, despite being a big name in the late 1990s, was totally a sweetheart. Her musical persona is every bit the person she is in real life. Soft spoken and shy, she came across to fans the only way she knew how.

She was apprehensive about wandering the streets of a strange country alone, so she grabbed the scariest looking guy on the production crew to accompany her. I guess she figured nobody would mess with her if she brought a goon. And I was her huckleberry.

It was a good day. We even ate in someone's private home. Not kidding! Cubans have a wonderful tradition. Some residents open their home in the evening to allow other folks to eat in their kitchen, as if it was a quaint restaurant. This is called a paladar, which translates to a small, family-run Latin restaurant. It comes from the Spanish word "palate", which (brace yourself), means "palate," or the roof of the mouth, in English. This practice tends to rotate among families in any given neighborhood.

I don't think Lisa knew who I was. Nor did anyone else, until right up to the night before the show.

On that night, I came into the hotel around two a.m. It had been a long day, but on my way to the room, I came upon Bonnie Raitt and Gladys Knight sitting in the hallway, singing.

It was a holy shit moment, for sure.

I asked if I could sit down and listen, and they kindly invited me to do so. A few songs in, I started singing along. Three or four songs later, they noticed I was pretty good, and asked if I had ever done this professionally.

I departed from the truth a little and said no. I was still masquerading in my non-superhero alter ego. I was "Ron, the production guy."

I even mentioned to Gladys Knight that, as a kid, I wanted to be a Pip. She was confused; a grimy, tatted-up, white guy wishing to be a regal Black guy in a shiny suit. After awhile, she understood my wish. Singing and chatting with those women was a dream come true for me.

But I had a show to do.

* * *

Because Peavey ran out of big mixers, I had to cobble together four smaller ones into a mega-mixer. Hartley brought smaller units for the recording studios but did not have a big one on hand to run the show in the Karl Marx Theater. I almost duct-taped my way to solving the final problem of our antiquated theater.

BRIDGE TO HAVANA

GLADYS KNIGHT EDESIO ALEJANDRO BONNIE RAITT PABLO MENENDEZ PETER FRAMPTON ALBERTO TOSCA MICK FLEETWOOD CARLOS VARELA JOAN OSBORNE MANOLITO SIMONET MONTELL JORDAN CARLOS ALFONSO BETH NIELSEN CHAPMAN AUGUSTO ENRIQUEZ N'DEA DAVENPORT RENE BANOS DAVE KOZ REY GUERRA PADDY MOLONEY

Except it wasn't the final problem. When we fired up the Frankenstein mixing board, the place went dark. There wasn't enough power in the entire building to run the mixer I had created. So, I did what anyone would do. I ran an extension cord and "borrowed" electricity from the neighbor.

Again, not kidding. At all. We ran a thick cable across the road and draped a few pieces of carpet over it. I am heart-attack serious when I say this. On our end, we hardwired the cable directly into the electric panel. I had no idea if it was going to work. I had a Moment of Truth when we flipped the switch. We had our fingers crossed, hoping the thing wouldn't blow up.

In the end, Cuban ingenuity was victorious. Their workers had a lot of experience dealing with situations where "shit didn't work and there wasn't any new shit to be found."

The show went well, despite a few technical hiccups along the way. Some artists understood and reacted with empathy and grace. Others were frustrated and angry. A group of artists is like any other group of people. Different personalities have a very diverse range of attitudes.

One of the coolest was Bonnie Raitt. When Bonnie was performing, her mic kept sagging on the mic stand. After a few rounds of her bowing her head and adjusting, bowing her head and adjusting some more, I grabbed a screwdriver and dragged my sorry ass onto the stage. In the background, I could hear the fans start to chant, "Ron Young! Ron Young! Ron Young!"

My ass puckered a little. I didn't want to upstage Bonnie Raitt. She didn't seem offended, but she did shoot me a quizzical glance.

"How do they know your name?"

I fiddled with the mic, "Umm, this is a Communist country and I'm a worker. They love the workers."

"That's bullshit!" She pointed at me. "You and I! We're going to talk when this thing is over."

She finished her set and we got together backstage.

"Okay, so tell me. What's your story?"

I gave her a little background. I told her about Little Caesar and our meteoric rise to mediocrity. She smiled and nodded through the whole thing.

"I knew it! I knew you had to be a pro. When you were singing with Gladys and me in the hallway, you didn't sound like a guy who's worn a tool belt his whole adult life."

She was now the Mary Jane to my Spiderman.

, *

On the night of the event at the Karl Marx Theater, the production crew was buzzing around, putting the finishing touches on everything we could think of. We noticed an uptick in the number of Cuban Secret Police that were entering the building, some with bomb-sniffing dogs.

Fidel Castro was on his way.

I don't remember who came and got me, but I was told the meet-and-greet was for artists only. However, it seemed that I was invited if I wanted to attend. You bet your sweet petunias I wanted to attend.

Inside his private box, there was an informal reception line. He and I chatted for a couple minutes; nothing too personal or memorable. Idle chit-chat from a couple guys who didn't know each other. He thanked me for building out the equipment and commented on how I made great use of their theater, which added to the cultural fabric of their country.

Not that I wasn't impressed. I kept thinking, *Holy shit...this is Fidel Castro!*

I don't think he was equally impressed to meet Ron Young, but I don't know. He was very charming and appreciative.

I shook his hand and moved on down the line. It was a surreal moment to punctuate a bizarre cultural experience.

To me, because I'm both decadent and truly fortunate to be born in American, I was amazed. The few minutes in El Presidente's private box put it all in stark contrast.

But that is how I met Fidel Castro.

* * *

The show was over, and we were in a celebratory mood. The crew got stir crazy, since they worked their asses off for several days. We were in Cuba, the land of incredible cigars, plentiful rum, and (oh, shit) beautiful women.

Remember my aluminum siding salesman, John Smith, and his lecture on Cuban prostitutes? That.

The entire crew went out to a discotheque. Of course, I was approached by the most jaw-droppingly beautiful woman I had ever seen. No joke; she was a cross between Selma Hayek and Maria Conchita Alonso in the prime of their careers.

She sat next to me at the bar and struck up a conversation.

I knew immediately that I still had game, man! Why else would she be here? My inner strength and outer beauty were undeniable beacons, drawing beautiful women like a tractor beam.

Either that, or she was a prostitute.

It was a coin toss, as far as I was concerned.

As the conversation wore on, she grew more flirty and more touchy-feely. She also spoke surprisingly good English. I thought nothing of it. My animal magnetism transcended such silly notions as ethnicity or language.

Either that, or she was a prostitute.

Again, a coin toss.

I learned that she was a doctor of botany. Like, she had earned a PhD in Botany. What are the odds of that!? I attracted a highly educated woman. She must have seen the intelligence in my eyes when she decided to approach me from across the room. She could sense my contemplative depths and the degree to which I could reduce all behavior down to its essential quantum equations, thus acquiring a true sentience when it came to understanding the world around me.

Either that, or she was a prostitute.

Not likely. But whatever.

At some point during this exchange of discourse regarding how the unseen world of microbiology affects the life of cruciferous trees, she leaned in and said, "Look, do you want to go back to my flat and have sex?"

Pfft. That sealed it for me. I was fucking irresistible.

She continued, "It'll only cost you a hundred and fifty dollars."

DAMNIT!

Turns out, she *was* a prostitute! I would have never guessed.

I was incredulous. "You've gotta be fucking kidding me. You're a prostitute?"

Before you judge, bear in mind that I know a lot about science. The conversation we had just left off was quite detailed. There was no way she could have held up her end without being highly educated in botany. Just like she said.

It was seriously confusing for me. She cleared it up.

"I'm not a full-time prostitute, but here's the deal. The Cuban economy is so bad that my job as a botanist pays the equivalent of about seven dollars per month. Don't get me wrong—many good things are provided for me by the government. My rent is free, as is most everything else when it comes to the basics of living."

She took a sip of her drink. Her was face was magic; formed from mahogany-colored cream.

"So, every couple of months, I supplement my income by coming to a place like this. I find a guy I think is attractive, and I approach him with an offer. Everyone wins!"

At this point, my fucking brain was exploding. This is a bona fide test from God. I was single and free to do whatever the hell I wanted to do—and this kind of opportunity NEVER HAPPENS TO ME. No strings, no mismatched expectations, no regrets.

But then there was John Smith. John. Fucking. Smith.

I echoed his words. She allayed my fears.

"Oh, no, no, no! I don't get involved enough for them to think I'm a prostitute. Believe me, they've been watching us this whole time. They've been watching you. If I only do this occasionally, they think we met and decided to spend the night together."

I looked around. She was right. I had been followed the entire time I was on the island. I would notice that whenever kids would run up to me for an autograph, those same kids would get pulled into a van and taken away afterwards. One morning at breakfast, our Cuban workers were sharing stories about how if anyone approached any of them and had a conversation, a van would take the civilian away.

The locals explained that the secret police would grab civilians so they could debrief them. They'd remind the civilian that they were not to speak to Americans. However, now that they *had* talked to the Americans, what did you people talk about? It was essentially reconnaissance for the Cuban government.

None of that mattered. I had Miss Universe sitting within arm's reach, making me an offer I could not refuse. I seriously considered pulling the trigger and taking this secret to my grave.

She sensed my hesitation, and then laid it out in more

pragmatic terms. After all, she was a doctor.

"Think about it," she began. "If we were back in the United States, we might have a mutual attraction, then date. We would go out a few times. You would take me for a few dinners and a few nights on the town before you would ever get my clothes off. It would cost way more than one hundred and fifty dollars."

I couldn't do it. Something inside of me said it wasn't right. Maybe it was the fear of a prison sentence. Maybe it was a moral thing. Maybe it was the notion of paying for sex.

Or maybe I chickened out.

I said no. She thanked me and walked away.

Fuckfuckfuckfuckfuckfuck!

I returned to the comfort of my half-empty virgin mojito. Some of the best limeade I've ever had in my life. And probably the only virgin in the room.

* * *

Coming home, most of the guys wanted to bring back some cigars. The problem was that nobody could give us a straight answer on how many we were allowed to take back through customs. This was almost unprecedented. No Americans had been allowed into Cuba since 1959, much less allowed to legally declare Cuban cigars.

As for me, I decided I wasn't taking any chances. Not that I wasn't going to bring back cigars. I think you know me better than that by now. Rather, I wasn't going to get *caught* bringing back cigars.

Montel Jordan, God love him, tried to cart a veritable mountain of cigars and rum through customs. He got stopped and almost all of his pirate's booty got confiscated. I think he walked away with one box of cigars and one bottle of rum.

I lined the big cable boxes with boxes of top-shelf Cuban cigars. Not the cheap knock-off, counterfeit cigars they sell to tourists; the ones with "real" bands around them.

**Yes, cigar workers steal the bands so they can peddle

cheap cigars as the real thing.

Anyway, on top of the cigar boxes, I coiled hundreds of pounds of cables. I knew the Customs Agents did a thorough job, but I also knew that nobody would want to lift those sons of bitches out of the boxes to inspect underneath.

Frankly, it all felt fair to me. We were leaving behind tens of thousands of dollars' worth of electronic gear and equipment. Included with that were batteries, flashlights, and toilet paper.

Nothing in Cuba had been given a fresh coat of paint since 1959. The citizens drove beautiful vintage cars, but they had no access to car parts to fix those beautiful cars because of the embargos placed upon their country.

The Cuban people are wonderfully resourceful. They were open and friendly to us, and I didn't detect even a hint of racism anywhere. It was a shame to see how the infrastructure had become so run down since 1959.

Man, it hurt like hell to see these good people struggle with poverty. Yet, it was inspiring to see how average people were able to keep their heads above water and remain optimistic about their future.

It helped me to understand the humility and the optimism I needed to heal. Thank you, Cuba!

CHAPTER 14:
BECOMING AN ADULT

Fred Saunders was an old friend of mine. He held a black belt in one of the martial arts (I can't remember which one), and was an absolute giant of a guy. Fred was about 6'5" and built like a brick shithouse. Plus, he was a big-time motorcycle enthusiast.

You don't fuck with Fred. Exactly my kind of dude.

Fred put his "no-fucks-given" attitude to work as the tour manager of Mötley Crüe throughout the 1980s. The Crüe's manager, Doc McGhee, warned Fred of the band's wild antics. He needed a security guy that would do whatever it took to keep the band members in line. Fred did exactly that. As a result, earned a lot of respect in the rock industry.

In 1992, Fred was in a horrific motorcycle accident. If memory serves, his spine dislocated from his pelvis, and he died a few times en route to the hospital. Fortunately, Fred is a fucking Viking; he pulled through. But he was exquisitely messed up, spending the next six months bedbound in a hospital.

A bunch of Fred's friends got together and held a benefit concert to help raise funds for his continuing treatment and physical therapy. Big names attended the benefit; it was an impressive list of rock and roll royalty. Motorhead was at the show, as was Guns 'n Roses and Mötley Crüe, among others.

Following the nice financial and spiritual boost provided by the benefit, Fred recovered. Being bedbound for six months was agonizing for a go-getter like him, so he made a career pivot. He decided to use of his impressive list of connections in the industry to start a production company, called Fred Saunders Production Services. The company basically provided all the scaffolding, lighting, staging, and video monitors for major concert tours. The company grew into a massive entity, employing up to 200 workers and putting on shows at enormous venues like Dodger Stadium and The Rose Bowl.

I worked for Fred off and on for many years. He put me to work whenever I needed some extra money. Early on, I used the money for dope, of course. But it was good work. He had me lay plywood or build scaffolding; blue collar work that put my hands to good use.

It started out as a tough pill for me to swallow. I wasn't a blue-collar worker. I was a singer, man. I was an ar-teest! I should have been singing on this stage, not bolting it together.

Don't these people know who I think I used to be?

But I'd do it. Like every other station I've passed through in life, I did what I had to do to survive. If nothing else, I was definitely good at that.

The last piece of my recovery journey was to find a real job. I needed to get back in the game and work out some sort of career-type job, rather than a "just getting by" type of job.

Naturally, I called Fred Saunders. In 1997, he was still the tour security manager for Mötley Crüe. And because he was still connected in the music industry, he was a great guy to know when it came to finding work. If I had to hang lighting rigs for a living, then so be it.

Fred took my call, and it changed my life.

Fred was the master of tough love, too. He laid it out for me. "Listen, dude. I don't need no dope-fiend bullshit. I don't need no rock star bullshit. I need motherfuckers that will work."

I was nothing if not that.

"If you're willing to show up, I'll give you work every fucking day. You gotta be on time and you gotta do the work."

"Dude, I'll do whatever it takes."

And I did.

I went to work for Fred, five or six days a week. Sometimes, I would sweep the stages on which I used to perform. It was humbling; exactly what my inflated ego needed.

My work became my life. I would put my nose to the grindstone by day, and then attend my meetings by night. It wasn't the glamorous lifestyle I had envisioned a decade earlier. Instead, it was way better. It was stripped down to the bare essentials.

In the immortal words of Janis Joplin, "Freedom's just another word for nothing left to lose."

I felt satisfaction with the work I did. I came to love my life and my sobriety.

I began to love myself…but not in my previously self-absorbed, selfish way. There is a huge difference.

That may sound cheesy, but I cannot stress enough how important that concept is for everyone. Love who you are; love who you have been and who you intend to be. Without that critical component in your psyche, you will never succeed in finding satisfaction with life.

Sometimes bad things happen to good people. The question becomes: What are you going to do about it? Stop blaming others. Become a good person, and that is good enough for now.

That was my life, man. And life was good.

Somewhere along the way, I became an adult. I took responsibility for my existence and the decisions I made. I took care of the people around me.

I was focused on my career and on building a good life for myself. Music was completely on hold during this time. Sure, I worked in the industry—but never told anyone who I used to be, or that I was on MTV. I was a production manager and didn't want to steal from my credibility in that arena.

Honestly, I missed singing. But I no longer possessed the burning desire to be on the stage as a "performer." The creativity required to do my production work kept my mind busy and made me feel a sense of satisfaction. I certainly didn't miss all the bullshit.

My life was simple. And I was happy.

I worked for a while and saved up some cash, which helped rescue my credit rating from the fiery pits of damnation it had previously been. Marlana and I had been quite a ways into arrears with the IRS, and I had finally cleaned up that tax burden.

The next step in my roadmap to adulthood was to purchase a home. I figured I would invest in some property. You know, like normal adults do.

I put together a down payment and bought a small house. I got lucky; this was right before the real estate market crashed from banks handing out super-risky mortgages to all the wrong people. My credit score improved, but it was nowhere near stellar. I squeaked in at exactly the right time.

I will add that I did not lose the house in the aftermath of the crash. I was lucky enough to pay every mortgage payment on time. When I sold the house, it was at a substantial profit.

God loves idiots, apparently.

I did do my homework before signing on the dotted line. No more recklessly impulsive decisions for this feral cat. I surrounded myself with level-headed, healthy people back then. I had some good guardrails around me when I needed to bounce ideas off friends.

Life became even better.

* * *

Yet another good thing happened. Fred called me with a new offer.

I don't remember what day of the week it was exactly, but I do remember it was raining—a curious oddity in Southern California. When the phone rang, I answered.

"Hello?"

"Hey man," it was Fred, "Do you know The Key Club? It used to be Gazzarri's?"

"Yeah, up on the Sunset Strip."

"Yeah, yeah. They're looking for a monitor engineer for the night. Can you mix?"

I enthusiastically blurted out, "Hell yeah! I went to production school. I know how to run a board."

That was a lie. Sort of. I definitely didn't have the savvy of full-time monitor guys, but I knew enough that I could fake it.

I went to the venue and did the show. Apparently, I was plenty good enough. The manager approached me and asked if I could work the next five nights. His regular monitor guy had quit or got fired or some such shit. I didn't care—I was happy to take over the job.

I called Fred, had him take me off the call sheet, and went to work mixing for The Key Club. At one point, the production manager, Jim O'Brien, came to me and said he was quitting in order to go on the road. Furthermore, he was recommending me as the guy to take his place. I would then be over the entire production staff, not just the monitors.

I said yes, and it was made official. I had a real, full-time job. I wasn't just a day laborer; I wasn't just a 1099 contract employee who showed up whenever they needed me. I was the production manager for The Key Club.

I supervised a staff of six, took care of the equipment, ran all the shows, provided equipment when a band asked for it, blah, blah, blah. It was a nice club with nice gear. I took to the job like a duck to water.

Because of my background, I knew what the artists wanted. My superpower became the ability to make the artists comfortable. When anyone played The Key Club, Ron took care of them. This led to rave reviews from tour managers and musicians alike.

* * *

During this era, I began to dabble with dating. It was fun, but crazy. I worked in a nightclub, which is the most polluted pond to fish in. Between female alcoholics and professional clubbers, I made a modest splash in the world of women. It was a start.

I was stepping into a new life. I knew I wasn't ready for anything long-term. It was time to explore the world with a healthier mindset. I was not about to make the same mistakes I made in my marriage.

My sobriety afforded me an opportunity to look back with eyes wide open. I began to fully understand the unhealthy dynamics between Marlana and me.

As I matured, our relationship did not. It was stuck in a surface-level trajectory that formed when we first got together at Stony Brook. We never had arguments, and this was not a good thing. We never could argue about anything because we never talked about anything deep, heavy, or meaningful. In 20 years, we never had one screaming match.

We just kind of…coexisted.

That's the downside of both partners being avoidant, nonconfrontational people. When things are going well, they cruise along, skimming the surface like a speedboat. When things grow troubling, they choose to go "radio silent" rather than strengthen their relationship through the richness of understanding and emotional intimacy. It's all very nice on the surface, but ultimately, it's not good. At all.

I had only recently begun to understand the value of confrontation. Each partner has to have a space within which to express themself, both positive and negative. Reinforce the traits you love in your partner. Ask for what you need if they have traits that leave you feeling unfulfilled. If they hurt your feelings, talk about it. Intimacy grows through risk; take the risk and express the things that make you feel insecure.

Screaming matches are not necessary; mature, healthy adults do not fight in a toxic manner. But intimate conversation is necessary.

In time, I got past the hurt and pain from the way Marlana and I broke up. I felt a tremendous amount of guilt, as well as some anger over how quickly she moved on. But I settled that part of my mind. Deep down, I finally got to where I could honestly be happy for her and wish her the best.

We have since rekindled and maintain a distant friendship. We are in touch occasionally on social media. She is a good person and I truly hope she lives her best life.

Those are my Dr. Phil two cents.

I soared through five or six years of dating and playing the field. I was able to have special friends and have some adult fun without the fear of too much emotional entanglement. That tendency was occasionally problematic. I would meet a woman, we would go out on a few dates, and then she would want to get serious. I wouldn't follow suit.

Truthfully, I *couldn't* follow suit. I knew I had to remain distant during this phase of my recovery. I wasn't spiritually capable for this type of relationship. We would break up and I would move on.

I wasn't ready for a romantic commitment.

Once I hit a level of equilibrium, I knew I was emotionally capable of entering a more committed relationship.

* * *

Because the universe tends to place opportunity in our path, it was not long after that realization that my phone rang.

It was a blast form the past: Little Caesar's former publicist, Renee.

Although I didn't know it at the time, she would eventually become my wife. And to our credit, she is still my wife…right up to this very moment.

It was so good to hear Renee's voice. While she was no longer affiliated with Little Caesar (we weren't even officially a band during that phone call in 2001), she and I had remained friends over the years. Renee would call me most every year on my birthday, just to say hi and catch up. It was all relatively innocent.

I wrote the word "relatively" because the end result was that we ended up marrying each other. To the outside observer, our continued friendship may seem a little specious, particularly in light of the fact that we were both married to other people at the time.

Anyway, she called, and we caught up over lunch. She mentioned that she had gotten out of the publicity game and started an ad agency. She felt her strong suit was best applied to marketing, so she took the plunge and opened her own shop.

Excellent for her.

The lunch hour flew by. We agreed to get together for a second lunch the following week. That was the big one.

"Listen, Ron, I have always been in love with you. I'm in a shitty marriage and I think it's time to get out of it."

That came as a shock to me. I had always found Renee to be extremely beautiful, both inside and out, as well as extremely intelligent. Like me, she was also a little nutty. We were two peas in a pod, as Forrest Gump would say.

Renee had been married twice, each time to a rather high-profile and powerful man in the music industry. I won't name either of them out of respect. I feel no sense of hubris knowing that I ended up with Renee and they didn't. From what I understand, neither relationship was a good match. They were both smart to end it. It all worked out the way it was supposed to.

From my perspective, an affair was out of the question at this point in my recovery. It was way outside of my moral compass and was told by my elder compatriots in Sobriety that such activities would probably lead me to getting loaded again.

That judgement call let me know that I had grown to be much

healthier than I had ever been before. I wasn't about to screw around with another man's wife. Even in love and war, it was neither fair nor right.

We waited. I was single and completely unattached, so I had no problem hovering in a fixed holding pattern while she went through the process of a divorce. I had recently decided that a long-term relationship was what I wanted again—and lo and behold, there it was.

A short time later, Renee called again.

"It's over. I told him I wanted a divorce, and we are officially separated."

And that was that. We started working on a relationship of our own. For the sake of complete transparency, her marriage at this point was "over enough" for me. The official court documents had not yet been signed, but both she and her soon-to-be ex-husband knew it was over. All that remained was the judge's ruling. No secrecy, no sneaking around. It was all above board.

We lived together from that moment forward. Not in a literal "we share an address" sense, but in the "you have space in my closet" sort of way.

I wasn't a kid anymore. I was north of 40 years old and felt no need to date forever and ever. We each knew who we were and what we wanted. And apparently, we knew a thing or two about ourselves. We have been together ever since.

A few years after her divorce finalized, we made plans to purchase a house together. I sold my house, she sold her house, and we used the proceeds to purchase one as a couple.

* * *

For the next five years, I lived the most pedestrian, mundane life of any human being on the planet. It was gloriously boring. I was with a woman with whom I felt a deep connection, I worked a job that gave me validation and personal satisfaction, and I was living my best life as a real functioning adult. No huge meteor strikes and no clashing with irreverent industry narcissists. Just me, her, and our pets…many, MANY pets.

We bought our place together in 2006. Situated in Calabasas, CA, we got a nice place on 1.5 acres. We lived near the coast because we loved the area, and because Renee was really into horses. She wanted to purchase a place that we could develop into a mini farm. That sounded okay to me. I had never dreamt of living in as nice of a place as we ended up buying, so I set out to make it as good as I could for the both of us.

The property we bought had been previously owned and developed by Bill Payne, the keyboardist and one of the founding members of the band Little Feat. Definitely a cool band with a cool vibe back in the 1970s. But the house didn't stand up to the test of time as well as Little Feat's music had. I gutted it to the studs and rebuilt the entire house from the ground up.

I also turned an already-existing pool house into a guest house and threw up a pole barn. I then created a space for the horses to roam. We are animal lovers at heart, which was a disadvantage for us. We began to accumulate more and more "pets" until our property looked like ten pounds of shit in a five-pound bag. We were bursting at the seams. It became clear that we were going to need more space.

In 2014, we looked around until we found the place where we currently live. It was a tidy tract of open land; unused, wild, and ready to get built into whatever animal paradise we wanted. Compared to Calabasas, the land was vast. Compared to proper farms, it was modest. It had 1200 Avocado trees and a small house we could live in—while I developed the property to her desires, and build a "dream home" from the ground up.

No matter how you sliced it, our new "little place" was not so damn little. I am a builder at heart, and Renee is a dreamer. Together, we are *dangerous*. Renee points to where she wants me to build something or add something on, and I dutifully grab my tools and get to work. A little hemming and hawing is involved, but that's what I do. I'm a curmudgeon in a hard hat.

The property has a small guest house where we lived while I oversaw construction of the bigger, main house. I reshaped the earth with heavy equipment, making it suitable for our mini-farm.

Over the next several years we acquired more horses, a miniature horse, and barn cats—all in addition to our previous menagerie. We recently added 5 mini-cows. Cutest damn things. We call the property The Rockin' R's Ranch. It takes up almost all of my time and energy to maintain, but I feel deeply at home here.

It must be because of all the blood, sweat and tears that goes into building a house from the ground up.

Our home is beautiful, but I have put over fifteen years of nonstop sweat equity into making this and the Calabasas property into our dream properties. It's been a slooooow go, as I've diligently added piece by frustratingly slow piece.

As a quick (and sad) follow up to our sweet Calabasas property, the entire parcel was purchased by a famous skateboard artist. I won't name him or her because of a dumbass move they made.

That buyer decided that fire insurance was too expensive.

Did you catch that? FIRE INSURANCE was too expensive. I *would* disclose what that person paid us for the property, but it would only serve to piss off both of us. Calabasas is an off shoot of Malibu. So that person must have literally thought, "A million for a house is fine, but a few thousand for insurance is a bridge too far."

Dumbass.

The person wrapped their Christmas tree in several strings of cheap fucking lights that year, which short-circuited and burned the entire house (and adjacent buildings) to the ground. If you drive past our old place today, you'll just see nothing but the concrete slab sitting there, bald-faced and depressed. Our former neighbor sent a cell-phone video of flames devouring the house.

After all the love I gave to that place, it's a real shame. It does serve as a stark reminder that there is no bottom when it comes to how stupid people can be. Net worth be damned; the face of "Stupid" covers all socioeconomic strata.

Speaking of stupid…

To build our current place, I had to fight with the morons who run the Ventura County department of Building and Safety. I was at least prepped for the battle because of all the years I fought the morons who run record labels. Same song, different verse.

I take back all my statements of no clashes and no meteor strikes. Fuck the assholes at the County level who are hell-bent on making it impossible for a normal person to build shit on *their own property*. It makes my blood pressure redline.

* * *

In 2006, before we purchased our first home together in Calabasas, Renee and I had a conversation over dinner. I was still working at the Key Club, allegedly happy as a clam. But she broached a topic that had been on her mind.

"Hey, have you thought about doing music again?"

I thought about it for a minute and then shook my head. I didn't think of myself in that way anymore. Another dive into music hadn't crossed my mind.

She continued, "The Key Club is nice, but it's a long drive and not a very functional place to work for a married man."

I nodded.

"Let's do this," she put down her fork, "Let's buy a property and develop it into a horse farm. You can work on that full time and get back to doing music part time. Would that be something you'd like?"

I almost gave Renee whiplash with how fast I said yes. I love to design and build stuff, but I was starting to feel the itch to get back to singing. Making another balls-out, full-time run at a career in music was not appealing to me on any level. But getting back on stage once in awhile, and feeling the rush of entertaining a fun crowd, was definitely something I could get behind.

I got back into music. I called everyone from Little Caesar and asked if they might want to start making music again. They all said yes.

We didn't have any real plans or goals at first. We were just a bunch of middle-aged dudes who sucked in their stomachs and jammed a few times. It was a shitload of fun; we still had the magic. Music was something we had been missing in our lives.

The old songs came back to us immediately, as did a desire to write some fresh new songs. I called a band meeting before we got started.

"Listen, whatever we end up doing, this is *not* going to be a business venture. This will be a journey of the spirit, not of the wallet."

Everybody was down for that. We approached it like we always had and hammered out some amazing tunes. The album is called *Redemption*, and the title could not have been more fitting.

For me, this marked the full circle of adulthood. I had overcome my disgust and rage against the music industry. I had made my peace with my life, and returned to my first love in a pure, unadulterated way. I could have a healthy relationship with music.

I loved it…and it could love me back.

The internet was going full force by then, which helped us promote and sell our music without the need for a label behind the album. We weren't going to get rich or famous, but those weren't the goals anymore. We had to self-fund the album, but we got to keep all the money from sales.

I fronted the money for the band. I committed $10,000 to restart Little Caesar. That money was to fund our production, our records, our travel, our bookings, and our merch. It would be replenished along the way by ticket sales, merch splits, record sales, and eventually royalties from downloads and streaming. Profits would be divided equally among the band members. Everyone has an even, 20% stake in our product.

We never got rich. But I can honestly say I have been playing off that original ten grand since day one. Little Caesar has been marginally profitable, and we have always managed to cover our costs.

Here's how old I am: *Redemption* came out when MySpace was still relevant. Social media was also its earliest stages in 2009. Don't laugh—that site allowed us to interact with fans, and it was fucking fantastic.

We received messages on our MySpace page from fans all over the world. They were so gracious, letting us know how much they loved our music and how delighted they were with our return.

Many of the people connecting with us were over in Europe. We hatched the idea to book an actual tour. We figured that we could go to Europe and recoup our expenses with no trouble at all. We were correct.

We played for the love the music, the love of the fans, and the love of each other. No pressure to perform like trained monkeys for a soulless record label. It was exactly what we needed.

Unfortunately, trying to make music late in adulthood creates an entirely different set of problems for musicians. As you can probably see from our Wikipedia page, there have been a number of personnel changes over the years. Apache first left the band after our debut album in 1991, and it didn't take long to lose him again in 2009.

CHAPTER 15:
WE, THE PEOPLE

Three of the original five members of Little Caesar are still together, 35 years after we first formed in Los Angeles. Managing the stresses and strains of running the band has been trying for me, but it has not driven me into the addictive cycle like it did back in 1992. Sometimes being an adult means you have to make hard decisions.

Here are the guys who played smaller, albeit important, roles in our band:

Marc Danzeisen played drums with us for a minute in 1992. He had previously played in River Dogs (with Vivian Campbell) and with Chris Latham (aka Beasto Blanco).

On lead guitar, we've had Joey Brasler, who had played with Cherie Currie and Bob Welch; Cary Baere, who played with Deanna Carter; Alex Kane, of Life Sex & Death and Anti Product; and Joey Malone, who has toured with Adam Ant. They all played with us for a brief stretch in the 2010s. I am forever grateful to them for filling in when we needed them.

It's been a challenge to field a consistent lead guitar player. Thank goodness we stumbled upon Mark Tremalgia. He has been perfect. He's a really great hang, a talented musician, and completely on board with the program.

When I use the phrase, "on board with the program," I'm referring to musicians who do not have the desire to earn a living with their craft. Since we reformed in the early 2000s, Little Caesar doesn't earn a living. Therefore, we need guys who lead a double life. Like the superheroes we are (HA!), we need players who maintain a day job in order to keep them afloat financially while we embark upon our side hustle.

At some point, most of our fill-in players had to grab a

different gig that paid better. I totally understood. There was never any bad blood. They simply had to make a move that allowed them to better take care of their families. The way Little Caesar operates financially played a key role in the way things went, with regard to personnel following our reunion in the 2000s.

I will give you a brief insight into how each of the original guys ended up leaving the band.

* * *

Apache and Fidel Paniagua are the two original members who are no longer with the band. I won't go into every gritty detail, but I will at least satisfy the curiosity of some of our fans.

Apache, for all his foibles, was a consummate rock star. He sported the "look": tall, lean, with the right amount of hair and a chiseled "don't give a fuck" face. If you called down to central casting and asked for someone to play the role of a rock and roll rebel, they'd send Apache. Incidentally, that is what he does these days for a living; he's now an actor.

He was as big a fan of R&B as I was. In fact, he had a very cool moment with The Temptations after he left Little Caesar the first time. It caused him to glow for several months.

When the money ran out and Apache walked out in 1991, he continued to work at SIR, a company that rents backline instruments and equipment (such as drums, amps, and monitors) to musicians and production staff. One day he was tapped to make a delivery to a private home. As it turned out, the home was owned by one of the original Temptations. When Apache brought the gear inside, he saw all of the Temptations gathered to rehearse for an upcoming show.

Apache chatted with the homeowner and brought up that he was in a band that covered the Temptations' song, "I Wish It Would Rain." I don't know which member it was; their line-up changed quite a bit through the 1990s. But this member was so impressed that he flipped out. He grabbed Apache by the arm and dragged him into the studio area.

"Hey everyone! This is the guy! He was in that band that did our song!" Turns out, The Temptations loved our version, a more rock and roll-tinged arrangement of their classic R&B tune.

The fucking Temptations knew about us!

Apache was a star struck teenager. He was over the moon.

But he wasn't just a music fan; Apache was also an amazing guitar player. I'm not well-versed in the art of guitar, so I may not be the most informed critic. But we have had five very capable guitar players in the band, two of which have toured the world with other big acts. I have heard many times how some of the licks Apache came up with are beautiful in their complexity. His tones were his own, and his style is difficult to duplicate. He brought a "sound" to Little Caesar that was easily identifiable to our fans. And I agree.

But underneath Apache's rock star exterior was a troubled dude with some tough issues. I saw his alcoholism. Like every addict, the alcohol was an attempt to manage, or self-medicate, all the demons that tortured him. Sadly, he wasn't able to quell his inner storm, thus making him one quirky motherfucker.

I'm sure he suffered from some serious anxiety and a few OCD-type behaviors. He had some rituals and routines that made his life far more difficult, yet he couldn't stop doing them.

I felt bad for the guy. But my empathy has its limits.

Apache had anger issues, too. He could present with any one of ten different personalities, from suave and charming to scary and aggressive. You never knew who you were going to get.

Not to mention, Apache clung to resentment. The guy could hold a fucking grudge like nobody's business.

I remember when Chuck Reed had a run-in with Apache. Chuck was the guy who "discovered" us for Jimmy Iovine. Not a slouch when it came to artist relations. He was no stranger to quirky musicians, either. Furthermore, Chuck understood artists in general; his father, Alan Reed, was in show business. He was the voice of Fred Flintstone for 20 years (1960-1977), and he appeared in several movies, including *Breakfast at Tiffany's*.

After we signed, Chuck became the guy we relied upon to get the day-to-day stuff we needed in order to operate as working musicians. At one point, Apache asked him to order some personalized guitar picks—a fairly standard request from guitar players. If you've ever been to a live show and were lucky enough to grab a pick tossed by the guitar player, odds are it was personalized to that guitarist.

I don't know exactly what went wrong, but the picks didn't show up when they were supposed to. It is unclear as to what happened, but Apache was incensed by the transgression. A grudge was formed. And to the best of my knowledge, it has never waned.

Apache never spoke to Chuck again. In fact, he told us he never even wanted to be in the same room with Chuck again. He went on to tell us to keep that fucking asshole away from him or else he was going to kick Chuck's ass.

Because of guitar picks.

Aside from the immediate, obvious problems, Apache's grudge made it incredibly difficult for the band to communicate with Chuck when we needed stuff. Apache cut off his nose to spite his face with that one. Or to spite the band's collective face.

We did our best to keep him between the lines. We'd tell him things like, "Dude, let it go. They're just fucking guitar picks." All to no avail.

I remember talking with him about his Chuck Reed grudge. Apache had it in his head that Chuck did it on purpose, just to fuck with him. It seemed totally delusional to me, but to Apache, it was cold reality. He was pissed to the point of spitting with rage.

When Apache finally quit in 1991, it was a relief. I hate to feel that way, but it really was. Drama followed Apache. It was nice to feel some calm after the storm.

A sweet guy hid inside that man somewhere. It was wrapped in a tortured soul.

Oh—and Apache hated my guts.

Can you imagine? Who could hate Ron Young?

It happened fast and it happened where I never saw it coming. We were never particularly close in the first place. We weren't friends; we were just two guys who worked together. What put me on his forever shit list happened in a Guitar Center store.

A new digital pedal had been developed for guitar players.

The old-school version of the pedal was manufactured by Bradshaw, and it was massively cool. A different company designed the same style of pedal, except it was one-fifth the size. Also, it was digital instead of analog.

I knew the artist rep from that company and talked to him at our local Guitar Center. He told me there was a ton of interest in the new pedal, so they were on backorder. It took a little schmoozing, but I told him I wanted to get my hands on two of them to give as gifts for my two guitar players.

The rep pulled some strings and found two of them for me. It was a coup, and I was thrilled to bring them to our next rehearsal.

Loren thought it was cool. It wasn't really his cup of tea; he wasn't a big "effects" guy when he played guitar. He thanked me anyway and accepted the pedal with grace.

When I presented the gift to Apache, he didn't interpret the gift as a nice gesture. Instead, he thought I bought him the pedal because I was trying to tell him what to play and how to play it. Like I was trying to control him or insult his playing or something. He lost his shit on me.

"Who the *fuck* do you think you are?!"

That was followed by radio silence for a couple of weeks. He wouldn't so much as look at me, much less speak to me. He was so offended.

I explained that I thought the pedal was cool. I wanted to be thoughtful and kind and buy one for him. He saw it as a power trip and wasn't going to stand for it.

That's what put me on his shit list forever. As it was with Chuck Reed, once you were on Apache's shit list, there was no turning back.

When we decided to reform in 2008, Loren found him. Obviously, I was banned from all contact him, so Loren placed the call.

At first, Apache was reluctant, "I don't want to play with fucking Ron."

Loren explained that I was sober now and much toned down from using "success" as my drug of choice. And Loren was right. I was dictatorial throughout our first run. I tried to not be a dick about it, but I would keep pushing until I got my way.

Unfortunately, Apache refuses to take diplomacy well. He was still bruised over so many things. It took some convincing before he finally agreed to join the rest of us and cut another album.

When he finally spoke to me, I validated that I understood his reluctance. The first run of our band nearly killed him. The drinking, the frustration…it was a spiritual death, if nothing else. I assured him that things would be different now. Our album was to be called *Redemption*, and we were approaching our "music" in an entirely different way with an entirely different mindset.

He agreed and wrote some amazing songs. One in particular, called "That Was Yesterday," spoke to his story about him having a breakdown over how fucked up the music business is. Truly fantastic song. In all, he had two songs on our album.

When we were in the final phases of mixing the album, Apache called and asked for money up front. He was angry, and felt he was being treated unfairly from a financial perspective.

We couldn't agree to pay him up front; I was personally funding the entire production myself. There simply was no money to front *anybody*. I was hoping to make my money back through sales proceeds, and then we had all agreed to split the remaining royalty profits equally.

He didn't like that answer and demanded that his songs get pulled from the album. We found a way to keep them on the album and let the attorneys take it from there. It would have been a ground-breaking case because these were the early days of the internet. There were some discrepancies over what we could and could not do when songs appeared on an artist's MySpace page.

I'd hope Apache wouldn't want to sue me over a 2008 album that sold a few hundred copies. Instead, we said "fuck it." Some *Redemption* CDs were manufactured before the cease and desist letter came from his attorneys, so his songs are on there. Some CDs were manufactured without his songs following the cease and desist, and some have been released digitally with the songs on them. Neither of his songs is available on YouTube. It's a mixed bag. I've already put it behind me and left it for dead.

Regardless, this is another example of how Apache could turn a warm, little project into a total fucking nightmare. He and I have not spoken since. I think he has played in some cover bands, and I heard he's had some health issues.

In all sincerity, I wish the best for him. I know the anger he feels; I hope he is able to overcome it before it overcomes him.

* * *

With regard to Fidel, I still feel really bad about the way things went down. It is what it is, but I'm sorry that things will never get worked out. Both of us are sitting pretty firm in our positions.

As with every family, there are boundaries. Some details can be shared with everyone, some are only shared with close friends, and then there are some aspects of a family that stay within the family. When I write or talk about band members, I am aware that I am talking about family.

Fidel is a very hard worker and a good provider for his family. He has worked in the same Los Angeles-area body shop for over 30 years; a shop he now owns.

His wife, Trace, tagged along on our tours, and we all love his wife. She's a great person and good to be around. However, as you can guess, adding his wife to the tour entourage added an odd dynamic to our touring life.

Still no real problems that we didn't try hard to work around. For awhile.

Things came to a head in 2014. We were getting ready to play the Hard Rock Hell festival in Wales. My intention was to do a one-off in front of their enormous crowd, and then use it to kick start interest so we could follow it up with a full European tour. We had played the festival in 2012 and it was fantastic.

Check the band listing for the 2014 festival. Little Caesar is not on it. Fidel got sick and had to pull out, leaving us over a barrel. Unfortunately, he didn't let any of us know he was sick until it was time to go to the airport, so it was too late to do anything about it. I was annoyed. From that day forward, the relationship between him and the band deteriorated.

I am not a tyrant or a monster. If it had only been a matter of Fidel getting sick, it would have been written off as "one of those things." Shit happens, right? It's all part of life. But things continued to roll downhill.

We moved forward, but tension was always percolating under the surface. Squabbles over rehearsal times (and Fidel being constantly late) reared their ugly heads on more than one occasion. Finally, the last turd hit the fan.

In 2015, we were preparing for another European tour. Europe has always been Little Caesar's "bread and butter." For two months leading up to the tour, Fidel had been negotiating to take over the autobody shop he had managed for three decades. He was anxious about the transaction and the transition, so didn't want to commit to the tour.

I needed to know what was up. I'm the one who puts up the money for flights, hotels, transportation, venues, merch, and so on— including constantly lending Fidel money to cover the expense of his wife coming along (to which, I have never been paid a dime back).

I also map out all the logistics and put up all the up front, out-of-pocket expenses. I don't know that the other guys fully understand the amount of work, energy, and anxiety that comes from managing the details of travel, logistics, and finances that develop when planning a tour or trip. It all suits my personality though, as I am far more obsessive about dotting I's and crossing T's than anyone else. It's a component of my addiction, and I try to use the formerly acquired skills to the benefit of our business. When *I* do it, I know it's done right. That tendency to want to be in control is an artifact of being an addict. I'm aware of it.

Anyway, Fidel, due to his potential purchase of the business, kept delaying and delaying, not wanting to fully commit to the tour. The crux of the issue was that he was nervous about the pending business transaction. I get it; the purchase was an immensely important thing in his and his family's lives. And honestly, Fidel didn't have a lot of experience in the purchase of a business. It all made him very anxious. He wanted to be present, in Los Angeles, to deal with anything that might potentially need his attention.

And that's where the vast difference in perceptions really began that led to the irreconcilable differences.

He could have easily used his phone to take care of any documentary needs. Not to mention the fact that the business was being purchased through a ghost buyer. In short, none of these matters couldn't be dealt with while we were in Europe, or have been put off for the three-and-a-half weeks we were over there. From signing documents to conducting meetings via FaceTime or Skype, he had options…but he felt he did not. Ultimately, he chose to back out of playing on the tour.

It was a shame. As it turned out, Fidel had nothing actually transpire while we were on tour. Although he didn't know it at the time, by the time of our meeting, his deal STILL had not been consummated.

We were never able to negotiate that difference in perspective, and I had to book the tour without him. I called an old friend to take over on bass (more on that in a moment), and off to Europe we went.

When we returned, we needed to sit down and air our resentments, and also get solid commitments moving forward. We needed to confront these matters with adult-like boundaries and communication. These issues were only going to get worse if not confronted. We needed to make sure that he was totally committed to showing up for the band's obligations—which get set *months* in advance.

At the meeting Fidel said his family and his business were the priorities, and that the band would always take the third back seat. Further, he said he would continue to play in the band if we understood that.

Then, he implied that no one else in the band could comprehend his priorities—and accused Loren of not putting his family first when it came to his musical commitments.

That's when the conversation took an ugly turn. Chests were beaten and personal space shrunk to just inches between Loren and Fidel.

When things calmed down a bit, we got back to trying to resolve it all. Lastly, Fidel kept saying that he would have more "free time" once he owned the business. He wanted us to understand that as well.

We did not. Or more specifically, I did not.

I know what it's like to own a business. It can be ALL consuming. You can't "punch the clock" when you are the last man in the "chain of command." When I pointed out that owning your own business can eat up way more time than you realize, he disagreed.

Look, Fidel knew how to *manage* a business, but never *owned* one. Ownership comes with a whole different set of engagements, obligations, pressures and relationships that are not afforded to a business's manager. Those are two VERY different things.

If he thought that now he would have more free time, he was truly delusional.

As you can imagine, the remainder of that meeting did not go very well either.

When the conversation and confrontations between Loren and Fidel got heated, it all became incredibly clear to me: This was no longer fun.

The continued delusions and avoidances of confrontations was never going to change. Watching the two of them nearly come to blows, I had an out of body experience. I was struck with a lightning bolt moment of insight.

I knew Fidel was moving toward owning his own business,

which I did not take for granted, and was really happy for him and his family. He had worked his ass off (for a tyrant) for decades and was finally seeing some great potential for him and the family he adored.

However, he needed to understand that we all had a ton of outside commitments and responsibilities. Each of us had a family to take care of and to spend time with. The difference was, the rest of us figured out how to show up for rehearsals on time and arrange our schedules to go on tour.

He wasn't hearing a thing I said. Furthermore, he was desperately clinging to a Truth that was a total Lie. I don't always have to be right in the eyes of my band mates, but I want reality to be accepted on reality's terms.

I couldn't change Fidel or open up his brain. As a part of my recovery, I learned to be okay with something being done and over. Sometimes you have to accept that something isn't going to work anymore. I can't change other people. I respect the futility.

For my own sanity and for the future of the band, I could not afford to remain delusional. I couldn't afford it financially or emotionally. It took a toll, and it was a toll I was no longer willing to pay. We were no longer going to put up with the dysfunction.

For Fidel, that was the end of his road with Little Caesar. I feel tremendous remorse over this but no guilt. I love Fidel and will always miss the part of him that was a part of me, but he never took ownership of reality. He couldn't reconcile this difference of reality. Pharaoh was an exceedingly capable replacement.

In a nutshell, a part Fidel was very angry about the band confronting him in the first place, especially about his future with Little Caesar. He could never bring himself to understand our point of view. He wanted the rest of us to suck it up and deal with it.

That was not going to cut it.

The chaos led us to eventually ask Pharoah (Barrett—who had filled in for Fidel on the 2015 tour) to become a permanent member of the band. At first, Pharaoh was just a substitute for Fidel on this tour.

* * *

I had first met Pharoah when I did a quick tour with The Horsemen way back in 1996. Their lead singer, Frank Starr, had fallen into a coma following a bad motorcycle accident, and I stepped in to take his place for their *Gettin' Pretty Good...at Barely Gettin' By* tour. Pharaoh and I got along great together.

I enjoyed the hell out of the Horsemen tour. My favorite story from those days involves a Little Black Book found stuffed into the back of a pawn shop guitar that Dave Lizmi, the guitar player, had bought on tour. It was like finding a fuckin' treasure chest. Apparently, a touring musician had owned the guitar and pawned it without removing his personal effects. The contact info was arranged alphabetically in the book, and listed dozens of women in different cities all over the United States.

We had a lot of fun utilizing phone numbers in the black book when we rolled into the different towns outlined in the index. It was a daily game to call the numbers of the women in that book and see who would show up in every town.

It ain't pretty, but that's rock and roll.

We tried to keep that lineup of the Four Horsemen together, but it wouldn't last. My addiction came back with a vengeance and I'm sure that didn't help. Our collaboration fizzled for the time being. When I called Pharoah in 2015, he was happy to step in for Fidel.

He has been with us ever since.

* * *

I will honorably mention Earl Slick. He was only with the band for a short time, but he is a big name and was the only other musician that was around for our original run.

Earl is an enormously talented guitar player. I think his track record with John Lennon and David Bowie speaks for itself. We were more than delighted to have him on board. Replacing Apache in 1991 was difficult, yet we struck oil when we landed Earl.

In reality, Loren landed Earl. I think Loren had known him from "back in the day," when the two of them were starving musicians knocking around in New York City. That was back when Earl was still known by his birth name, Frank Madeloni.

Little Caesar was signed to a major label, which interested Earl. Plus, our music was totally up his alley. He loved rockabilly, and played a genre of music that resembled our guitar-driven, old school rock and roll. He had creative freedom to contribute to the songwriting process, which made him very happy. Heck, even his look was a throwback to the style we loved.

We got Earl Slick.

Unfortunately, we got him at exactly the wrong time. Little Caesar was at an all-time low, both spiritually and financially. He stepped aboard a moving train, only it wasn't going to better places. It was going straight to hell.

You'd think that would be a plus for him. Earl was one cranky motherfucker who was getting sick of all the industry bullshit. He had just left two projects that seemed to have huge potential, only to see each of them fall apart.

In 1985, he'd joined Slim Jim Phantom and Lee Rocker, who had just been orphaned when Brian Setzer left The Stray Cats. They formed the super group Phantom Rocker & Slick. That group released two albums, the second of which bombed pretty hard. As a result, Phantom and Rocker got back together with Brian Setzer. Earl went back to session work.

He then joined another super group, Dirty White Boy, and signed with Geffen. The group included David Glen Eisley, who had recently been fired from the band Giuffria (by Gene Simmons, no less). This lead to Giuffria's reformation as House of Lords. Keni Richards of Autograph and Pete Comita, who was briefly with Cheap Trick, were the other half of Dirty White Boy. That group released one album, *Bad Reputation*, in 1990 to high expectations. It was produced by legendary hair metal producer, Beau Hill.

This all happened about the time grunge had begun its takeover. Geffen was in corporate disarray. Dirty White Boy's album fell into the same black hole as our debut.

Earl was already frustrated when he got to Caesar. However,

he was hopeful that we were going to be a thoroughbred racehorse, breaking from the gate of a storied career. What he got instead was a sway-backed nag headed for the glue factory.

Between he and I, the days surrounding the second Caesar album became a gigantic pity party. He realized soon enough that he had jumped aboard a sinking ship. I was in the throes of addiction and had stopped giving a fuck.

When we got back from Europe that year, a dark cloud hung over everyone in the band. We did one last show in Las Vegas, which was the climax of an already miserable tour. All of us got into a big screaming match before the show. I honestly can't remember what we were all so angry about. My guess is that it was something minor that built up and unleashed after months and years of pent-up frustration.

We played the show as scheduled. Then we all got into separate vehicles and went home, never to play together again.

Earl went back to some session work and released a solo record, In Your Face. He also worked on movie soundtracks, landing songs in *Hudson Hawk* and *Nothing but Trouble*.

As a silver lining, we ended with no bad blood between us and Earl. Before Earl reunited with David Bowie in the late 1990s and early 2000s, he was nice enough to take us onto his record label. As a result, we were able to release an album consisting of demos and songs that never made it onto Little Caesar albums. The album, *This Time It's Different*, originally came out in 1998. In 2022, that record was re-released under the Deko Music label.

* * *

Let me round out the band and tell you about Tom and Loren.

I cannot say enough about how wonderful of a human being Tom Morris is. Not only is he the warmest and most genuine person I know, he is also fiercely intelligent when it comes to musical history, trivia, and obscure anecdotes. That guy is a walking encyclopedia of music.

I first met Tom when I arrived in Los Angeles and answered

an ad in a periodical called *LA Weekly*. This was pre-internet, of course. The paper had a Classifieds section and a category called "Music Connection." Tom had placed the ad because he was getting a band together.

I gave him a call to find out what he was looking for. We got to chatting and I was struck by how knowledgeable he was regarding music. In addition to history and trivia, Tom was a complete audiophile. He knew a shit ton about gear and equipment, which appealed to the scientific engineer part of my brain.

We put together the band, Smilin' Jacks—which I can honestly say was a damn good band. We were too eclectic for any label to sign, which is an unfortunately common occurrence in the music industry. Labels want bands (and music) that are easily pigeon-holed into a category. Our music was mostly on brand, but we didn't meet their specs to be a marketable band. We had a huge, 6'3" black dude on bass guitar, a surfer dude on lead guitar, and a Robert-Smith-from-The-Cure looking dude on rhythm guitar. With Tom behind the kit and me on vocals, we were a random bag of chaotic awesomeness, to say the least.

We had good record company interest. We played in several showcases and got our demo tapes placed in some powerful hands. But they all passed because of the photograph on our eventual album cover. We looked crazy and disjointed.

That issue from many record execs, "the way you look is a big problem," would continue to haunt me for the rest of my career.

From the wreckage of Smilin' Jacks, Tom and I became the core of Little Caesar. He remains one of the longest-standing friends I have had in my life. It feels like there hasn't been a time when he *hasn't* been in my life.

Tom, like the rest of us, also had some idiosyncrasies that I always wondered about. Little quirky tendencies that he quietly carried throughout his life.

For example, he used to tie his sticks to his hands so he would never drop one during a performance. It made perfect sense for him to do it, but I have no idea why he would. I never asked him, so it's not my place to judge his methods. I think I filed that information away under "because he's Tom."

Also, Tom prefers a particular kick pedal on his bass drum—one that hasn't been manufactured since the 1970s. He owns about six of them; he probably grabbed every single one he could find during the great "Kick Pedal Famine" of 1981.

Despite owning several, he still uses the original one he acquired back in the Paleolithic Era. He even took it to a machine shop to get it re-tooled and bolstered when it started to fall apart.

It's not a big shameful trade secret—it's just Tom. Every fucking drummer we've come across who's laid eyes on that thing will exclaim, "Whoa, dude! Did you get that from one of the guys on The Mayflower?"

Yet, Tom owns it. He knows who he is and he is at one with his quirks.

As I've alluded to, Tom Morris decided to quit the band in 1992, right before our European tour for *Influence*. Tom had a real, bona fide phobia of flying, as many people do. It paralyzed him. Not the best complication to have for a touring musician. He was too embarrassed to tell any of us about how badly he suffered when we boarded a plane.

Unfortunately, Little Caesar's Geffen mess, combined with the prospect of another fifteen-hour flight, pushed Tom over the edge. He decided it was easier to quit for a short while in 1992 than to endure flying in another airplane. So he removed himself from the equation.

I know first-hand, man. Irrational fears are a motherfucker. And a half.

These days, Tom has gotten a good handle on his fear of flying. He still doesn't like it—that would be a bridge too far. But he is able to manage his thoughts and emotions to the point that he can cope with a trans-Atlantic flight. He's still a bit of a self-proclaimed hypochondriac, but it's best to fight one battle at a time.

I can't imagine my life without Tom in it. He has a heart of gold and would never do anything immoral or unscrupulous. And when you are in a band, there is no better personality type to be around.

Loren Molinare has always tried to prioritize the needs of the band, but he too has faced issues with alcoholism. At some point early in the band's existence, he became worried about it…as did the rest of us.

Eventually, we had to sit Loren down and have a conversation. Loren would have rather taken a bullet than do anything to hurt the band. He took our concern to heart and went immediately to clean up. We're all proud of his decades-long sobriety.

This guy is the absolute epitome of rock and roll. Loren is one cool-ass motherfucker. It's like he was torn from another era, back when being "punk rock" actually meant something.

Loren grew up in the Detroit music scene (Lansing, Michigan, actually), finding influence and a bunch of success when he was a young man. He has been in bands that opened for MC5 and Bob Seger. Then he got swept into the punk rock movement and became a punk rocker before it hit the New York underground.

Loren is the elder statesman of our group and has balls of steel. I remember one story he told about the old days, when his band, The Dogs, opened for Seger.

The producer of the show was jacking around with something, and the curtain didn't go up until well after the advertised start time. Loren was approached and told that they were going to be cut out of the bill because there was no longer enough time for them to go on stage and perform. The venue had a curfew, and Seger needed his time.

Loren replied, "Fuck that. We're playing."

His band jumped up on stage and started playing, so the promoter had them arrested. The cops proceeded to drag their asses off the stage. I think Loren still has photos from that crime scene somewhere lying around. It nearly caused a riot and his band got black-balled from the area.

Fuckin' rock and roll, man.

It's funny how life lines up. Now that his band was ostensibly dead in Detroit, they moved to New York and squatted into the scene there. While there, he ran into a young Gene Simmons (no shit!). Kiss was brand new at the time, rising from the ashes of a band called Wicked Lester.

Loren told Gene he wanted his band to open for Kiss. Gene told him that if Loren's band provided the backline and took responsibility for setting up and striking the set, they were welcome to open. Loren Molinare's band opened for Kiss in a tiny club somewhere on Long Island in 1974.

The Dogs also opened for AC/DC at The Whiskey (in Los Angeles) when AC/DC first came to tour the US. Lorne actually got to drink shots of Jack Daniels with Bon Scott.

Fucking balls of titanium.

He is like Iggy Pop and Keith Richards rolled into one. The dude has boundless, punk rock, up-on-the-beat energy, along with a very clear idea of what music is and what it means. He is the preacher in the Church of Rock and Roll. His excesses may have gotten the better of him for awhile, but he got them under control and emerged a better man and musician for it.

That energy, by the way, was critical for creating the signature sound of Little Caesar. We would have been a markedly different band without him.

Just like Tom, Loren is integrated into my life in such a way that I almost don't remember life before him. One of my closest friends and my musical confidant, Loren has been the only member of our band that has never left my side.

No bullshit; no posing; Loren is the beacon of proper rock and roll attitude. He's The Dude and represents the true spirit of what music is all about.

I've seen that guy pogo around the stage like a possessed spider monkey. He'll fall down and get back up like nothing happened. Later, he'd show me a huge bruise when we get back to the dressing room.

Tom and Loren have been my partners in crime since Day One. Both are sober now, and I can't tell you how proud I am of them both.

The show goes on, all in the name of rock and roll.

CHAPTER 16:
PRESENT TENSE

In addition to Little Caesar, I currently sing for The Cruzados, a band founded in the 1980s by bassist Tony Marsico. They grew out of a Los Angeles-based Latino punk band called The Plugz and were signed by Arista Records. The Cruzados released albums in 1985 and 1987; tours with Fleetwood Mac and INXS followed. The band did pretty well before going their separate ways.

Loren used to roadie for them when he needed some extra cash back in the mid-1980s. Small world.

Tony Marsico is a monster bass player and one of the nicest guys from the early-to-mid-80s era of music. Hollywood was split in two during those days: on the West side, the Sunset Strip scene was the genesis of Hair Metal. On the East side, the California alternative scene formed, boasting genres like punk, cow punk, and post-new wave. It was a more eclectic scene on the East side, and a lot more fun, in my opinion. But it didn't generate the commercial success as their brethren on The Strip.

A few bands were able to straddle the line between both scenes and find a few scraps of success nationally: Little Caesar, Junkyard, and Rhino Bucket, to name a few. The Cruzados were on the next tier down; enormously popular on the local scene but struggled to break out in a significant way nationally.

The Mecca of the East side music scene was a club called Raji's. In fact, Guns 'n Roses got their start in Raji's. If you look at very early pix of GnR, they looked more like a hair metal band. Axl had his hair blown out, back-combed, and teased. Then when GnR saw the influence and popularity of bikers and grittier audiences in the East side clubs, they toned it down and really found their stride.

The Cruzados were among the biggest bands coming out of Raji's and the other popular clubs on that side of town—Club

Lingerie, Madame Wong's, and The Music Machine. These places were all packed every night to see them or The Blasters or whoever was tearing it up.

As a result, Tony was pretty well-known around town back then. I knew him from working the clubs. Obviously, Loren knew him from being an employee. But Tony also had the full attention of big names in the industry. When the Cruzados broke up, he ended up recording and touring with legendary artists like Bob Dylan, Willie Nelson, Neil Young, and Roger Daltrey. The dude was on point when he played.

One day in 2020, I was on the phone with Mark Tremaglia, talking about getting together for a Little Caesar rehearsal. Mark told me he couldn't make it that night because he was doing a project with the aforementioned Tony Marsico. He told me that Tony was resurrecting The Cruzados because a couple of early members of the band had recently passed away. Founding member and original drummer, Charlie Quintana, and lead guitar player Marshall Rohner (who replaced original guitar player, Steven Hufsteter in 1986) had both died in the past five years. Tony wanted to do something in their honor. Getting the band back together and maybe cutting an album seemed like a perfect gesture to show some respect to their legacy.

I said, "Wow, that sounds great. Who's doing vocals for them?"

Mark chuckled, "It's funny. We were just talking about that. Tony has a few guys in mind. You want me to throw your hat into the ring?"

I said what I always say. "Fuck yeah, dude! That'd be great."

I've always been a fan of the band and a fan of the songs. Plus, I love Tony. Yeah, I'm totally interested if he wants me.

Twenty minutes later, my phone rang. It was Tony.

"Aw Ron, I didn't think you'd be able to do it."

I repeated what I said to Mark. "Fuck yeah, dude. Are you crazy? I'd be totally into this."

He was delighted. We talked for a few more minutes, reminiscing about the old days on The Strip. And then the conversation turned to business.

"Yeah man. We actually need another guitar player too."

He started throwing out a few names. I could tell there was something he wanted to say, but wasn't saying it. Finally, he brought it up.

"Would you feel weird if I called Loren? I'm a big fan of his playing, and have been a big fan for years."

I said, "Yeah, of course that would be okay."

"That would make three guys from Little Caesar." He paused, sounding very cautious. "Is that going to weird you out?"

Pfft. Nothing about making good music weirds me out. I had zero problem with it. The bands have different styles of music and different histories. There was plenty of room for both bands.

Loren was all-in. I don't think he took more than a second or two to think about the offer. He agreed before the question got out of Tony's mouth.

Tony needed a drummer. I recommended Rob Klonel, who got the gig. I had known Rob from a soul cover band we were in. He also filled in for Little Caesar when Tom declined an opportunity to play some live streaming dates because of his COVID concerns.

Loren Molinare   Tony Marsico   Ron Young   Mark Tremalgia   Rob Klonel

CRUZADOS

Photo Credit: Heather Harris

271

Tony has been great to work with. He struggles mightily to catch up and keep up with 20th century technology. Hell, sometimes it seems like he struggles to keep up with 15th century technology. But that guy is a prolific and fantastic writer; he can deliver his musical ideas by carrier pigeon and smoke signals, for all I care. I thoroughly enjoy working with him.

We did a few rehearsals to tighten up the band, and then went into Bruce Witkin's place, Unison Studios in Los Angeles, to cut the record. Consistent with Tony's sensibilities, we did the whole thing old-school. It was mostly recorded live; very few overdubs. We were all in the same room playing the songs as they were recorded; none of this "record each part separately and then paste them together" bullshit that we had gotten used to with major labels.

A lot of old friends from the Los Angeles punk scene wanted to be a part of the album. They either dropped by the studio or sent their contribution over the internet, when COVID was still raging. Each artist was eager to add their own flair to the recording and production. It was like a homecoming of sorts, an absolute blast down memory lane.

Old friends and classic music. Right up my alley, man.

I love the band! It's a great fucking project. I sometimes resent being painted into a corner by virtue of Little Caesar being a "Sunset Strip era" band. My musical taste is far more varied than that. The Cruzados allows me access into another musical classification altogether. It's easier on my voice to sing Cruzados songs than some of the stuff I sing with Caesar. Less battle fatigue on the vocal cords.

It has been so much fun. The album, *She's Automatic*, came out in 2021. Our tour manager in Europe called and said there was a lot of interest in his country for a tour. We hopped aboard the idea. COVID threatened to shut down our plans, so we pushed the tour to 2022 to create enough distance in order to make it happen. People are hungry for live music.

Photo Credit: Reynald Reyland

Joining The Cruzados has been revitalizing for me. I believe it has been for the rest of the band members as well, but I am personally grateful to Tony for inviting me into his dream.

* * *

These days, I live a quiet life at home. I make time to relax and enjoy my ranch, although I'm still busy and constantly entangled in band stuff. I still build custom cars and motorcycles, as my need for speed and unique vehicles in life are so very dear to me.

Little Caesar recently hired a manager, but I still take care of many business-related odds and ends. I work hard to make it as easy as possible for my guys to just show up and play the gigs.

I'm no altruistic saint. Making my band mates' lives easier ultimately makes my life easier. If there is a problem—and there always seems to be in this business—I am the one on site who steps forward and deals with it.

Back in California, Renee and I have built a life and a home where we are comfortable. She and I are a good team when it comes to creating a working homestead and a fun, exciting life together. She likes to point to open areas of land and then tell me what she wants built. I like to strap on a tool belt and make it happen. I'm starting to slow down as I get older and creakier, but I love Rockin' R's Ranch.

It is a farm, but not a "thousands of acres of corn" farm you see in the American Midwest. It's more of a gentleman's farm, compete with a modest avocado grove and 23 animals. And because I love our animals, here's what we have:

Four horses

Two pigs

Two mini-donkeys

A mini-horse

Five mini-cows

Five cats

Four dogs

We have ponds on property, too. I have a "decoy pond" in the front yard (stocked with Koi, Goldfish and Bass) to give the herons and cranes something to do. It keeps them busy enough that they don't venture into the backyard. I don't grow attached to the fish in the front yard pond. I just wave goodbye when I see a heron take off with one of those brave soldiers in its mouth.

In the back, under a cover, we've got a decent-sized pond which is home to some very large Koi. Those fish are my buddies. I care for them like they are members of our family.

All of the animals, fish included, require upkeep and maintenance. So Renee and I stay extremely busy.

* * *

I wish I could say I'm a simple man, but my mind is constantly abuzz with this or that. I like to keep my hands busy because I need to keep my mind busy. A blessing and a curse, my mental horse needs to get out for a run every now and then.

My core personality hasn't changed…but as I grow older, I am more aware of its different facets. Just like the events that have shaped me into the man I have become, the ride is wilder than anything Mr. Toad could have imagined.

So, I continue to get older; happy birthday to me. I never thought I'd live to the ripe old age of 62. Not that it's been all fun and games.

I've had a spinal fusion, I have arthritis in many places of my body—various motorcycle accidents didn't help. I have had 2 inguinal hernia's and have a hiatal hernia that has me living on stomach pills. I've had kidney stones. No way I'm going to suffer through that fucking nightmare again, so I take supplements to help prevent their formation. Also, I take Melatonin to get to sleep (really helps with jetlag when we go on tour). And multi-vitamins.

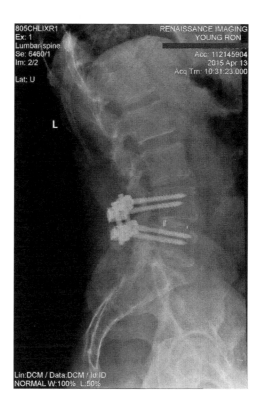

I'm old, but I'm a little wiser than I was yesterday.

Along those same lines, I find myself in surreal arguments with my peers on Facebook. When aging rockers try to hang onto the same hair and clothing they wore in the late 1980s or early 1990s, they end up looking pathetic. Dyed hair and Affliction jeans? Who do they think they're fooling?

So now, I'm *that* guy. Wearing comfortable shoes and yelling at birds in the park. When did Ron Young become the voice of reason? The guy who tells rebellious teen-age 60-somethings to go back in and change their stupid outfits?

I embrace my age and grow old with dignity. That guy on the Dos Equis commercials seems to have figured it out.

That image of the Dos Equis "World's Most Interesting Man" creates a nice metaphor for the current bend in the road I've traveled. It's who I've tried to become. Just call me Mister Rock and Roll. From crazy mom to crazy potential to crazy record execs to crazy failure to crazy addict to crazy recovery to the crazy old, social media nut-job.

All wrapped into one guy.

Life is so…*weird*.

EPILOGUE

Writing this book has been a good exercise for me. Going through recovery has taught me to take a step back and recognize how the stories I tell and the decisions I make can be warped. It's not that I'm operating the machinery incorrectly, it's that the machinery itself is kinda fucked up.

It is rare that I'm afforded an opportunity to slow down my day-to-day brain and really take a look at the big-picture tapestry of my life. I have a drive to do that: create comfort and forgiveness for my past, but also accept responsibility for being a caring adult in the present and future.

As far as this book goes, I have enjoyed doing it.

A secondary motivation for writing this book was to demonstrate that you, the reader, do not have to be afraid of the mistakes you've made or the difficulties you've had with yourself or others. You can learn to walk with your limp.

My best advice is to surround yourself with people you trust and those that you can engage in healthy, loving relationships. Healthy people who can point out that something in the way you make decisions isn't right. Then you can accept what they tell you is the truth. If they tell you, "Dude, you're walking with a limp," don't immediately respond with, "What're you talking about? I'm not limping at all! That's totally a normal gait. Everybody does this shit."

Defensiveness does not give way to growth. It keeps you stuck in an endless cycle of avoiding your stress in ways that will invariably damage you over time. Whether it's booze, drugs, gambling, shopping, fucking, or isolating and watching Pornhub all day long, we do what we have to do in order to keep our head above the water. Why not become more buoyant by accepting your foibles and working to smooth them out? That way, you connect more solidly to the people around you. You drive off those ne'er-do-wells, and hang onto a crowd who will triumph your successes and grieve for your failures.

It's how I have come to live my best life. So far.

REFERENCES

National Center for Biotechnology Information. (2022). *PubChem Compound Summary for CID 6292*. https://pubchem.ncbi.nlm.nih.gov/compound/Methaqualone.

Tiebout, H. M. (December 1954). Ego Factors in Surrender in Alcoholism. *Quarterly Journal of Studies on Alcohol*, (15)4, 610-621. doi:10.15288/qjsa.1954.15.610.
Reprinted in *Harry Tiebout: The Collected Writings*

PHOTO CREDITS

I have included photo credits for everyone that I could remember and find for this book. Photographers are artists too and I want to give credit to anyone whose art is included in this book. Being that a lot of my life was in the "public eye" and photographers were hired to capture my likeness for public consumption by "entities outside of my control," I am relying on my memory or where credits were published on the initial published works. If I have left your photo credit out of this book, please reach out to me and I will correct that omission. Thanks.

Made in the USA
Columbia, SC
21 December 2022

73510541R00154